Science Foundations

G000149196

NEW EDITION

Chemistry

Jean Martin
Bryan Milner

CAMBRIDGE
UNIVERSITY PRESS

Series Editor	Bryan Milner
Chemistry Editor	Ray Oliver
Authors	Peter Evans
	Helen Norris
	Ray Oliver
Consultants	Nigel Heslop
	Martyn Keeley
	Helen Norris
Authors for	Jean Martin
Second Edition	Bryan Milner

PUBLISHED BY THE PRESS SYNDICATE OF THE UNIVERSITY OF CAMBRIDGE
The Pitt Building, Trumpington Street, Cambridge,
United Kingdom

CAMBRIDGE UNIVERSITY PRESS
The Edinburgh Building, Cambridge CB2 2RU, UK
40 West 20th Street, New York, NY 10011-4211, USA
477 Williamstown Road, Port Melbourne, VIC 3207, Australia
Ruiz de Alarcón 13, 28014 Madrid, Spain
Dock House, The Waterfront, Capetown 8001, South Africa

© Cambridge University Press 1997, 2001

First edition published 1997
Second edition published 2001
Reprinted 2002

Printed in the United Kingdom at the University Press, Cambridge

A catalogue record for this book is available from the British Library

Typeface Stone Informal *System* QuarkXpress

ISBN 0 521 00891 3 paperback

Designed and produced by Gecko Ltd, Bicester, Oxon

Contents

■ Structure and bonding

■ Patterns of chemical change

■ Handling data   **204**

■ Revising for tests and examinations   **207**

■ How to write good answers in GCSE Science examinations   **208**

■ Chemical data   **211**

■ What you need to remember: completed passages   **214**

■ Glossary/index   **224**

■ Acknowledgements

12, 13c, 15, 18t, ct, cb, b, 19c, b, 20, 21, 23lc, 25, 28b, 30, 42r, 43t, 46l, r, 51, 52cl, c, cr, b, 53, 59r, 68, 77t, 79, 104, 111c, b, 112, 113, 114, 115, 141, 144r, 148, 151c, r, 152, 156 (except t), 157b, 159, 160, 167bl, br, 168, 171t, 171b, 175t, Andrew Lambert; 13t, 59l, Werner Reith/Photo Images; 13b, 52tr, Malcolm Fife; 14, 133, 167t, Graham Portlock/Pentaprism; 19t, TRH Pictures/Boeing; 23t, The Art Archive/Private Collection/Dagli Orti; 23cc, courtesy of the Trustees of the Wedgewood Museum, Barlaston, Staffordshire, England; 23cl, The Art Archive/British Museum/Eileen Tweedy; 23cr, The Art Archive/Victoria and Albert Museum London; 23b, Ammonia 4 Plant, Terra Nitrogen (UK) Limited, Billingham; 28t, TRH Pictures/MoD; 31, D Dennis; 32, The Natural History Museum, London; 35, Favre Felix, Jerrican/Science Photo Library; 38, Kathie Atkinson/www.osf.uk.com; 41tl, Jim Winkley/Ecoscene; 41tr, Susan Cunningham/Panos Pictures; 41bl, 72b, Erik Schaffer/Ecoscene; 41br, Bridget Hodgkinson/Ecoscene; 42l, courtesy of Ford Motor Company Limited; 42b, artwork of zinc blocks on steel based on photo from Corrintec Limited; 43b, 97, Roger G. Howard; 87t, 87b, Corbis; 55, Ben Osborne/www.osf.uk.com; 56, courtesy of British Cement Association; 72t, Adrian Davies/Bruce Coleman Ltd; 75t, John Reader/Science Photo Library; 75b, 76, 78tr, 82c, b, 128, Geoscience Features Picture Library; 78tl, Science Photo Library; 82t, Genevieve Leaper/Ecoscene; 106, 174, Mary Evans Picture Library; 111t, TRH Pictures/US Navy; 130, Martyn F Chillmaid/www.osf.uk.com; 134, courtesy of Manchester City Engineers; 144l, Chinth Gryniewicz/Ecoscene; 144c, Michael Brooke; 151l, 172, 173, 175b, 192, Nigel Cattlin/Holt Studios International; 156t, The Kobal Collection/©1982 Paramount Pictures Corp.; 157t, 158, Biophoto Associates; 163, James King-Holmes/Science Photo Library

How to use this book

An introduction for students and their teachers

The four main sections of this book, *Metals*, *Earth materials*, *Structure and bonding* and *Patterns of chemical change* contain three different types of material:

- ideas from your previous studies of Science at Key Stage 3;

- scientific ideas that all Key Stage 4 students are expected to know, whether they are entered for the Foundation Tier or the Higher Tier of GCSE Science tests and examinations;

- scientific ideas that only candidates entered for the Higher Tier GCSE tests and examinations need to know.

Ideas from your previous science studies at Key Stage 3

You need to understand these ideas before you start on the new science for Key Stage 4.

But you will <u>not</u> be assessed <u>directly</u> on these Key Stage 3 ideas in GCSE Science tests and examinations.

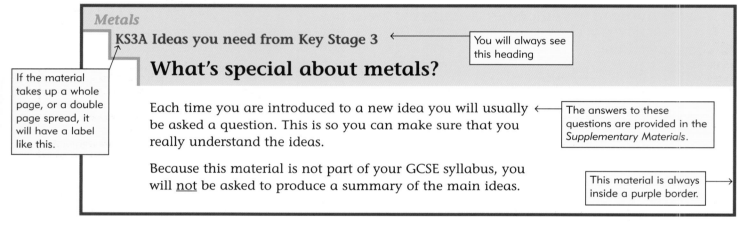

Metals

KS3A Ideas you need from Key Stage 3 ← You will always see this heading

What's special about metals?

If the material takes up a whole page, or a double page spread, it will have a label like this.

Each time you are introduced to a new idea you will usually be asked a question. This is so you can make sure that you really understand the ideas. ← The answers to these questions are provided in the *Supplementary Materials*.

Because this material is not part of your GCSE syllabus, you will <u>not</u> be asked to produce a summary of the main ideas.

This material is always inside a purple border. →

Occasionally, the Key Stage 3 ideas will take up less than one whole page.

In such cases, the Key Stage 3 material will be included in a box at the start of the Key Stage 4 topic.

Ideas you need from Key Stage 3

Science that all Key Stage 4 students need to know

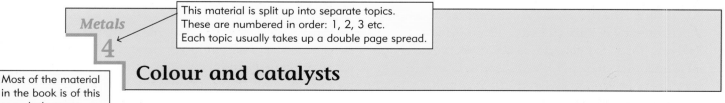

Metals

4

This material is split up into separate topics. These are numbered in order: 1, 2, 3 etc. Each topic usually takes up a double page spread.

Colour and catalysts

Most of the material in the book is of this type. It does not have any special border or heading.

Each time you are introduced to a new idea you will be asked a question. This is so you can make sure that you really understand the ideas ← The answers to these questions are provided in the *Supplementary Materials*.

At the end of each topic you will find a section like this.

→

What you need to remember [Copy and complete using the **key words**]

You should keep your answers to these sections in a separate place.

They contain all the ideas you are expected to remember and understand in tests and examinations. So they are very useful for revision.

It is very important that these summaries are correct, so you should always check your summaries against those provided on pages 214–223 of this book.

At the bottom of some pages, you will find a note for Higher Tier students.

These ideas are extended, for Higher Tier students, in Metals H1 on page 47.

■ Science that only Higher Tier students need to know

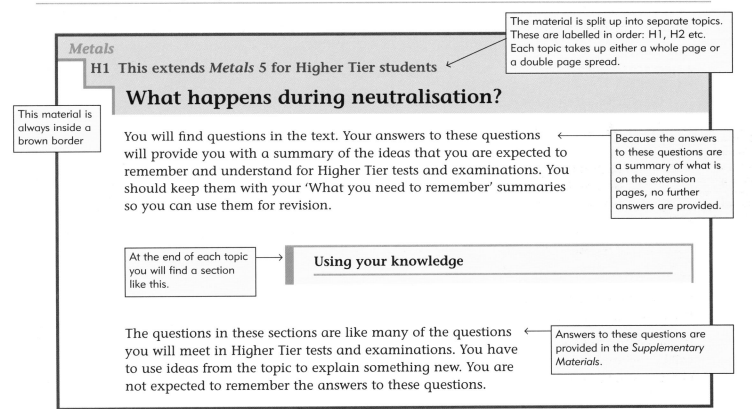

The material is split up into separate topics. These are labelled in order: H1, H2 etc. Each topic takes up either a whole page or a double page spread.

Metals

H1 This extends *Metals 5* for Higher Tier students

This material is always inside a brown border

What happens during neutralisation?

You will find questions in the text. Your answers to these questions will provide you with a summary of the ideas that you are expected to remember and understand for Higher Tier tests and examinations. You should keep them with your 'What you need to remember' summaries so you can use them for revision.

Because the answers to these questions are a summary of what is on the extension pages, no further answers are provided.

At the end of each topic you will find a section like this.

→

Using your knowledge

The questions in these sections are like many of the questions you will meet in Higher Tier tests and examinations. You have to use ideas from the topic to explain something new. You are not expected to remember the answers to these questions.

Answers to these questions are provided in the *Supplementary Materials*.

■ A note about practical work

Practical work, where you observe things and find out things for yourself, is an important part of Science. You will often see things in this book which you have yourself seen or done, but detailed instructions for practical work are not included. These will be provided separately by your teacher.

The *Supplementary Materials* contain many suggestions for practical activities.

■ A note about Ideas and Evidence

All GCSE Science syllabuses must now assess candidates' understanding of what the National Curriculum calls *Ideas and Evidence*. Those parts of this book which include material about this aspect of Science are indicated on the contents page like this:

Drawing diagrams of chemical apparatus

You will find the information on these pages useful throughout this book.

When we do an experiment, we often need to draw a diagram. Adding a diagram to our written notes makes it easier to show what happened in the experiment.

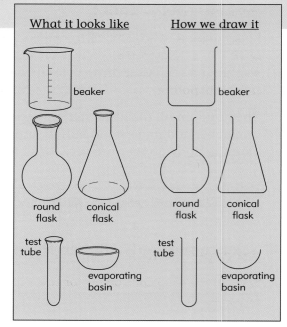

What it looks like   How we draw it

beaker   beaker

round flask   conical flask   round flask   conical flask

test tube   evaporating basin   test tube   evaporating basin

■ Drawing diagrams of containers

The simplest container we can use is a **test tube**.
We can heat solids or liquids in a test tube.
For bigger volumes of liquid we use a **beaker** or a **flask**.
We can use round flasks or conical flasks.
We can use an **evaporating basin** to grow crystals from a solution.

■ Measuring the liquids we need

Most beakers have a scale marked on the outside.
This gives a rough idea of the volume of liquid inside.
We can use a **measuring cylinder** if we need to measure liquids more carefully.
A **burette** lets us measure liquids very accurately.

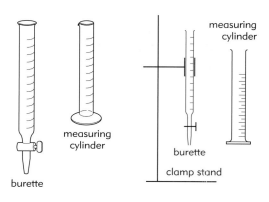

measuring cylinder

measuring cylinder

burette

burette

clamp stand

■ Special apparatus that we use with gases

We can collect many kinds of gas in a **gas jar**. If we want to measure an amount of gas, we can use a **gas syringe** which has a scale on it.

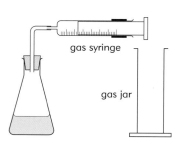

gas syringe

gas jar

■ Filtering mixtures to separate them

We need a **filter funnel** and some **filter paper** to separate sand from a solution. The solution goes through the filter paper but the sand does not. The job of the filter funnel is to support the filter paper.

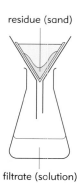

residue (sand)

filtrate (solution)

Making things hotter

Many experiments need a **Bunsen burner** to make them work. We can use the gas burner to heat test tubes or to set things on fire, such as magnesium ribbon. We also need a **tripod** and a metal **gauze** to hold beakers or flasks.

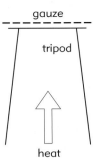

Distilling liquids

We need a **condenser** to turn steam back into water. It also works with other liquids such as alcohol.

This is how we draw the distilling apparatus.

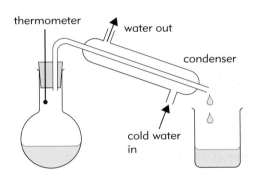

An experiment shown in diagrams

Look at the diagrams below for the experiment to separate a mixture of water, sand, salt and iron filings.

1 Write down the names of the <u>six</u> pieces of apparatus that have a mark like this *.

2 Draw a diagram, using the six pieces of apparatus from question 1, to show how you could produce salt and water from a salt solution that also contained sand.

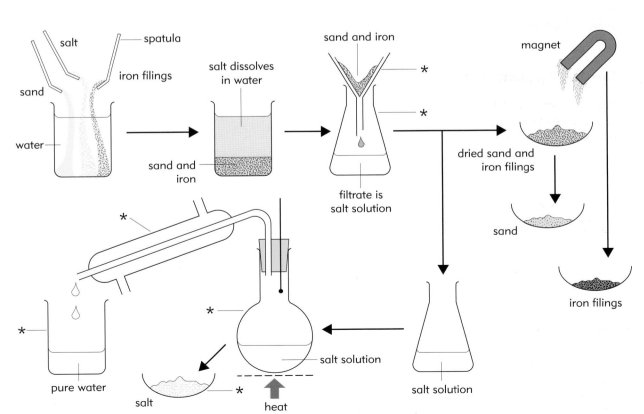

Knowing when to be careful

We have to be careful when we use some substances. This is because the substances may harm us in some way. When we use harmful substances, we need to look for warnings on the labels. The labels usually have **hazard symbols**. There are different hazard symbols for substances that harm us in different ways.

> You need to be able to handle chemicals safely throughout your Science course. Your knowledge of hazard symbols will be assessed with Patterns of chemical change.

■ Starting a fire

Some substances catch fire very easily. We call these **highly flammable** substances.

1 The label on a bottle of methylated spirits says:

Keep container tightly closed. No smoking.

Why does the label say this?

highly flammable

This symbol appears on labels for substances like methylated spirits.

■ Helping it burn more fiercely

When things burn they use up oxygen from the air. Some substances contain oxygen, which lets other materials burn even better. We say that substances like this are **oxidising** substances.

2 Sodium chlorate is a strong weedkiller. It can kill all the weeds on a garden path.

A gardener may store sodium chlorate in a garden shed near dry sacks and wood. Why is this a bad idea?

oxidising

This symbol appears on labels for substances like sodium chlorate.

■ Don't take chances with these materials

Pirate flags used to have a skull and crossbones. Pirates were dangerous and could kill you! Substances that can kill you are called **toxic** substances.

We use <u>tiny</u> amounts of chlorine to kill dangerous bacteria in our drinking water. We also use chlorine to treat the water in swimming pools. But if you breathe in a <u>lot</u> of chlorine it can kill you.

3 Why do we add a little chlorine to the water in a swimming pool?

toxic

This symbol appears on labels for substances like chlorine.

■ Still bad, but at least it won't kill you

Some substances are **harmful**, but they are not as dangerous as toxic materials.

Copper sulphate forms beautiful blue crystals, but if you swallow solid copper sulphate or some of its solution, it is harmful.

4 A student used copper sulphate to grow crystals. Why should she wash her hands before eating food?

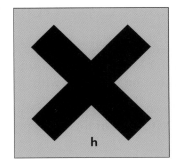
harmful

This symbol appears on labels for substances like copper sulphate.

■ There is more than one way to get burned

If you touch the inside of a hot oven you will burn yourself. There are chemicals that can destroy your skin and damage your eyes. We call these **corrosive** materials. Corrosive materials can give skin burns.

5 Sulphuric acid is used in experiments and to fill up car batteries. Why should you use safety glasses when using sulphuric acid?

corrosive

This symbol appears on labels for substances like sulphuric acid.

■ Some substances are irritants

Some substances can make your skin go red or form blisters. If the substance is a dry powder it may make you cough. We call substances like this **irritants**. They are less dangerous than corrosive materials but you must still take care.

Copper carbonate is a beautiful green colour. We can use copper carbonate to make copper metal. If you spill the green powder and breathe it in, it can make you cough. We call the powder an irritant.

irritant

This symbol appears on labels for substances like copper carbonate.

What you need to remember [Copy and complete using the **key words**]

Knowing when to be careful

Some substances have warning signs on them called

.

If a material catches fire easily it is _____ _____.

If a material helps other substances to burn by supplying oxygen, we say it is an

_____ substance.

We say that substances that can kill you are _____.

Less dangerous substances are called _____.

The skin can be destroyed or burned by _____ substances.

Substances that can redden your skin or make you cough are _____.

[You will find the completed version of this passage with Patterns of chemical change

KS3A Ideas you need from Key Stage 3

What's special about metals?

We use metals for lots of different things.
Our lives wouldn't be the same without them.

It is not always easy to tell whether something is a metal or not. We have to look at lots of its <u>properties</u>.

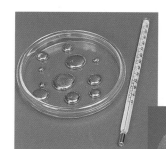

Mercury is a liquid metal.

■ Metals don't usually melt easily

Metals are usually <u>solids</u>. Only one metal is a liquid at room temperature, but we can melt all metals if we heat them enough. Metals usually have <u>high melting points</u>.

Look at the photographs and the table.

1 (a) Which metal is a liquid at room temperature?

(b) Write down <u>one</u> use for this liquid.

2 Which metal is used to make lamp filaments?

3 Which metal has a low melting point, but is a solid at room temperature (20°C)?

Temperature of filament is about 2000°C.

Metal	Melting point in °C
mercury	−39
gold	1063
iron	1535
sodium	98
tungsten	3410

■ Metals let heat and electricity pass through them

Both <u>heat</u> and <u>electricity</u> flow easily through all metals. We say that metals are good <u>conductors</u> of heat and electricity. This is a good way to tell the difference between metals and non-metals. If we know that a substance conducts electricity, then we are almost sure that it is a metal. The only non-metal that conducts electricity well is a type of carbon called graphite.

4 Is the substance in the diagram a metal?
Give a reason for your answer.

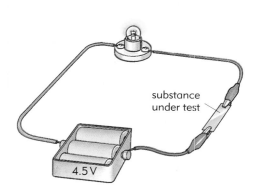

substance under test

4.5 V

■ Metals are usually strong

Most metals are <u>strong</u>. They can hold large weights without snapping.

5 Why do tall buildings have steel frameworks?

Metals can take a hammering

Metals are <u>tough</u>. They do not shatter easily. They do not crack when we hit them or squeeze them. But we can force a metal to bend into a different <u>shape</u>. This is easier if the metal is thin.

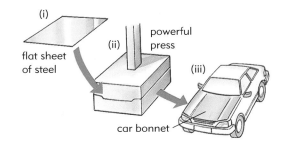

flat sheet of steel

powerful press

car bonnet

6 Look at the diagram. Why is steel useful for making car body parts?

Using the properties of metals

The pictures show how we can use the <u>properties</u> of metals.

7 Copy out each of the properties (a) to (g) listed below. Then write down the numbers of the pictures that show the property being used. You will need to write down each number more than once.

(a) Most metals are solids at room temperature.

(b) Most metals have high melting points.

(c) Most metals are tough.

(d) Most metals are strong.

(e) We can hammer metals into shape.

(f) Metals conduct heat.

(g) Metals conduct electricity.

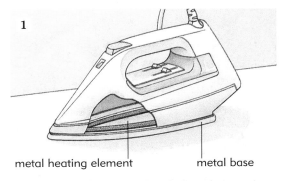

1

metal heating element   metal base

2

The steel is shaped to fit the horse's hoof.

3

The kettle is made from a metal called copper.

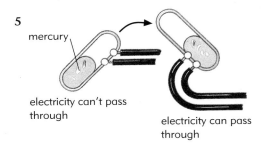

4

metal crane   metal demolition cube

5

mercury

electricity can't pass through

electricity can pass through

This switch goes on and off when you tilt it.

13

Acids, alkalis and indicators

■ Acids

All acids <u>dissolve</u> in water to give colourless and <u>corrosive</u> solutions. Strong acids will harm most living tissue and dissolve or corrode most metals and rocks.

1 Car batteries contain sulphuric acid. This is a very strong acid. Write down <u>two</u> reasons why you must take care not to spill it.

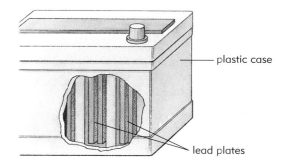

A lead–acid battery.

This warning sign tells you that a substance is corrosive.

■ Alkalis – the opposites of acids

<u>Alkalis</u> also dissolve in water to form <u>colourless</u> solutions.

Like acids, strong alkalis attack living tissue. But unlike acids, they would turn bits of you to soap.

2 Why is it important to wear safety spectacles or goggles when using alkalis?

3 What other protection do you need when using an oven cleaner?

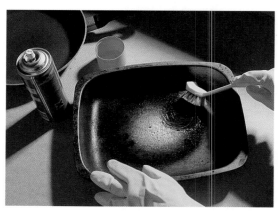

Many powerful oven cleaners contain strong alkalis.

■ Not an acid, not an alkali

Water is not an acid and not an alkali. Water is <u>neutral</u>.

When a substance dissolves in water, it makes an <u>aqueous</u> solution. Aqueous means 'watery'. We have seen that we can have aqueous solutions of acids and alkalis. Salt, sugar, alcohol and many other substances dissolve in water to give solutions that are not acidic or alkaline. They are neutral.

4 Look at the three liquids. Explain why you cannot tell which is which just by looking.

The labels have fallen off these three bottles.

Indicators

Indicators are dyes that change <u>colour</u> with acids and alkalis. They tell us whether the solution is <u>acidic</u> or <u>alkaline</u> or neutral.

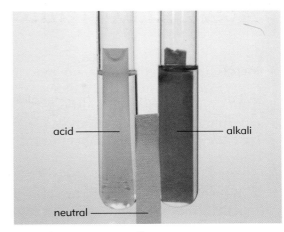

Using litmus as an indicator.

5 Copy and complete the following sentences.

Acids turn litmus _____.

Alkalis turn litmus _____.

6 What colour does litmus give with a neutral liquid like water?

How strong is my acid or alkali?

Strong acids have a pH of 0–1

Neutral solutions have a pH of 7

Strong alkalis have a maximum pH of 14

| 0 | 1 | 2 | 3 | 4 | 5 | 6 | 7 | 8 | 9 | 10 | 11 | 12 | 13 | 14 |

← increasingly acidic ——————— increasingly alkaline →

We use a scale of numbers called the <u>pH</u> scale (the 'pee-aitch' scale) to tell us how strong an acid or alkali is.

7 Make a table with these headings.

Substance	pH

Put the substances from the list into your table in order of their pH numbers. Start with the highest pH and go down to the lowest.

Substance	pH
ammonia cleaning liquid	11.5
blood	7.5
coffee	5
liquid X	7
liquid Y	8.5
liquid Z	4
orange juice	3
oven cleaner	14
stomach acid	1.5
urine	6

Universal indicator – a chemical rainbow

Universal indicator is a mixture of dyes. Each dye changes colour at a different pH so the mixture gives us different colours as we go through the pH range. We add the indicator in drops, so the chemical we test must be colourless for us to see the proper colour change.

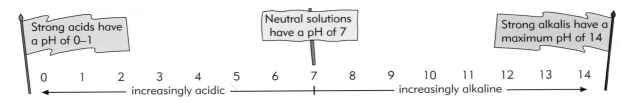

Colour	red			orange		yellow		green	blue		navy blue			purple	
pH	0	1	2	3	4	5	6	7	8	9	10	11	12	13	14

increasingly acidic ←   neutral   → increasingly alkaline

8 Show on your table, what colour each substance would turn universal indicator. (Use actual colours if you can. Otherwise use words.)

How many metals are there?

Metals, like everything else, are made of very small particles called atoms. A substance that contains just one type of atom is called an element. For example, iron is an element as it contains only iron atoms.

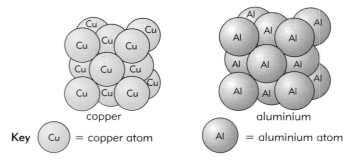

copper   aluminium

Key (Cu) = copper atom   (Al) = aluminium atom

1 Write down the names of <u>two</u> other metals that are elements.

■ How many metal elements are there?

The table shows all of the different elements we find in the natural world around us.

2 (a) How many elements are there altogether?

   (b) How many of these elements are metals?

   (c) Would you say that about a quarter, about a half or about three-quarters of the elements are metals?

A table of elements set out in this way is called the Periodic Table.

3 What do you notice about where the non-metals and metals are in this table?

H
hydrogen

Key

Group 1   Group 2

Transition Elements

Group 1	Group 2							
Li lithium	**Be** beryllium							
Na sodium	**Mg** magnesium							
K potassium	**Ca** calcium	**Sc** scandium	**Ti** titanium	**V** vanadium	**Cr** chromium	**Mn** manganese	**Fe** iron	**Co** cobalt
Rb rubidium	**Sr** strontium	**Y** yttrium	**Zr** zirconium	**Nb** niobium	**Mo** molybdenum	**Tc** technetium	**Ru** ruthenium	**Rh** rhodium
Cs caesium	**Ba** barium	*	**Hf** hafnium	**Ta** tantalum	**W** tungsten	**Re** rhenium	**Os** osmium	**Ir** iridium
Fr francium	**Ra** radium	**Ac** actinium	**Th** thorium	**Pa** protactinium	**U** uranium			

*
La lanthanum	**Ce** cerium	**Pr** praseodymium	**Nd** neodymium	**Pm** promethium	**Sm** samarium

Alloys – mixtures of metals

We don't use just the metals that are elements. We also mix metals together to get the properties we want to use. These mixtures of metals are called alloys.

Alloys are usually harder and stronger than the metals from which they are made. For example, aluminium is often alloyed with magnesium.

4 How is the aluminium alloy different from aluminium?

		Group 3	Group 4	Group 5	Group 6	Group 7	Group 0
							He helium
		B boron	**C** carbon	**N** nitrogen	**O** oxygen	**F** fluorine	**Ne** neon
		Al aluminium	**Si** silicon	**P** phosphorus	**S** sulphur	**Cl** chlorine	**Ar** argon
Cu copper	**Zn** zinc	**Ga** gallium	**Ge** germanium	**As** arsenic	**Se** selenium	**Br** bromine	**Kr** krypton
Ag silver	**Cd** cadmium	**In** indium	**Sn** tin	**Sb** antimony	**Te** tellurium	**I** iodine	**Xe** xenon
Au gold	**Hg** mercury	**Tl** thallium	**Pb** lead	**Bi** bismuth	**Po** polonium	**At** astatine	**Rn** radon

Gd gadolinium	**Tb** terbium	**Dy** dysprosium	**Ho** holmium	**Er** erbium	**Tm** thulium	**Yb** ytterbium	**Lu** lutetium

About the Periodic Table

During the nineteenth century, chemists discovered how to compare the weights of different atoms. These are called relative atomic masses.

The Periodic Table was first produced by listing the elements in order, starting with the element that had the lightest atoms.

The list of elements was then arranged in rows as shown on this page. Each column in the table contains similar elements. These columns are called **Groups**.

Note
Potassium atoms actually have a smaller relative atomic mass than argon atoms. But we still put potassium <u>after</u> argon in the Periodic Table. We do this because potassium is similar to the elements in Group 1 and argon is similar to the elements in Group 0.
[You will find more about the Periodic Table on pages 116–117 and 120–121.]

What you need to remember [Copy and complete using the **key words**]

How many metals are there?

About three-quarters of the elements are _____.
Metals are mainly in _____ 1 and 2 of the Periodic Table and in the block of elements called _____ elements.
[You should also know the information in the box about the Periodic Table.]

Making things from metals

Most of the metals that you meet in everyday life are transition elements. These metals are useful for making many things because of their **properties**.

Transition metals are good conductors of heat and electricity. All of them except **mercury** are hard, strong, tough solids that can be hammered or bent into shape. Mercury is the odd one out because it is a liquid at room temperature.

Two transition metals that we use a lot are iron and copper. Iron is usually turned into steel before we use it.

Some of the ways we use copper.

Electrical **cables.**

■ Using copper

Here are some of the facts about copper:

- ■ copper is easy to shape into pipes and wires

- ■ copper pipes and wires are easy to bend

- ■ copper is a better **conductor** of heat and electricity than most other metals

- ■ copper does not corrode as quickly as iron or steel

- ■ copper is a fairly expensive metal.

Water pipes.

1 (a) Write down <u>three</u> uses for copper everyday life.

    (b) In each case give a reason for using copper.

1p and 2p coins are made from steel coated with copper. The copper gradually goes duller and darker.

■ Using steel

We use more **steel** than any other metal. Millions of tonnes are used every year. Steel is **strong**, tough and easily shaped. It is also cheaper than most other metals. Many structures, including vehicle bodies, are made of steel.

2 Look at the picture below. Write down <u>five</u> things in the picture that are usually made from steel.

3 Why is steel used so much as a structural material?

Steel rusts quite quickly in damp air.

steel supports

steel railway lines

Using aluminium

Another metal that we use a lot of is **aluminium**. It is not a transition metal, but it is still really useful. Aluminium is a very **lightweight** metal, and it does not easily corrode. These two properties make aluminium an important metal.

But pure aluminium is weak and soft and easy to bend. This means that we can't use it for many jobs. We can mix aluminium with another light metal called magnesium. We get an alloy that is **stronger**, **harder** and **stiffer** than aluminium.

4 Write down <u>one</u> use of aluminium

  (a) that depends on aluminium being easy to bend

  (b) that depends on aluminium being lightweight

  (c) that needs an alloy of aluminium.

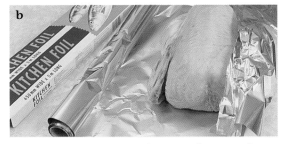

a An aeroplane made mainly from aluminium to make it lighter.

b The metal foil used in cooking has to bend easily.

c A ladder needs to be strong and stiff.

Aluminium conducts electricity

Aluminium is a very good **conductor** of electricity. It isn't quite as good as copper but it is much lighter than copper. So it is used for overhead power cables. Steel is much stronger than aluminium, but doesn't conduct electricity so well.

5 What are overhead power cables made from

  (a) on the outside?   (b) in the centre?

6 Why are the cables made like this?

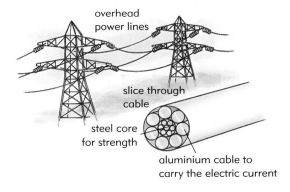

overhead power lines

slice through cable

steel core for strength

aluminium cable to carry the electric current

What you need to remember [Copy and complete using the **key words**]

Making things from metals

Many things are made from transition metals because they have all the usual _____ of metals. Copper, for example, is used to make electrical _____.
This is because it is a good _____ of electricity and is easily shaped into wires.
The most widely used structural metal is _____.
This is because it is tough, _____, cheap and is easily shaped.
(One transition metal, however, is a liquid at room temperature. This is _____.)
A widely used metal that is <u>not</u> a transition metal is _____.
It is a very _____ metal and is also a very good _____ of electricity.
Aluminium can be mixed with other metals such as magnesium.
This makes an alloy that is _____, _____ and _____ than aluminium.

The alkali metals – a chemical family

The metals lithium, sodium and potassium are all very much alike. So we say that these elements are all part of the same chemical family. We call this family the **alkali metals**.

The diagram shows part of the Periodic Table of elements.

1 The alkali metals are all in the same Group of the Periodic Table. Which Group is it?

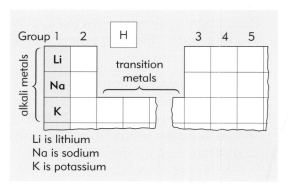

Li is lithium
Na is sodium
K is potassium

What are the alkali metals like?

Alkali metals are like other metals in many ways. There are also some differences.

2 Write down <u>two</u> ways in which alkali metals are the same as other metals.

3 Write down <u>three</u> ways in which alkali metals are different from other metals.

Alkali metals are also very **reactive**. They are so reactive that we have to store them under oil, away from the air and water. The properties of alkali metals mean that they are unsuitable to use for making things like pans, cars and bridges.

4 Write down <u>two</u> properties of alkali metals that make them unsuitable as structural materials.

Most metals are hard, but your teacher can cut alkali metals with a knife, as easily as cutting cheese.

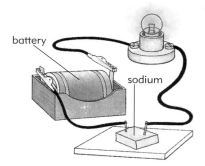

Like other metals, alkali metals conduct electricity and heat, but they melt more easily than most other metals.

Why do we call them alkali metals?

Alkali metals all react very fast with cold water. They fizz and move around on the water as they react. A gas called **hydrogen** is produced.

This is the word equation for the reaction of potassium with water:

potassium + water ⟶ hydrogen + potassium hydroxide

The potassium **hydroxide** dissolves in the water as the potassium reacts. Potassium hydroxide solution is **alkaline**.

Potassium, like lithium and sodium, is lighter (less dense) than other metals. It is so light that it floats on water. The potassium darts about as it reacts with the water, making it fizz.

The diagram shows what happens when sodium reacts with water.

The sodium moves about on top of the water, making it fizz. A colourless solution is left behind.

5 Why does the water fizz as it reacts with the sodium?

6 How do we know that the colourless solution is alkaline?

7 Sodium reacts with cold water in the same sort of way as potassium. Write a word equation for this reaction.

8 Sodium gives an alkali with water. What is the name of this alkali?

dropper containing universal indicator

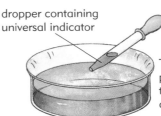

The indicator turns purple, which shows that the solution is alkaline.

All alkali metal hydroxides dissolve in water to give alkaline solutions. This is why we call these metals the alkali metals.

Do alkali metals react with other elements?

Not all of the elements are metals. Oxygen is an example of a non-metal. Some **non-metals** will react with metals to make compounds.

Hot sodium metal reacts violently with oxygen gas. This is the word equation for the reaction.

sodium + oxygen $\longrightarrow$ **sodium oxide**

The other alkali metals react with oxygen in the same way.

9 Write down the word equation for the reaction between lithium and oxygen.

Alkali metals also react with the family of non-metal elements called the halogens in Group 7 of the Periodic Table.

oxygen gas

hot sodium metal

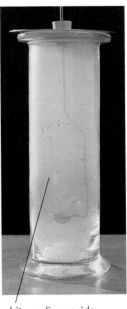

white sodium oxide fumes fill the jar

What you need to remember [Copy and complete using the **key words**]

The alkali metals – a chemical family

The elements in Group 1 are called the _____ _____.
We need to keep them under oil because they are very _____.
Alkali metals react with water to produce _____ gas.
A colourless solution of the alkali metal _____ is also produced.
An indicator shows that the solution is _____.
Alkali metals react with some _____, such as oxygen.
For example: sodium + oxygen $\longrightarrow$ _____ _____

21

Colours and catalysts

■ Looking at transition metal compounds

Like alkali metals, nearly all of the transition metals will react with non-metal elements to form compounds.

For example, they react with oxygen to form oxides and with chlorine to form chlorides. The diagram shows some alkali metal compounds and some transition metal compounds.

1 Write down the differences that you notice between alkali metal compounds and transition metal compounds.

Alkali metal compounds

lithium oxide	**colourless** solution
sodium oxide	colourless solution
potassium oxide	colourless solution
lithium chloride	colourless solution
sodium chloride	colourless solution
potassium chloride	colourless solution

Transition metal compounds

copper oxide	does not dissolve
iron oxide	does not dissolve
lead oxide (2 forms)	does not dissolve
zinc oxide (cold / hot)	does not dissolve
copper chloride	coloured **solution**
cobalt chloride (on paper) (dry / wet)	

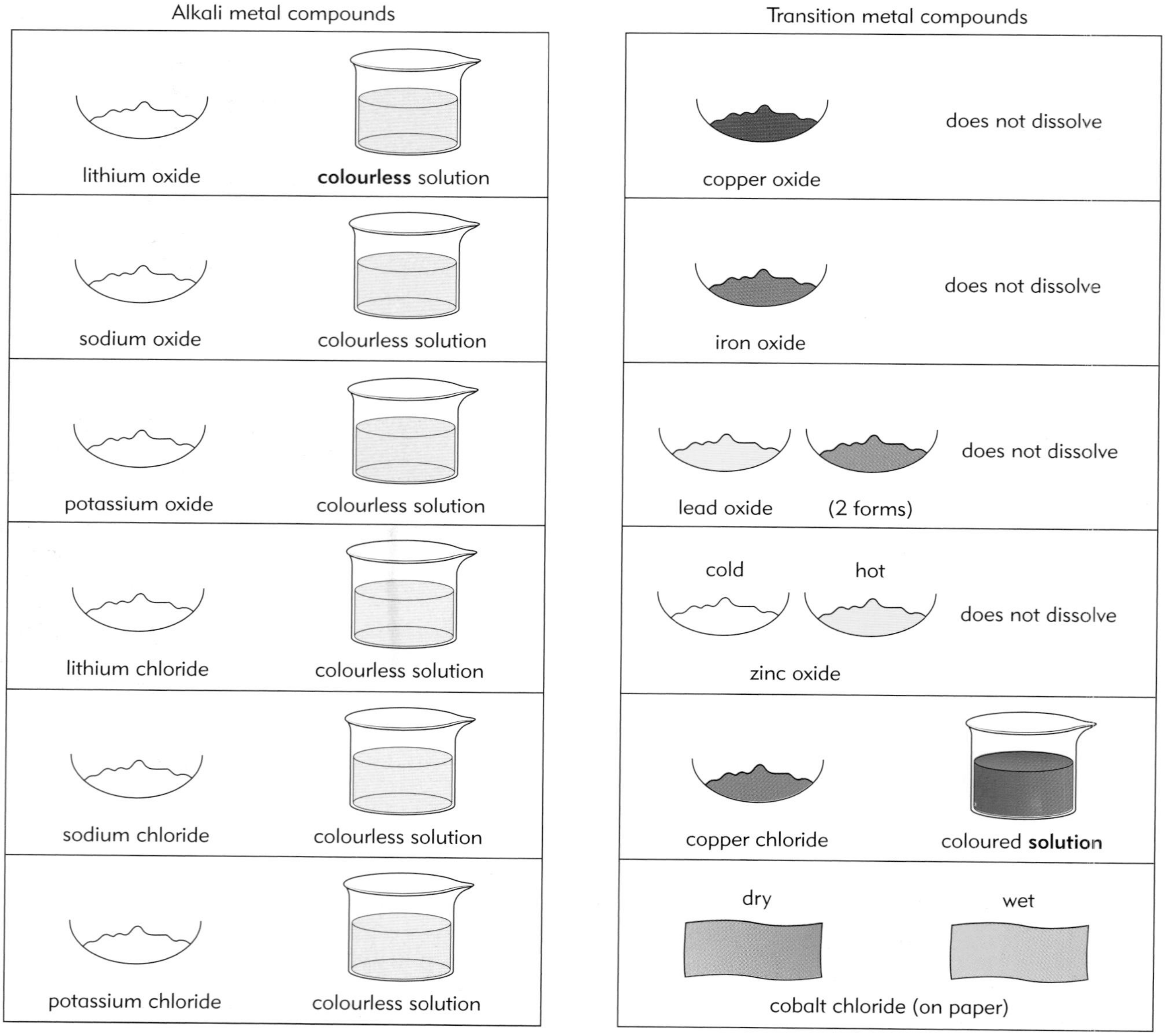

Using transition metal compounds

Because they are **coloured**, we use transition metal compounds to colour glass. We also use them to produce coloured **glazes** on pottery.

When copper is used on the roof of a building it eventually goes green. This happens because of the copper compounds produced when copper reacts with substances in the air.

This glass is coloured using cobalt oxide.

2 Copy the table. Then use information from the photographs to complete it.

Transition metal compound	Colour(s)	Where the colour is used

The copper compound that gives this roof its green colour is called verdigris.

3 A particular metal oxide doesn't always give a the same colour in a pottery glaze. Explain why.

iron oxide glaze

copper oxide glaze

cobalt oxide glaze

The colours that you get with pottery glaze vary a lot. They are affected by other chemicals in the glaze and by the conditions in the kiln when they are fired.

Another use for transition metals

Some transition metals can also be used to speed up chemical reactions. Substances that are used in this way are called **catalysts**.

The Haber process for making ammonia from nitrogen and hydrogen uses an iron catalyst. To make nitric acid the ammonia is first reacted with oxygen using a platinum catalyst.

4 Copy the table, then complete it.

Catalyst	One reaction that is speeded up
iron	
	the reaction between ammonia and oxygen

What you need to remember [Copy and complete using the **key words**]

Colours and catalysts

Most transition metal compounds are _____.

If a transition metal compound dissolves in water it forms a coloured _____.

Alkali metal compounds are white. They dissolve to form _____ solutions.

Transition metal oxides are used to make coloured glass and pottery _____.

Some transition metals are used as _____. They speed up chemical reactions.

Making salts of alkali metals

Alkali metals react with water to produce alkaline solutions.
If you add acid to these alkaline solutions, you can make new compounds.
These compounds are called salts.

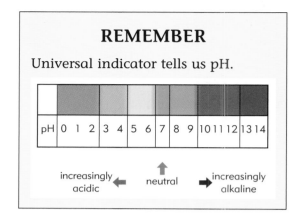

REMEMBER

Universal indicator tells us pH.

pH	0 1 2 3 4 5 6 7 8 9 10 11 12 13 14

increasingly acidic ← neutral → increasingly alkaline

Adding acid to alkali

The diagrams show what happens as you add more and more <u>acid</u> to an <u>alkali</u>.

1 What colour is the indicator in diagram B?

2 Is the solution in the flask in diagram B acidic, alkaline or neutral?

If you add just the right amount of acid to an alkali you get a solution that is neutral. We say that the acid and alkali **neutralise** each other. We call the reaction between an acid and an alkali **neutralisation**.

3 The solution in diagram C is acidic.
Explain why, as fully as you can.

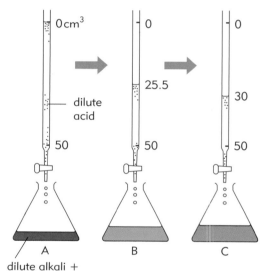

dilute alkali + universal indicator

A B C

What happens to the acid and the alkali during neutralisation?

When you mix some acid with just the right amount of alkali you get a neutral solution. But all the particles from the acid and alkali are still there. They have reacted to make new substances. The diagram shows how you can obtain some of the new substance made in a neutralisation reaction. The reaction also produces more water.

4 Copy and complete the word equation for this reaction.

$$\text{sodium hydroxide} + \text{hydrochloric acid} \longrightarrow \underline{\hspace{2cm}} + \underline{\hspace{2cm}}$$

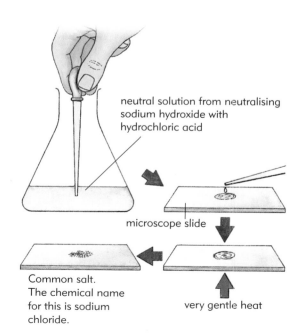

neutral solution from neutralising sodium hydroxide with hydrochloric acid

microscope slide

Common salt.
The chemical name for this is sodium chloride.

very gentle heat

Different kinds of salt

Sodium chloride is the salt you put on your food. But it isn't the only kind of salt. Whenever you neutralise any acid with any alkali you get a **salt** and **water**.

5 Look at the photograph. Write down the names of <u>two</u> different kinds of salt besides common salt.

Some salts.

How do you know which salt you have made?

When you neutralise **hydrochloric** acid, the salt you make is always a chloride. The salt takes the first part of its name from the metal in the alkali you use.
So neutralising **sodium** hydroxide with hydrochloric acid gives you sodium chloride.

6 What salt do you get if you neutralise potassium hydroxide with hydrochloric acid?

The salts of **nitric** acid are nitrates.
The salts of **sulphuric** acid are sulphates.

7 Copy and complete the word equations.

(a) potassium hydroxide + sulphuric acid ⟶ _____ + water

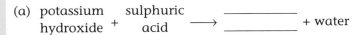

(b) _____ hydroxide + _____ acid ⟶ sodium nitrate + water

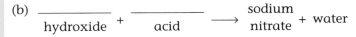

8 The diagrams show how to make potassium chloride.

(a) Why is litmus added to the acid?

(b) Why is the neutral solution boiled with charcoal and then filtered?

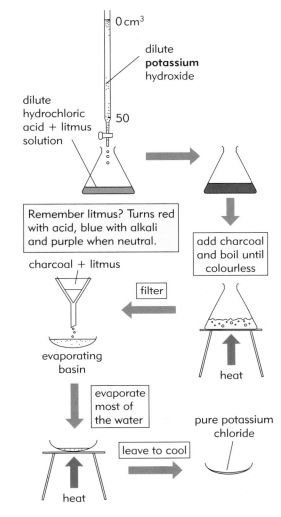

What you need to remember [Copy and complete using the **key words**]

Making salts of alkali metals

Acid + alkali ⟶ _____ + _____
The acid and alkali _____ each other. This is called a _____ reaction.
To make: ▪ a sodium salt you neutralise _____ hydroxide with an acid
▪ a potassium salt you neutralise _____ hydroxide with an acid
▪ a chloride you neutralise _____ acid with an alkali
▪ a nitrate you neutralise _____ acid with an alkali
▪ a sulphate you neutralise _____ acid with an alkali.

These ideas are extended, for Higher Tier students, in Metals H1 on page 47.

Making salts of transition metals

Transition metal oxides and hydroxides do not dissolve in water. They are **insoluble** in water. So they can't be used to make alkaline solutions.

This means that you can't use acid + alkali reactions to make salts of transition metals.

> ### REMEMBER
>
> You can make an alkali metal salt using a neutralisation reaction:
>
> acid + alkali $\longrightarrow$ salt + water
>
> You can use an indicator to tell when an acid and an alkali have neutralised each other.

■ How can you make transition metal salts?

Even though they do not dissolve in water, transition metal oxides (or hydroxides) can still neutralise acids to make **salts**.

The diagram shows a reaction of this kind.

1 Why can copper oxide not be used to make an alkaline solution?

2 How do you know that the copper oxide reacts with the hydrochloric acid?

3 Why do you think that the mixture of copper oxide and hydrochloric acid is heated and stirred?

4 What <u>two</u> new substances are produced in the reaction between copper oxide and hydrochloric acid?

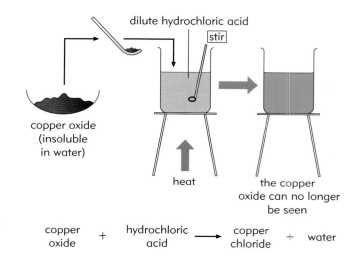

copper oxide
(insoluble
in water)

the copper
oxide can no longer
be seen

copper oxide + hydrochloric acid $\longrightarrow$ copper chloride + water

■ A new name for anti-acids

All substances that react with acids to produce a salt and water are called **bases**.

So we can say:

acid + base $\longrightarrow$ salt + water

Alkalis are bases that dissolve in water. They are **soluble** bases.

5 The diagram shows another reaction between an acid and a base.

Write down a word equation for this reaction.

> ### REMEMBER
>
> Neutralising hydrochloric acid $\longrightarrow$ a chloride
> Neutralising nitric acid $\longrightarrow$ a nitrate
> Neutralising sulphuric acid $\longrightarrow$ a sulphate

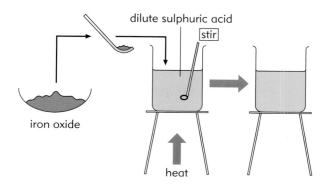

iron oxide

How can we tell when all the acid has been neutralised?

When we neutralise an acid with an alkali, we use an indicator. This tells us when all the acid has been neutralised so that we add just the right amount of alkali.

When we neutralise an acid with an insoluble base, we don't need an indicator. The diagrams explain why.

6 (a) How do you know when all the acid has been neutralised?

(b) What do you then do to separate the salt solution from any insoluble metal oxide that is left over?

(c) How can you get <u>solid</u> salt from the salt solution?

(d) What is the name of the salt produced from the acid and base used in the reaction shown in the diagrams?

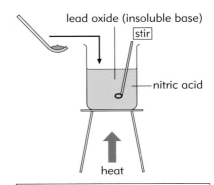

lead oxide (insoluble base)

stir

nitric acid

heat

Keep adding the insoluble base until no more will **react**, this tells you that all of the acid has been neutralised.

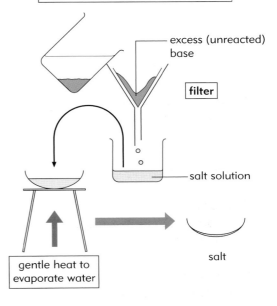

excess (unreacted) base

filter

salt solution

gentle heat to evaporate water

salt

Alkalis and salts that don't contain metals

Ammonia is a gas made from nitrogen and hydrogen. It dissolves in water to produce an alkaline solution called ammonium **hydroxide**.

ammonia + water ⟶ ammonium hydroxide
  (gas)   (liquid)   (solution)

Ammonium hydroxide can be used to neutralise an acid and produce an **ammonium** salt.

7 The box shows how you can make ammonium chloride.

Write down a word equation to show how you can make ammonium nitrate.

ammonium hydroxide + hydrochloric acid ⟶ ammonium chloride + water

---

What you need to remember [Copy and complete using the **key words**]

Making transition metal salts

Transition metal oxides and hydroxides are _____ in water so they cannot produce alkaline solutions. But they can still neutralise acids to produce _____ and water. All substances which can do this are called _____. Alkalis are _____ bases. To make sure that all of an acid has been neutralised, you must keep on adding an insoluble base until no more will _____.

You can then _____ off any unreacted base.

Ammonia dissolves in water to produce an alkaline solution of ammonium _____.

This will neutralise acids to produce _____ salts.

Comparing the reactivities of metals

■ Burning metals

Many metals burn. But some metals burn more easily than others.

Magnesium burns quickly in the oxygen in the air with a brilliant white flame. The picture shows how we can use this white light.

1 Copy and complete the word equation for the reaction.

magnesium + _____ ⟶ magnesium oxide + energy

2 When you burn magnesium, a white powder is left behind. What is it?

Zinc doesn't burn as easily as magnesium.
The photographs show how you can make it burn.

We can heat up iron filings in the same way as the zinc powder and put them into oxygen. They may glow red-hot and produce a few sparks. Iron oxide powder is produced. Iron burns much less easily than zinc.

If we do the same thing with copper powder there is very little reaction. It just glows a little. Afterwards we see that the surface of the copper has changed from brown to black copper oxide.

■ Putting the metals into order

Magnesium burns easily. We say that it is very <u>reactive</u>.
Zinc does not react so easily with oxygen.
It is less reactive than magnesium.

3 Write down the metals copper, iron, magnesium and zinc in order. Start with the most reactive and end with the least reactive.

A list of metals in order of their reactivity is called a <u>reactivity series</u>.

Magnesium is used in flares.

zinc powder

zinc oxide is produced

oxygen

Making zinc oxide.

most reactive

metal A

metal B

metal C

metal D

least reactive

How to make a reactivity series.

Reacting metals with water

The diagrams show calcium and magnesium reacting with water.

4 Which metal reacts faster with water?

If you put some zinc into cold water you cannot see any reaction.

The reaction between sodium and water is so fast that it is dangerous. Potassium reacts even more quickly with water. (See page 114.)

5 Using the information above, add calcium, sodium and potassium to your reactivity series.

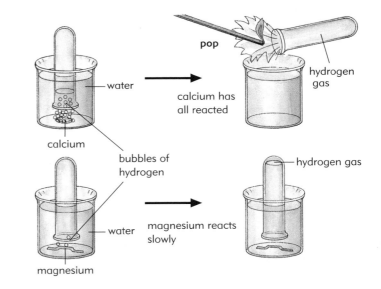

Reacting metals with dilute acids

The diagrams show how four different metals react with dilute acid. The metals are all in powder form.

Silver is less reactive than copper and gold is less reactive still.

6 Using the above information, add silver and gold to your reactivity series.

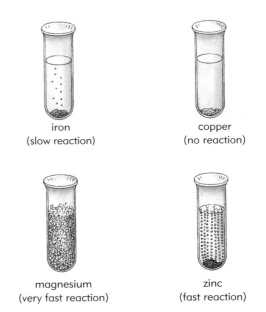

iron
(slow reaction)

copper
(no reaction)

magnesium
(very fast reaction)

zinc
(fast reaction)

Word equations

Instead of describing a chemical reaction in sentences, you can use a word equation.

Here is the word equation for the reaction between magnesium and hydrochloric acid.

magnesium + hydrochloric acid ⟶ magnesium chloride + hydrogen

Another way of writing chemical equations

Instead of writing the names of all the elements in chemical compounds we can use their <u>symbols</u>. We then get a <u>symbol equation</u>. For example:

$$Mg(s) \quad + \quad 2HCl(aq) \quad \longrightarrow \quad MgCl_2(aq) \quad + \quad H_2(g)$$

| magnesium (a <u>s</u>olid) | hydrochloric acid (<u>a</u>queous – this means dissolved in water) | magnesium chloride (<u>a</u>queous) | hydrogen (a gas) |

[Don't worry, for the present, about what the numbers mean.]

Competing metals

The photographs show what happens when you put an iron nail into copper sulphate solution.

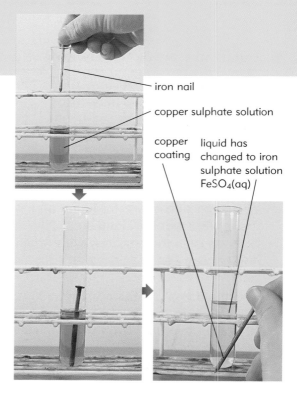

iron nail

copper sulphate solution

copper coating | liquid has changed to iron sulphate solution FeSO₄(aq)

magnesium   copper   no change

1 Copy and complete the following sentences.

The iron nail becomes coated with _____.
The liquid changes colour from _____
to _____.
The liquid has changed from _____ sulphate
solution to _____ sulphate solution.

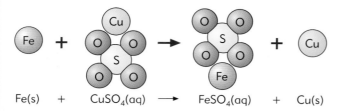

$$Fe(s) \quad + \quad CuSO_4(aq) \longrightarrow FeSO_4(aq) \quad + \quad Cu(s)$$

2 Write down a word equation for this reaction.

Iron is more <u>reactive</u> than copper. The iron pushes the copper out of the copper sulphate solution.
We say that the iron has displaced the copper.

■ Which metals compete best?

A more reactive metal usually **displaces** a **less** reactive metal from a solution of one of its compounds.

3 Look at the photographs.
Which is the more reactive metal?

4 We say that the magnesium _____ the copper from the copper sulphate.

5 Write a word equation to describe this reaction.

■ Using the reactivity series

You can use the reactivity series to predict whether a displacement reaction will happen.

6 Copy the table. Use the short reactivity series to decide whether a displacement reaction will happen. Fill in the missing ticks and crosses.

Put a tick if you think a reaction will happen and a cross if you think it won't.

copper sulphate | magnesium sulphate | now magnesium sulphate solution

most reactive

magnesium   Mg
iron   Fe
copper   Cu

least reactive

	Magnesium sulphate solution	Iron sulphate solution	Copper sulphate solution
Mg			✓
Fe			✓
Cu	✗		

Pushing a metal out of its solid compound

Aluminium is more reactive than iron. So if you heat up aluminium powder with iron oxide there is a reaction.

$$2Al(s) + Fe_2O_3(s) \longrightarrow Al_2O_3(s) + 2Fe(l) + energy$$
[l = liquid]

7 Write a word equation for this reaction.

When the reaction starts, it makes so much heat that the iron is melted. The photograph shows this reaction being used to weld together railway lines. The welders build a small mould around the gap between the railway lines. The molten iron runs down into the gap and welds the two sections together.

8 The welders who carry out this reaction stand back at a distance from the reaction and wear thick heatproof gloves. Why is this?

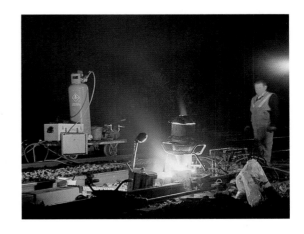

The reactivity series for metals.

most reactive

potassium	K
sodium	Na
calcium	Ca
magnesium	Mg
aluminium	Al
carbon	C (a non-metal)
zinc	Zn
iron	Fe
tin	Sn
lead	Pb
hydrogen	H (a non-metal)
copper	Cu
silver	Ag
gold	Au
platinum	Pt

least reactive

A non-metal that can push out metals

Carbon isn't a metal, but if we heat it up, it can displace some metals from their oxides. Some metals can also be displaced from their heated oxides by passing hydrogen over them.

Even though carbon and hydrogen are not metals, they will displace some metals from their oxides. So we can put them into the **reactivity** series of metals. Carbon and hydrogen will only displace metals that are below them in the reactivity series.

9 Will carbon displace:

(a) aluminium from aluminium oxide?
(b) iron from iron oxide?
(c) copper from copper oxide?

10 Which of the metals in question 9 will hydrogen displace from its oxide?

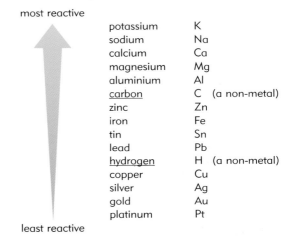
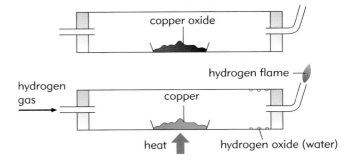

Using hydrogen to displace a metal.

What you need to remember [Copy and complete using the **key words**]

Competing metals

A more reactive metal will push a _____ reactive metal out of its compounds. We say that it _____ the less reactive metal.

We can also put carbon and hydrogen into the _____ series because they can displace a metal less reactive than themselves from a metal oxide.

8 Where do metals come from?

■ Where do we find metals?

We find metals mixed with rocks in the Earth's **crust**. We find gold in the Earth's crust as the metal itself. The pieces of gold in rocks contain just gold and nothing else. You can collect lots of small pieces of gold, heat them until they melt and then pour the molten gold into a mould. The gold sets hard as it cools. Gold is a very rare metal. Many other metals are much more common than gold.

1 Which are the <u>two</u> most common metals in the Earth's crust?

2 Why don't we show gold in the pie chart?

We find most metals, including iron and aluminium, as metal **ores**. In the ore, the metal is joined with other **elements**. Metals are often joined with oxygen in compounds we call metal **oxides**. For example, most iron ores contain iron oxide. Metals may also be joined with sulphur in compounds we call metal sulphides.

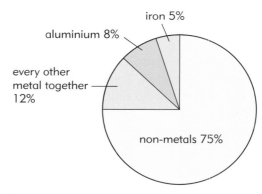

Elements in the Earth's crust. Gold makes up only three parts in every billion (thousand million) parts of the Earth's crust.

Iron ore often contains haematite, a type of iron oxide.

haematite

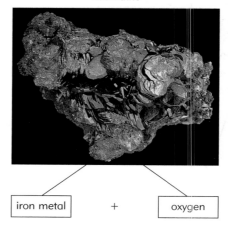

| iron metal | + | oxygen |

■ Looking at ores

The photograph shows a common iron ore.

3 (a) What is the name of this iron ore?

(b) There are <u>two</u> elements in the ore, what are they?

Look at the photographs showing two other metal ores.

4 Copy the headings and then complete the table.

Name of the ore	Metal in the ore	Other elements in the ore

Malachite is copper carbonate.

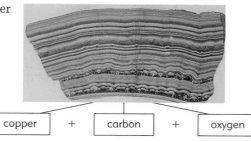

| copper | + | carbon | + | oxygen |

Galena is lead sulphide.

| lead | + | sulphur |

How much metal is there in metal ores?

Metal ores contain rock as well as the valuable metal compounds. Different ores contain different amounts of rock.

5 How much metal compound is there in 100 g of each of the ores shown? An ore that only contains a small amount of metal may still be worth mining if the metal is valuable enough.

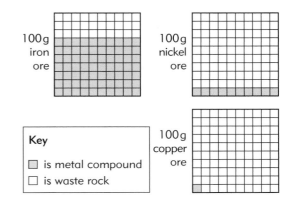

Key

☐ is metal compound
☐ is waste rock

How can we extract metals from their ores?

To get pure metals from ores you must split up the metal compound in the ore. You can release, or extract, some metals by heating the metal oxide with **carbon**. We can extract copper by heating copper oxide with charcoal, a form of carbon. The charcoal reacts with the oxygen in the copper oxide. This leaves copper metal.

6 (a) What other substance is produced?

(b) Write a word equation for this reaction.

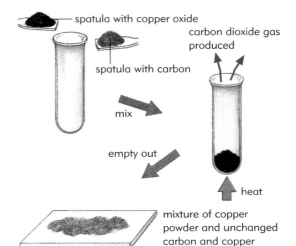

spatula with copper oxide

carbon dioxide gas produced

spatula with carbon

mix

empty out

heat

mixture of copper powder and unchanged carbon and copper oxide

Removing oxygen from a metal oxide is called **reduction**. So carbon has reduced the copper oxide. Reducing iron oxide with carbon needs a much higher temperature than for copper. Aluminium oxide cannot be split using carbon. Aluminium oxide can be reduced to aluminium metal only by using **electricity**.

7 Use the reactivity series to explain why:

(a) You can't reduce aluminium oxide using carbon.

(b) Gold is found as the metal itself in the Earth's crust.

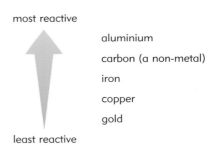

most reactive

aluminium
carbon (a non-metal)
iron
copper
gold

least reactive

What you need to remember [Copy and complete using the **key words**]

Where do metals come from?

Metals are found in the Earth's _____.

Most metals, except gold, are found joined with other _____ as compounds.

Compounds of metals and oxygen are called _____.

Rocks containing metal compounds are called _____.

Copper and iron are extracted from their oxides by heating them with _____.

Removing the oxygen from a metal oxide is called _____.

Aluminium oxide can only be reduced using _____.

How do we get all the steel we use?

Steel is a strong and tough material. It is also cheap to make. Steel is mostly iron, so to make steel, we must first extract iron from iron ore. The commonest iron ore is called **haematite**.

■ How can you get iron from iron ore?

We extract iron from iron ore in a **blast** furnace.

1 Look at the diagram of the blast furnace.

(a) Write down the <u>three</u> things that go into the top of the blast furnace.

(b) What goes into the blast furnace near to the bottom?

■ Why is coke needed in the blast furnace?

First the **coke** reacts with oxygen from the **air** to make carbon **dioxide** gas. This reaction releases lots of heat.

$$C(s) + O_2(g) \longrightarrow CO_2(g) + energy$$

2 Write down a word equation for this reaction.

Next the carbon dioxide reacts with hot coke to give carbon **monoxide** gas.

$$CO_2(g) + C(s) \longrightarrow 2CO(g)$$

3 Write down a word equation for this reaction.

4 What are the <u>two</u> different jobs that coke does inside the blast furnace?

The carbon monoxide removes oxygen from the haematite (iron oxide) to give iron metal. Carbon **dioxide** gas is also made at the same time.

carbon + iron → iron + carbon
monoxide oxide   dioxide

The iron in the iron oxide <u>loses</u> oxygen.
So we say that it is **reduced**.
The carbon in the carbon monoxide <u>gains</u> oxygen.
So we say that it is **oxidised**.

> **REMEMBER**
>
> Carbon is more **reactive** than iron.
>
> most reactive
>
> aluminium
>
> carbon
>
> zinc
>
> iron
>
> least reactive
>
> So carbon can be used to reduce iron oxide.

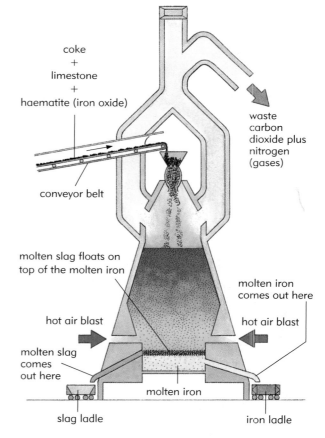

A blast furnace

What happens to the air that is blasted into the furnace?

The hot air that is blasted into the furnace contains both oxygen and nitrogen gases. Nitrogen is not a reactive gas, so it goes through the furnace without changing. The oxygen from the air ends up in carbon dioxide.

5 What are the <u>two</u> main gases in the waste that comes out of the top of the furnace?

Iron has to be poured into a mould when molten to make the shape we want.

Why is limestone needed in the blast furnace?

Iron ore contains solid waste, such as sand, as well as the useful iron oxide. This waste would make the iron weak so it must be removed. **Limestone** reacts with the solid waste to produce **slag**. The blast furnace is so hot that both the iron and slag **melt** and trickle down to the base where they collect.

6 How are the molten iron and slag removed from the base of the furnace?

7 Why is it easy to keep the iron separate from the slag?

8 Iron made in the blast furnace is often turned into steel. Why do you think that mild steel is a more useful material than iron from the blast furnace?

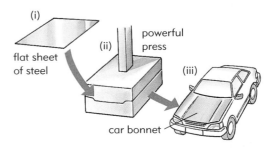

Steel can be rolled into thin sheets then pressed into the shapes we want.

Material	% carbon	Properties
iron from the blast furnace	4.0	brittle
mild steel	0.4	tough

What you need to remember [Copy and complete using the **key words**]

How do we get all the steel we use?

Iron is extracted from iron ore in a _____ furnace. The ore is called _____.
The high temperature needed is produced by burning _____ in the hot _____
that is blasted into the furnace. This makes carbon _____ gas.
The carbon dioxide then reacts with more carbon to make carbon _____ gas.
Carbon is more _____ than iron, so carbon monoxide takes the oxygen from iron
oxide. This gives the metal iron and a gas called carbon _____.
The iron oxide has been _____. The carbon monoxide has been _____.
Solid waste materials in the iron ore react with _____ to make _____.
The furnace is so hot that the iron and slag both _____ and run down to the
base of the furnace.

These ideas are extended, for Higher Tier students, in Metals H2 on pages 48–49.

Using electricity to split up metal compounds

We can get some metals from their ores by heating them with carbon.

Another way to get metals from their compounds is to pass **electricity** through the compound.

1 What is the problem with trying to pass electricity through metal compounds?

To make a metal compound conduct electricity we must either **melt** it or **dissolve** it.

> **REMEMBER**
>
> Solid metals let electricity pass through them.
>
> Solid metal <u>compounds</u> such as metal ores do not conduct electricity.

■ Getting copper from copper chloride

Copper chloride is a metal compound that dissolves in water. The diagram shows what happens when an electric current passes through copper chloride solution.

2 Copy and complete the word equation for this reaction.

copper chloride $\xrightarrow{\text{electricity}}$ _____ + _____

3 Copy and complete the following sentences.

Copper is produced at the _____ electrode.

Chlorine gas is produced at the _____ electrode.

The electricity has split up the copper chloride. We say that the copper chloride has been **decomposed**.

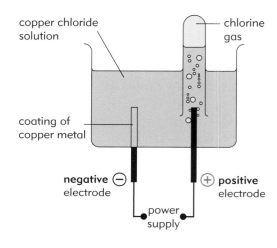

$$CuCl_2(aq) \xrightarrow{\text{electricity}} Cu(s) + Cl_2(g)$$

■ Getting lead from lead bromide

Lead bromide is another metal compound, but it does not dissolve in water. To make electricity pass through lead bromide you must first melt it.

The diagram shows what happens when you melt lead bromide and pass an electric current through it.

4 Write down a word equation for this reaction.

Splitting up a compound by passing an electric current through it, is called **electrolysis**.

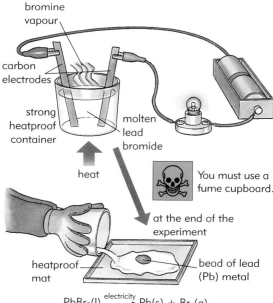

$$PbBr_2(l) \xrightarrow{\text{electricity}} Pb(s) + Br_2(g)$$

How does electrolysis work?

In copper chloride solution:

- the copper atoms have a positive (+) charge
- the chlorine atoms have a negative (−) charge.

Electrically charged atoms are called **ions**.
When we dissolve solid copper chloride in water, the ions can **move** about.

Look at the diagrams.

5 Copy and complete the following sentences.

The copper ions have a _____ charge.

They move to the _____ electrode.

The chloride ions have a _____ charge.

They move to the _____ electrode.

This shows that opposite charges _____.

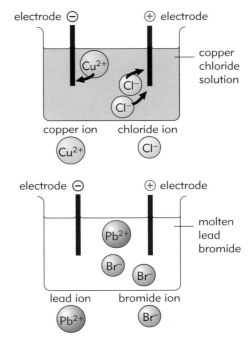

The ions move to the electrode with the opposite charge. Opposite charges attract.

Lead bromide is made of charged ions. We call it an ionic compound. When we melt solid lead bromide, the ions can then move about.

6 Copy the diagram showing lead bromide. Mark on the diagram the way that the ions move during electrolysis.

Metal compounds are ionic. Look at the table of ions.

7 Copy and complete the following sentence.

During electrolysis metals are always formed at the _____ electrode.

Metal ions	Non-metal ions
sodium Na^+	chloride Cl^-
copper Cu^{2+}	bromide Br^-
lead Pb^{2+}	oxide O^{2-}
aluminium Al^{3+}	

Metal ions always have a positive charge.

What you need to remember [Copy and complete using the **key words**]

Using electricity to split up metal compounds

Electrically charged atoms are called _____.
You can split up a metal compound by passing _____ through it.
You can do this only if you _____ the compound by heating it, or
_____ the compound in water.
This means that the ions in the compound can _____ about.
Using electricity to split up a compound is called _____.
We say that the compound has been _____.
The metal ions in a compound have a _____ charge.
During electrolysis, the metal ions always move towards the _____ electrode.

These ideas are extended, for Higher Tier students, in Metals H2 on pages 48–49.

11 How do we get all the aluminium we need?

Aluminium is the most common metal in the Earth's crust. But you never find pieces of natural aluminium. This is because aluminium is a very reactive metal. Aluminium combines with other elements to form compounds.

Look at the photograph.

1 What is the name of natural aluminium ore?

2 Which aluminium compound do you find in aluminium ore?

3 Clay is very common and contains plenty of aluminium compounds. So why don't we extract aluminium from clay?

■ How do we get aluminium from its ore?

We use carbon to extract iron from iron oxide, but we cannot use carbon to extract aluminium from aluminium **oxide**. It doesn't work.

Look at the reactivity series.

4 Why can't carbon push aluminium out of aluminium oxide?

We must extract aluminium in a different way. We need to use electricity to extract aluminium from its oxide. We must make the aluminium ore conduct electricity to do this.

■ How to make aluminium oxide conduct electricity

Aluminium oxide does not dissolve in water to give a solution, so to make it conduct we have to **melt** it.

Look at the diagrams.

5 What is the problem with melting aluminium oxide?

6 How can we solve the problem?

When we have melted aluminium oxide we can use electricity to split it up. This is called electrolysis.

REMEMBER

Solid metal compounds will not conduct electricity. We have to melt them or dissolve them in water.

We get aluminium from an iron ore called **bauxite**. Bauxite is mainly aluminium oxide.

| aluminium | + | oxygen |

A lot of aluminium in the Earth's crust is in clay. It is very hard to get the aluminium from the clay.

most reactive

aluminium

carbon

zinc

iron

least reactive

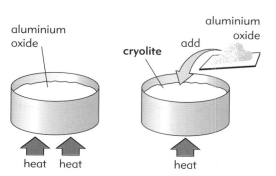

To melt the aluminium oxide you need to heat it to a high temperature, more than 2000 °C. This is much hotter than a Bunsen burner flame.

A mixture of cryolite and aluminium oxide melts at a lower temperature of 950 °C.

Using electrolysis to split up aluminium oxide

The diagram shows how aluminium is made from melted aluminium oxide.

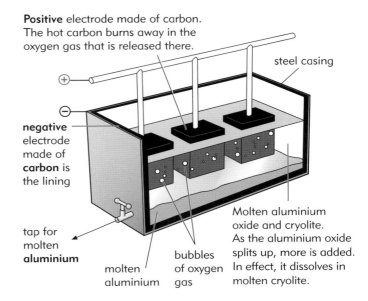

Positive electrode made of carbon. The hot carbon burns away in the oxygen gas that is released there.

steel casing

negative electrode made of carbon is the lining

tap for molten aluminium

molten aluminium

bubbles of oxygen gas

Molten aluminium oxide and cryolite. As the aluminium oxide splits up, more is added. In effect, it dissolves in molten cryolite.

7 (a) What <u>two</u> materials does aluminium oxide give when it splits up?

(b) Write down where each of these materials is formed.

8 (a) What do we use to make the electrodes?

(b) The positive electrode burns away and we must replace it with a new one. Write down why it burns away.

Why does electrolysis work?

In aluminium oxide both the aluminium and the oxygen have electrical charges. We call them aluminium ions and oxide ions. If you melt aluminium oxide, the ions can move about in the liquid.

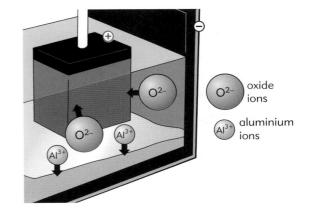

O^{2-} oxide ions

Al^{3+} aluminium ions

9 Copy and complete the following sentences.

Aluminium ions have a _____ charge.

They move to the _____ electrode.

Oxide ions have a _____ charge.

They move to the _____ electrode.

What you need to remember [Copy and complete using the **key words**]

How do we get all the aluminium we need?

We can extract aluminium from an ore called _____.
This contains the compound aluminium _____.
To pass electricity through aluminium oxide we need to _____ it.
This only happens at a very high temperature.
So that we can use a lower temperature, the aluminium oxide is added to molten _____.
The electrodes are made of _____.
Since the temperature is high and oxygen is given off, the _____ electrode burns away. Aluminium is produced at the _____ electrode.
Molten _____ collects at the base.

These ideas are extended, for Higher Tier students, in Metals H2 on pages 48–49.

Which ores should we mine?

Many rocks contain metals, usually in the form of metal **compounds**. But most rocks are no use as ores. If a rock does not contain enough metal it costs too much to extract the metal. We say that it is **uneconomic** to use the rock as an **ore**.

1 Look at the information on the bar charts.

Then copy and complete the table.

Metal	What 1 kg of the metal is worth	Amount of metal in ore worth using
lead		
copper		
gold		

The more **valuable** a metal is, the less there needs to be in rocks to make them worth using as ores.

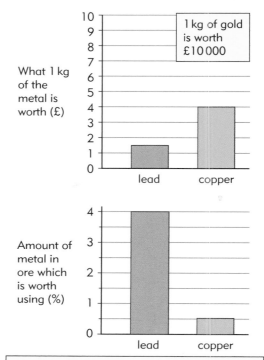

What 1 kg of the metal is worth (£)

1 kg of gold is worth £10 000

Amount of metal in ore which is worth using (%)

Gold is worth mining even if there are only 10 parts in every million. This is about the same amount as 2 wedding rings in a truck-load of rock.

■ Concentrating the metal compounds in ores

Some ores contain only a small amount of metal compound. This needs to be separated from the rest of the rock before the metal can be extracted from it. The diagram shows one way of doing this.

2 Copy and complete the following sentences.

A crusher breaks the ore up into bits of _____ and bits of _____ _____.

The crushed ore is then churned up with _____, _____ and _____.

The bits of metal compound are carried away mainly by the _____.

The bits of waste rock are carried away mainly by the _____.

The metal can then be extracted from the **concentrated** ore.

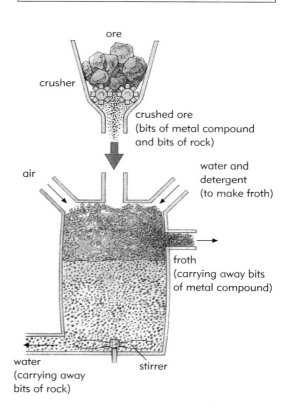

ore

crusher

crushed ore (bits of metal compound and bits of rock)

air

water and detergent (to make froth)

froth (carrying away bits of metal compound)

water (carrying away bits of rock)

stirrer

■ Metals and the environment

Iron ore mine in Australia.

Gold mine in Brazil.

Mining metals and metal ores can make huge holes in the Earth's crust.

Huge heaps of waste rock may be left behind. Wastes still contain metal compounds. These can pollute streams and harm living things.

Without metals, our lives would be very different. There would be no cars, televisions, fridges and many other things. There wouldn't be any electricity either.

But producing these useful metals also causes problems.

Metal compounds are often heated with carbon to extract the metal. This can pollute the air.

3 Write down:

(a) <u>three</u> problems that mining metal ores can cause;

(b) <u>one</u> problem that extracting metals from their ores can cause.

What you need to remember [Copy and complete using the **key words**]

Which ores should we mine?

Many rocks contain metal, usually in the form of metal _____.

If a rock contains enough metal it can be used as an _____.

If a rock contains too little metal, it is _____ to extract the metal from it.

A rock containing only a small amount of metal may still be used as an ore if the metal is _____ enough.

The metal compound in the ore may need to be _____ before the metal is extracted.

[You should also be able to comment on the environmental aspects of producing metals, just like you have on this page.]

Preventing corrosion

Ideas you need from Key Stage 3

Iron and steel are cheap and strong. This makes them really useful structural materials.

But iron and steel tend to corrode (rust) quite quickly when water and oxygen are both present.

When this happens, the metal changes back into its ore.

We can stop this happening to iron and steel by painting them or by covering them with a layer of plastic, oil or grease. This works because it prevents water or oxygen (or both) from reaching the iron or steel.

This car body is painted.

This bicycle chain is oiled.

■ How do other metals affect the corrosion of iron?

Iron and steel (which is mainly iron) **corrode** more quickly than most other transition metals. The diagrams show how the rate of corrosion is affected when the iron or steel is connected to other metals.

1 How is the rate of corrosion of iron related to the reactivity of the metals to which it is attached?

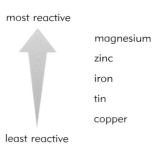

most reactive

magnesium

zinc

iron

tin

copper

least reactive

Key ▨ = rust

When a more **reactive** metal is in contact with iron, this metal corrodes instead of the iron.

The more reactive metal is sacrificed to protect the iron. This method of protection is called **sacrificial protection**.

2 Describe and explain how:

(a) gas and oil pipelines, made from steel, are protected against corrosion in the ground;

(b) the steel hulls of ships are protected against rusting.

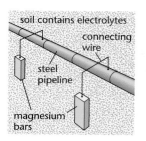
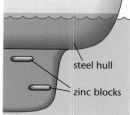

Examples of sacrificial protection.

What is stainless steel?

Stainless steel is a special type of steel that does not go rusty. We can make stainless steel (an alloy) by mixing iron with two other metals called **nickel** and **chromium**. Stainless steel does not rust but it is expensive.

3 Write down <u>three</u> things that we make from stainless steel.

4 Car exhausts made from stainless steel last a lot longer than car exhausts made from ordinary (mild) steel.

Why do you think all exhausts are not made from stainless steel?

Why aluminium doesn't corrode

Metals corrode by reacting with oxygen or water (or both). Aluminium is a much more reactive metal than iron so you would expect it to corrode more quickly. The pictures show why this doesn't happen.

5 Copy and complete the following sentences.

A tough, thin layer of _____ _____ forms on the surface of the aluminium. This prevents any further corrosion.

Sometimes things made from aluminium are deliberately given a layer of aluminium oxide. This is called anodising.

Stainless steel in the kitchen.

When iron (or steel) corrodes rust (iron oxide) is produced. This is very weak. It also lets oxygen and water get to the metal. So the iron keeps on rusting.

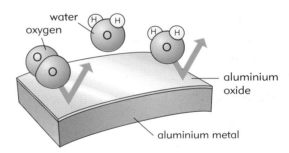

A **tough**, thin layer of **aluminium oxide** protects the metal underneath. Water and **oxygen** cannot get through this layer.

What you need to remember [Copy and complete using the **key words**]

Preventing corrosion

Iron and steel tend to _____ (rust) quite quickly.

One way of preventing this is to connect the iron or steel to a more _____ metal.

This method of preventing corrosion is called _____ _____.

Steel which doesn't rust is called _____ steel.

It is an alloy of iron, _____ and _____.

Aluminium is a reactive metal but it does not corrode very quickly because a layer of _____ _____ forms on the surface. This is _____ and prevents water and _____ from reaching the aluminium underneath.

These ideas are extended, for Higher Tier students, in Metals H3 on page 50.

Metal through the ages

The diagram shows lots of different things about metals.

1 Copy and complete the following sentences.

The first metal that people found and used was _____.

This metal is the _____ reactive.

2 How long ago were copper, iron and aluminium first used?

Explain your answer.

The alkali metals sodium and potassium were first discovered by Sir Humphry Davy in 1807.

3 Why do you think the alkali metals were not discovered much earlier?

Most metals react with oxygen or water.
This makes them corrode.

4 Copy and complete the following sentences.

The most reactive metals usually corrode _____.

The least reactive metals usually corrode _____.

5 (a) Which metal corrodes more slowly than you would expect?

(b) Explain why this happens.

Dates	Metals and their use
about 50 years ago (plenty of cheap electricity)	Aluminium is used to make many things, including aeroplanes. 
about 200 years ago (Volta invented the battery, which produced an electric current)	[Alkali metals discovered]
IRON AGE	 Steel is harder and tougher than bronze.
4000 years ago	
BRONZE AGE	 Bronze is mainly copper, with tin added to make it harder.
6000 years ago	 Jewellery and coins were made from gold.
STONE AGE	
10000 years ago	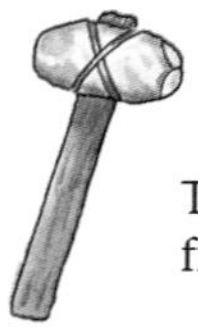 Tools were made from stone.

How the metals are extracted	Reactivity	How quickly the metals corrode in damp air
	MOST REACTIVE	FASTEST CORROSION
By passing an electric current though the molten metal compound.	alkali metals	alkali metals

Freshly cut sodium or potassium … … starts to corrode in seconds.

	aluminium	
	[carbon]	
By heating iron oxide with carbon in a very hot furnace.	iron	iron

A shiny, new iron nail … … starts to corrode in hours or days.

| By heating copper oxide with carbon. | copper | copper |

A shiny, new copper coin … … starts to corrode in weeks or months

| | | aluminium |

Aluminium quickly gets a coating of aluminium oxide, which is very tough and stops further corrosion

| You find gold as the metal in the ground. | gold | gold |

Gold does not corrode.

| | LEAST REACTIVE | SLOWEST CORROSION |

What you need to remember

Metals through the ages

There are no new things to remember on these two pages.
They bring together ideas from a lot of other pages.

Making very pure copper

Why we need pure copper

We all use many different electrical appliances such as computers, CD players, TVs and electric kettles. We need copper to make these appliances. We also need copper to be able to use them. The diagrams show why.

1 Write down <u>two</u> reasons why a mains TV set depends on copper.

The copper that is produced from copper ore in a furnace is 98–99% pure. But this is not pure enough to make cables or electric circuits. The copper that we use for these jobs must be very pure indeed.

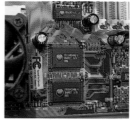

Copper is used to make the printed circuits inside TVs, CD players and computers.

Copper is used inside the cables that carry electricity to electrical appliances.

How to make copper very pure

The impure copper from the furnace is made into 99.98% pure copper by a process called **electrolysis**. The diagrams show how this is done.

2 Copy and complete the following sentences.
At the positive electrode, copper _____ become copper _____.
At the negative electrode, copper _____ become copper _____.

3 (a) What happens, over a period of two weeks, to all of the copper from the positive electrode?

 (b) What happens to the impurities?

In this electrolysis reaction, the copper sulphate is <u>not</u> decomposed. It remains unchanged. Copper ions enter the solution at the positive electrode and leave the solution at the negative electrode.

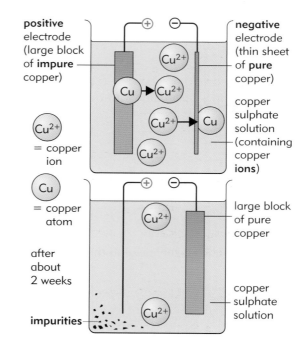

What you need to remember [Copy and complete using the **key words**]

Making very pure copper

Copper is purified by a process of _____.
The positive electrode is a large block of _____ copper from a furnace.
The negative electrode is a thin sheet of _____ copper.
The electrodes are placed in a solution containing copper _____.
During the electrolysis, copper is transferred from the _____ electrode to the _____ electrode. The _____ in the copper fall to the bottom of the container.

These ideas are extended, for Higher Tier students, in Metals H4 on page 51.

What happens during neutralisation?

Acidic solutions are acidic because they contain hydrogen atoms that have a positive (+) electrical charge.
These are called hydrogen ions.
The symbol for a **hydrogen ion** is **H⁺**.

Alkaline solutions are alkaline because they contain hydroxide ions.
These have a negative (–) electrical charge.
The symbol for a **hydroxide ion** is **OH⁻**.

When an acidic solution and an alkaline solution are mixed, each hydrogen ion joins up with an hydroxide ion to form a water molecule.

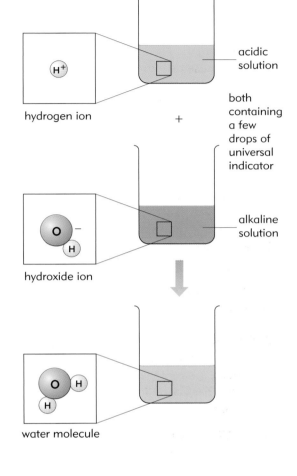

hydrogen ion

acidic solution

+

both containing a few drops of universal indicator

hydroxide ion

alkaline solution

water molecule

1 Copy and complete the following.

Hydrogen _____, H^+, make solutions _____.

_____ ions, OH^-, make solutions _____.

In <u>all</u> acid + alkali neutralisation reactions:

_____ (aq) + _____ (aq) ⟶ H_2O(l)

  hydrogen ions   hydroxide ions   water
    (in water)   (in water)

Using your knowledge

1 This page describes what is the <u>same</u> about <u>all</u> acid + alkali neutralisation reactions.

These reactions also produce another product which is <u>different</u> in different reactions.

(a) What is the general name for this product?

(b) Explain, using examples, why this product is different in different reactions.

2 'Water is neutral in two different senses.' Explain this statement.

3 Use the idea of hydrogen ions and hydroxide ions to suggest an explanation for the difference:

(a) between solutions with pH 1 and pH 5

(b) between solutions with pH 8 and pH 13.

H2   **This extends *Metals* 9, 10 and 11 for Higher Tier students**

Oxidising and reducing

When oxygen <u>combines</u> with elements or compounds, converting them into other substances, it <u>oxidises</u> them. The process is called **oxidation**.
The picture shows one example.

When some or all of the oxygen is <u>taken away</u> from a compound, this is **reduction**. For example:

copper oxide + hydrogen → copper + water
$$CuO + H_2 \rightarrow Cu + H_2O$$

We say that hydrogen is the <u>reducing agent</u> here.

1   The box shows how iron oxide is reduced to iron in a blast furnace.

   (a) Copy and complete the sentences.

   In the blast furnace, _____ is removed from iron oxide to leave _____. The iron oxide is _____ to iron. The carbon monoxide has been oxidised to _____.

   (b) What is the reducing agent in this reaction?

■ **Redox reactions**

In the blast furnace, iron oxide is reduced and carbon monoxide is oxidised. This is just one of many examples of reactions in which one substance is oxidised and another is reduced. We call them **redox reactions**.

REDuction + OXidation = REDOX

2   (a) Explain why the reaction between copper oxide and carbon is a redox reaction.

   (b) What is the reducing agent in this reaction?

When zinc reacts with copper oxide, zinc oxide and copper are produced. The box on the right gives more details of what happens in this reaction.

3   Copy and complete the sentences.

   When atoms of an element are oxidised they _____ electrons. When atoms of an element are _____, they gain electrons.

An oxidation reaction.

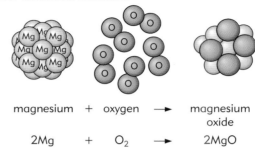

magnesium + oxygen → magnesium oxide

$$2Mg + O_2 \rightarrow 2MgO$$

Reducing iron oxide to iron

The following reaction occurs in a blast furnace.

iron oxide + carbon monoxide → iron + carbon dioxide

$$Fe_2O_3 + 3CO \rightarrow 2Fe + 3CO_2$$

Reducing copper oxide to copper

copper oxide + carbon → copper + carbon dioxide

$$2CuO + C \rightarrow 2Cu + CO_2$$

Using zinc to displace copper

zinc + copper oxide → zinc oxide + copper

$$Zn + CuO \rightarrow ZnO + Cu$$
$$[Cu^{2+}O^{2-}] \rightarrow [Zn^{2+}O^{2-}]$$

The zinc atoms combine with oxygen.
So they are oxidised.
But zinc atoms also become zinc ions.
To do this they lose two electrons (e^-).
So oxidation is <u>losing</u> electrons.

Oxygen is taken from the copper ions.
So they are reduced.
But copper ions also become copper atoms.
To do this they gain two electrons.
So reduction is <u>gaining</u> electrons.

Oxidation without oxygen

Oxidation and reduction involve **electron transfer**, i.e. atoms losing and gaining electrons. So the terms oxidation and reduction are also used in other reactions, even if oxygen does not take part.

4 In the reaction between iron and copper sulphate, which substance is oxidised and which substance is reduced? Give reasons for your answers.

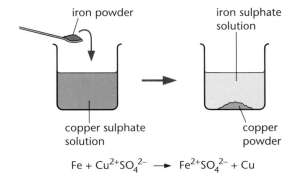

iron powder

iron sulphate solution

copper sulphate solution

copper powder

$Fe + Cu^{2+}SO_4^{2-} \longrightarrow Fe^{2+}SO_4^{2-} + Cu$

To help you remember	
OIL RIG	**O**xidation **I**s **L**oss (of electrons).
	Reduction **I**s **G**ain (of electrons).

Electrolysis

Metal compounds, when molten or in solution, will conduct electricity. We call the liquid an **electrolyte**. When we split up a compound by passing electricity through it, we call this **electrolysis**.

In the electrolysis of copper chloride solution:

- at the negative electrode, copper ions <u>gain</u> electrons to form copper atoms:
  $Cu^{2+} + 2e^- \rightarrow Cu$

- at the positive electrode, chloride ions <u>lose</u> electrons to form chlorine molecules:
  $2Cl^- - 2e^- \rightarrow Cl_2$

5 Copy and complete the sentence.

In electrolysis:
- at the negative electrode, positively charged ions _____ electrons. This is _____.

- at the positive electrode, negatively charged ions _____ electrons. This is _____.

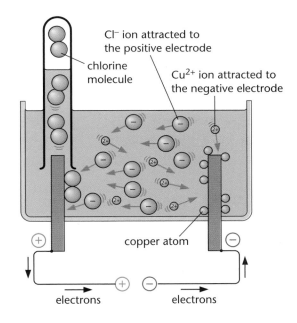

Cl^- ion attracted to the positive electrode

chlorine molecule

Cu^{2+} ion attracted to the negative electrode

copper atom

electrons

electrons

Using your knowledge

1 What is meant by a redox reaction? Use an example to explain your answer.

2 Aluminium is made by the electrolysis of molten aluminium oxide. These are the reactions that take place at the electrodes:

- at the positive electrode:
  $2O^{2-} - 4e^- \rightarrow O_2$

- at the negative electrode:
  $Al^{3+} + 3e^- \rightarrow Al$

Describe this reaction in terms of oxidation and reduction.

Explaining sacrificial protection

It is easy to understand why a metal that is more reactive than iron might corrode more quickly than iron. But it isn't so easy to understand why connecting a more reactive metal to iron should slow down the corrosion of iron.

This happens because when you put two different metals, such as iron and zinc, into a solution containing ions you make a simple electric cell.

An electric cell is basically an electron pump. The diagrams show how a zinc–iron electric cell can prevent the iron from rusting.

1 Draw and label a similar diagram to explain why connecting iron to a less reactive metal such as copper makes the iron rust faster.

> ### REMEMBER
>
> You can protect iron (or steel) from corrosion by connecting it to a more reactive metal.
>
> Because the more reactive metal is sacrificed to protect the iron, this is called sacrificial protection.

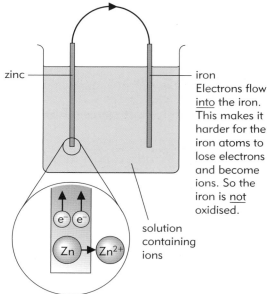

electrons flow through this connecting wire from the zinc to the iron

zinc

iron
Electrons flow <u>into</u> the iron. This makes it harder for the iron atoms to lose electrons and become ions. So the iron is <u>not</u> oxidised.

solution containing ions

Metals in cell	Potential difference
zinc + iron	0.4 volts
magnesium + iron	2.0 volts

Using your knowledge

1 You can measure the potential difference (voltage) across the two different metals in a simple cell using a voltmeter.

   (a) Which metal, zinc or magnesium, would be better at preventing iron from rusting?

   (b) Which of these two metals would itself corrode most quickly when connected to iron?

(c) Use the idea of electron transfers to suggest an explanation for each of your answers.

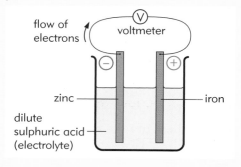

flow of electrons

voltmeter

zinc

iron

dilute sulphuric acid (electrolyte)

Electron transfers when purifying copper

Oxidation and reduction can be understood in terms of **electron transfer** (see Box).

We can also use the idea of electron transfer to understand what is happening when copper is purified.

When an electric current flows through a circuit connected by wires to a battery or power supply:

■ electrons flow <u>into</u> the positive (+) terminal;

■ electrons flow <u>out of</u> the negative (−) terminal.

In the electrolysis that is used to purify copper, the flow of electrons has the following effects:

■ at the positive electrode, copper atoms lose two electrons (e^-) and become copper ions (Cu^{2+}). These go into the solution (electrolyte);

■ at the negative electrode, copper ions gain two electrons and become copper atoms. These are deposited on the electrode.

1 Use the ideas of oxidation and reduction to describe what happens at each electrode.

> **REMEMBER**
>
> Oxidation Is Loss (of electrons).
> Reduction Is Gain (of electrons).

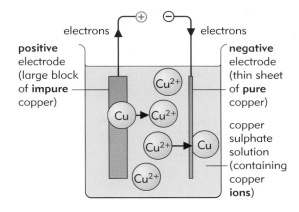

Cu^{2+} = copper ion Cu = copper atom

Using your knowledge

1 The process that is used to purify copper can also be used to give objects made from a cheaper metal a thin coating of copper, chromium or silver. We say that the object has been plated with one of these metals.

In silver plating, for example:

■ the positive electrode is made of silver;

■ the object being plated is the negative electrode;

■ the electrolyte is a solution containing silver ions (Ag^+).

Use the ideas of electron transfer, oxidation and reduction to describe what happens during silver plating. Use a labelled diagram as part of your answer.

Sports cups are usually silver plated.

Limestone – a useful rock

The ground under our feet is made of **rock** but you don't always see it. This is because the rock is often covered with soil. We also cover the ground with roads, pavements and buildings. If you dig down far enough you always reach solid rock. There are many different kinds of rock. One common rock is called limestone.

The diagram shows how we get limestone from the ground.

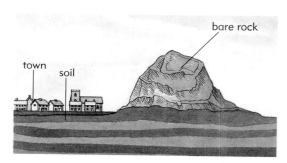

1 Copy and complete the following sentences.

We get limestone rock from places called _____ .

Large chunks of rock are blasted off using _____ .

We get limestone from **quarries**. Rock is blasted off the quarry face using explosives.

■ Looking at limestone

The pictures show some pieces of limestone.

2 Describe carefully what each piece of limestone looks like.

Some types of limestone.

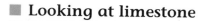

Chalk is a soft white limestone.

We cannot always tell if a piece of rock is limestone just by looking at it.

3 Look at the picture.

How can we test a rock to see if it really is limestone?

Drops of acid fizz when they are added to a lump of limestone.

Using limestone

Limestone is not a very hard rock so we can cut limestone into blocks and slabs quite easily.
This makes limestone very useful for **buildings**.
But there is a problem with using limestone for buildings as the picture shows.

4 Why is limestone a useful building material?

5 What is the problem when we use limestone for buildings?

6 Why is this problem worse today than it was hundreds of years ago?

Weather changes limestone. Acid rain makes it change even faster.

Heating limestone

We can use limestone to make other materials.
If we make limestone really hot we can change it into **quicklime**. We use a lime kiln to do this.

7 A lime kiln is heated in <u>two</u> ways. Write them down.

A word equation for the reaction is:

limestone + energy ⟶ quicklime + carbon dioxide

The chemical name for limestone is **calcium carbonate**.
The chemical name for quicklime is **calcium oxide**.

8 Write down the word equation using the chemical names.

A reaction that uses heat or thermal energy to break down a substance into different substances is called **thermal decomposition**.

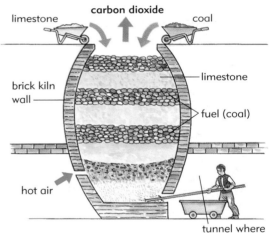

An old-fashioned lime kiln.

What you need to remember [Copy and complete using the **key words**]

Limestone – a useful rock

Limestone is a common _____. We get limestone from _____.
Limestone is very useful for _____ because it is easy to cut into blocks.
The chemical in limestone is _____ _____.
When we heat limestone strongly in a kiln it breaks down into _____ and
_____ _____. We call this kind of reaction _____ _____.
The chemical name for quicklime is _____ _____.

What can we do with quicklime?

If you heat a piece of limestone strongly, it changes into a new material called quicklime.

1 (a) What is the chemical name for quicklime?

(b) What other substance is produced when you heat limestone to make quicklime?

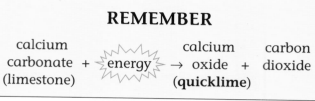

REMEMBER

calcium carbonate (limestone) + *energy* → calcium oxide (**quicklime**) + carbon dioxide

pieces of limestone (calcium carbonate)

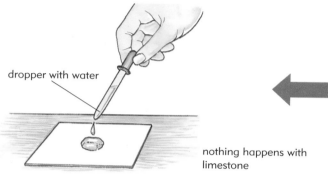

dropper with water

nothing happens with limestone

limestone

Bunsen flame

wire support

limestone changes into quicklime (calcium oxide)

Many other **carbonates** also split up (decompose) when you heat them.

2 What <u>two</u> substances are produced when you heat copper carbonate?

Quicklime looks almost the same as limestone, but when you add a few drops of water you can see the difference.

3 What happens when you add a few drops of water to limestone?

4 What happens when you add a few drops of water to quicklime?

The quicklime **reacts** with the water to form a new material.

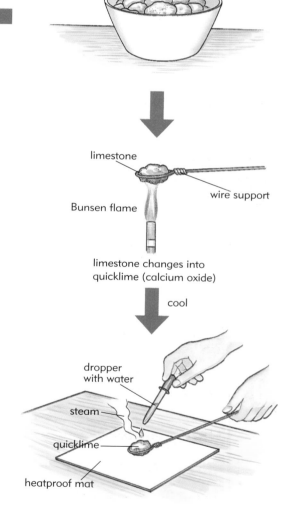

cool

dropper with water

steam

quicklime

heatproof mat

■ What is the new material?

The new material formed from quicklime is called **slaked lime**.

5 Copy and complete the word equation.

quicklime + _____ ⟶ _____ + *energy*

The chemical name for slaked lime is calcium hydroxide.

6 Write down the word equation using the chemical names for quicklime and slaked lime.

What is so special about slaked lime?

Slaked lime dissolves just a little in water.
We call this solution lime water.

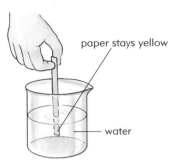
paper stays yellow
water

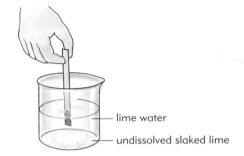
lime water
undissolved slaked lime

7 What happens when we test lime water with indicator paper?

8 What does this tell you about lime water?

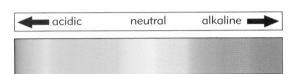
acidic   neutral   alkaline

Using slaked lime

Soil in fields and gardens may be too acidic for some plants. We can use an **alkali** to neutralise the acidity. We need to add just the right amount of alkali.

Look at the photograph.

9 What is the farmer spreading on the field?

10 Write down <u>two</u> reasons why lime helps the soil.

11 Why must the farmer be careful not to add too much lime to the field?

Fish don't like acidic water. So we can also use lime to neutralise the **acidity** of some lakes.

Spreading slaked lime. The lime neutralises soil acid. It also makes clay soil less sticky.

What you need to remember [Copy and complete using the **key words**]

What can we do with quicklime?

When you heat limestone, it decomposes into _____ and carbon dioxide.
Many other _____ decompose in a similar way when you heat them.
Quicklime (calcium oxide) _____ with cold water to form _____ _____
(calcium hydroxide). Slaked lime is an _____, it can neutralise acids.
We can use slaked lime to neutralise the _____ in lakes and soils.
Most plants do not grow well in acidic soils.

Other useful materials made from limestone

Many of the things we build today are made from concrete. When wet concrete sets, it becomes as hard as stone. When we mix concrete it can be poured into moulds. This is how we make concrete into lots of different shapes.

1 Write down <u>two</u> things we can make using concrete.

2 Write down <u>two</u> reasons why concrete is useful for making these things.

To make concrete you need **cement**.
Cement is made from limestone.

These objects were made using concrete.

■ Making cement

We need to use two materials from the ground to make cement.
These are the raw materials.

3 What <u>two</u> raw materials do you need to make cement?

4 What do you have to do to these raw materials to turn them into cement?

5 Write down <u>two</u> reasons why the kiln rotates all the time.

■ Making concrete

The diagram shows how you can make **concrete**.

6 What <u>four</u> things must you mix together to make concrete?

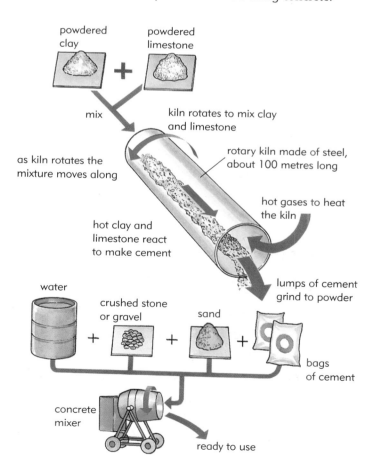

powdered clay + powdered limestone

mix

kiln rotates to mix clay and limestone

as kiln rotates the mixture moves along

rotary kiln made of steel, about 100 metres long

hot gases to heat the kiln

hot clay and limestone react to make cement

lumps of cement grind to powder

water + crushed stone or gravel + sand + bags of cement

concrete mixer

ready to use

Using concrete

Once you have mixed some concrete you need to make it the right shape. The diagrams show how you can do this. The water **reacts** slowly with the cement to make the concrete set hard as stone. This can take a few days.

7 How can you keep the sides of the new concrete step straight?

8 Why should you wait a few days before removing the wooden frame?

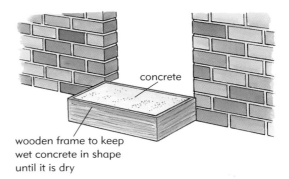

concrete

wooden frame to keep wet concrete in shape until it is dry

Making a concrete step for a house.

Making glass

Glass is another very useful material that we make using limestone.

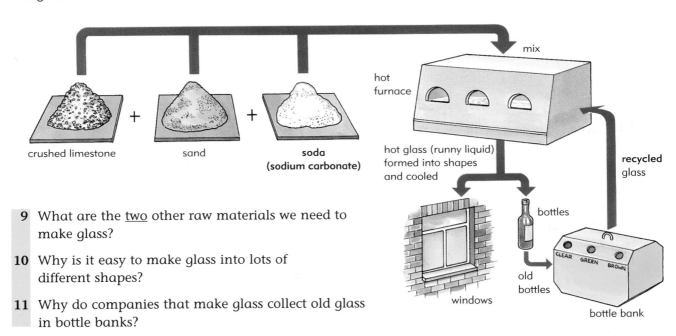

crushed limestone   +   sand   +   **soda (sodium carbonate)**

hot furnace

mix

hot glass (runny liquid) formed into shapes and cooled

windows

bottles

old bottles

recycled glass

bottle bank

CLEAR   GREEN   BROWN

9 What are the <u>two</u> other raw materials we need to make glass?

10 Why is it easy to make glass into lots of different shapes?

11 Why do companies that make glass collect old glass in bottle banks?

What you need to remember [Copy and complete using the **key words**]

Other useful materials made from limestone

We heat limestone and clay together in a hot kiln to make _____ .

A mixture of cement, sand, rock and water gives _____.

The water _____ with the cement and makes the concrete set solid.

Glass is a very useful material. You need to heat a mixture of limestone, sand and _____ to make glass.

Soda has the chemical name _____ _____.

We can melt old glass and use it again. We say that the glass has been _____.

Where does oil come from?

Things we make from crude oil.

We find many useful substances in the Earth's crust.
One of these substances is oil.
We call the oil that comes out of the ground crude oil.

1 Write down some of the things that we can make from crude oil.

■ How did the crude oil get there?

The story of oil starts millions of years ago in the sea.
Large numbers of animals and plants died and fell to
the sea bed. If the remains were buried quickly, other
animals could not eat them. If there was no oxygen,
they did not decompose fully. The organic remains
turned into oil.

2 Put these sentences into the right order to explain
how oil was made.
The first sentence has been put in place for you.

Millions of tiny plants and animals lived in the seas.

- ■ The pressure and heat of the rocks turned the
  remains of the dead plants and animals into oil.

- ■ As the dead plants and animals decayed they were
  covered with layers of mud and other sediments.

- ■ When the plants and animals died their bodies fell
  to the bottom of the sea.

- ■ The layers of mud and other sediments slowly
  changed into layers of sedimentary rock.

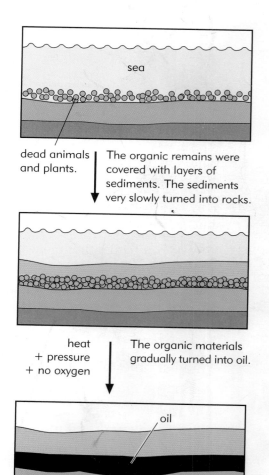

dead animals and plants.

The organic remains were covered with layers of sediments. The sediments very slowly turned into rocks.

heat + pressure + no oxygen

The organic materials gradually turned into oil.

oil

58

How do we get oil from the ground?

Oil forms in small drops which are spread through lots and lots of rock. Luckily for us, the oil doesn't stay like this. A lot of oil often collects together in one place, as you can see in the diagrams.

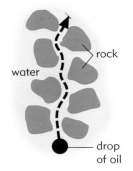

Many rocks have lots of tiny spaces. Oil and water can move through these spaces. We say the rocks are permeable. Oil floats on water. So oil rises to the top of the permeable rocks.

3   Copy and complete the following sentences.

Oil rises up through _____ rock because it floats on _____.

It collects underneath a layer of _____ rock.

4   What must you do to collect the trapped oil?

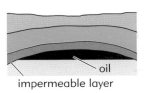

When the oil reaches an impermeable layer it can't rise any further. The oil is trapped under the rock. (Impermeable means <u>not</u> permeable.)

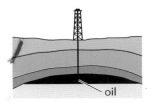

To get the oil you have to drill down through the impermeable layer.

What are fossil fuels?

Fossils are the remains of plants and animals that we find in sedimentary rocks. Oil is also the remains of plants and animals from millions of years ago. So we call it a <u>fossil</u> fuel.

coal

fossil fuels

oil

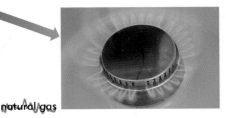
natural gas

5   Why do we call crude oil a fossil fuel?

6   Write down the names of <u>two</u> other fossil fuels.

How crude oil is split up into parts

Crude oil is a mixture of <u>lots</u> of different liquids. These liquids are very useful, but we can't use them until we have separated them from each other.

1 Write down the <u>two</u> main uses for the liquids in crude oil.

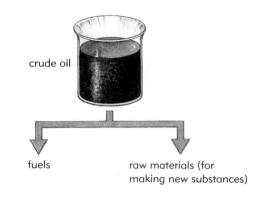

crude oil

fuels   raw materials (for making new substances)

■ How to separate a mixture of liquids

If you heat up a liquid it changes to a vapour. We say it **evaporates**. If you make the liquid hot enough, it boils. A boiling liquid evaporates very quickly.

If you cool a vapour it changes back into a liquid. We say it **condenses**.

2 Copy the diagram on the right. Then complete it.

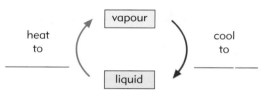

vapour

heat to _____

cool to _____

liquid

Evaporating a liquid and then condensing it again is called **distillation**.

We can use this idea to separate a mixture of liquids.

The diagram shows how brandy is made from wine.

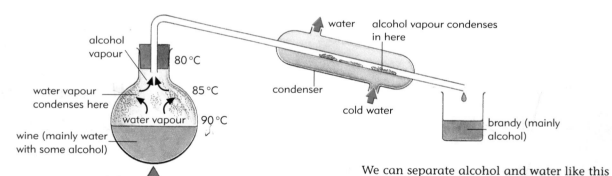

alcohol vapour

80 °C

water vapour condenses here

85 °C

water vapour 90 °C

wine (mainly water with some alcohol)

gentle heat

water   alcohol vapour condenses in here

condenser

cold water

brandy (mainly alcohol)

We can separate alcohol and water like this because they have different **boiling points**. Water boils at 100 °C, alcohol boils at 78 °C.

3 Copy and complete the following sentences.

The wine contains two liquids called _____ and _____.

The liquid alcohol boils at _____.

It turns into alcohol _____.

Droplets of alcohol form in the _____.

Water boils at _____.

Any water vapour _____ in the neck of the flask.

Separating a mixture of liquids into parts or fractions like this is called **fractional distillation**.

wine

Wine is a mixture of water, alcohol and small amounts of other chemicals.

Separating crude oil into fractions

We use fractional distillation to separate crude oil into different parts or fractions. The different fractions boil at different temperatures.

Fraction of crude oil	Boiling points in °C
dissolved gases	below 0
petrol	around 65
naphtha	around 130
kerosene	around 200
diesel oil	around 300
bitumen	over 400

4 (a) Which fraction of crude oil has the highest boiling point?

(b) Which fraction has the lowest boiling point?

5 Explain why crude oil can be separated by fractional distillation.

6 Why is separating crude oil into fractions more difficult than making brandy?

An oil fractionating tower

In Britain, 250 000 tonnes of oil are produced every day! To separate all of this oil into its fractions we use enormous **fractionating towers**.
The diagram shows one of these.

7 Copy and complete the following sentences.

Crude oil is heated to about _____ °C.

Bitumen has a _____ boiling point so it falls straight to the bottom of the tower.

Methane has a _____ boiling point so it goes straight to the top of the tower.

Fractions with in-between boiling points _____ partway up the tower.

The lower the boiling point of a fraction, the _____ it goes up the tower before it condenses.

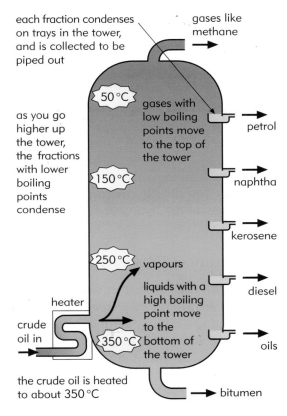

each fraction condenses on trays in the tower, and is collected to be piped out

gases like methane

50 °C — gases with low boiling points move to the top of the tower — petrol

as you go higher up the tower, the fractions with lower boiling points condense

150 °C — naphtha

kerosene

250 °C — vapours
liquids with a high boiling point move to the bottom of the tower

heater

crude oil in

350 °C

diesel

oils

the crude oil is heated to about 350 °C

bitumen

A fractionating tower to separate crude oil.

What you need to remember [Copy and complete using the **key words**]

How crude oil is split up into parts

When you heat a liquid it _____ to form a vapour.
When you cool a vapour it _____ to form a liquid.
Evaporating a liquid and then condensing it again is called _____.
Separating a mixture of liquids like this is called _____ _____.
The liquids in the mixture must have different _____ _____.
Crude oil is separated into fractions in _____ _____.

What are the chemicals in crude oil?

In nature, there are about 90 different kinds of atom, which we call the elements. Substances that contain more than one kind of atom joined together are called **compounds**. Most of the substances in crude oil are compounds that are made from just two kinds of atom. The smallest part of each compound is a **molecule**. The diagram shows two of the molecules you find in crude oil.

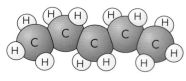

This molecule has 5 carbon atoms and 12 hydrogen atoms. We write this C_5H_{12}. This is the formula of the compound.

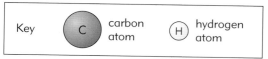

Key — carbon atom — hydrogen atom

1 Which <u>two</u> kinds of atom do these molecules contain?

2 What is the difference between the two molecules?

3 Write down the formula of

 (a) the smaller molecule

 (b) the larger molecule.

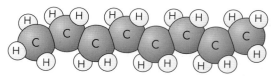

This molecule has 8 carbon atoms and 18 hydrogen atoms.

Molecules made only of **hydrogen** atoms and **carbon** atoms are called **hydrocarbons**. Most of the molecules in crude oil are hydrocarbons.

■ Differences between hydrocarbons

Crude oil is a mixture of many different hydrocarbons. The hydrocarbon molecules are all different sizes and masses. The boiling point of a molecule depends on its size and mass. This means that the hydrocarbon molecules all boil at different temperatures.

4 Copy and complete the table.

Hydrocarbon	Formula	Boiling point in °C
butane		
hexane		
decane		

5 Copy and complete the following sentence.

The hydrocarbon with the biggest molecules boils at the _____ temperature.

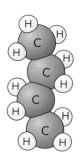

butane
boiling point
0 °C

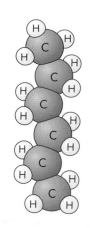

hexane
boiling point
70 °C

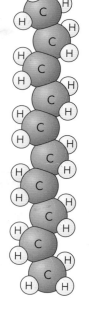

decane
boiling point
175 °C

■ Which hydrocarbons are in which fractions?

Hydrocarbons with the **largest** molecules have the highest boiling points. These large molecules condense to liquids lower down the fractionating tower.

6 Which fraction of crude oil has the smallest molecules?

7 Which fraction of crude oil has the largest molecules?

8 Copy and complete the following sentences.

Diesel fuel has _____ molecules than kerosene.
Naphtha has _____ molecules than kerosene.

A simple way to say how big hydrocarbon molecules are is to count how many carbon atoms they have.
The diagram below shows the hydrocarbons in some of the oil fractions.

9 How many carbon atoms are there in:

(a) the hydrocarbon molecules in petrol?

(b) the hydrocarbon molecules in diesel?

(c) the hydrocarbon molecules in bitumen?

10 How many carbon atoms would you expect to find in the hydrocarbon gases?

The crude oil fractions are different in more ways than their different boiling points. This is why we can use them for different jobs.

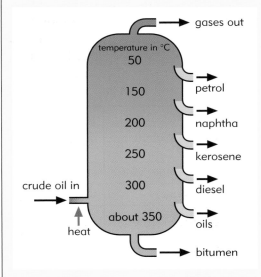

REMEMBER

The different fractions in crude oil condense to liquids at different temperatures.

Each fraction contains more than one hydrocarbon compound. The hydrocarbons in a fraction have a similar number of carbon atoms and similar boiling points.

| petrol | diesel | | bitumen |

1 2 3 4 5 6 7 8 9 10 11 12 13 14 15 16 17 18 19 20 21 22 23 24 25 26 27 28 29 30 31 32 33 34 35 36 37 38 39 40 41 42 43 44 45 46 47 48 49 50 51 52 53 54 55

Number of carbon atoms in a molecule

What you need to remember [Copy and complete using the **key words**]

What are the chemicals in crude oil?

Substances that contain more than one kind of atom are called _____.
Most of the compounds in crude oil are made from two kinds of atoms.
These are _____ atoms and _____ atoms.
We call these compounds _____.
The smallest part of each hydrocarbon is called a _____.
Hydrocarbons with the highest boiling points have the _____ molecules.

Different hydrocarbons for different jobs

Different hydrocarbons have molecules of different sizes. This gives them different **properties**. One example is their boiling points. Hydrocarbons with smaller molecules have lower boiling points. The properties of different hydrocarbons make them useful for different jobs.

> **REMEMBER**
>
> The compounds in crude oil contain hydrogen and carbon atoms.
> They are hydrocarbons.

Oil fraction	petrol	diesel	lubricating oil	bitumen
Number of carbon atoms	5 to 12	15 to 25	26 to 50	more than 50
Size of the molecules	small	fairly small	big	very big
Boiling point	low	fairly low	fairly high	high
Appearance				
A few drops left in the open air.	Quickly changes to a vapour. We say it is very **volatile**.	Slowly changes to vapour.	Very slowly changes to vapour.	Hardly changes to vapour at all.
A few drops soaked into glass wool.	Catches fire very easily. We say it is very **flammable**.	Catches fire quite easily.	Hard to light.	Hard to light.
How easy is it to pour?	Easy to pour.	Easy to pour.	Not easy to pour, it sticks to the sides.	Almost solid, very slow to pour. We say it is **viscous**.

1 Petrol and diesel are both used as fuels in engines.
Which properties make them useful for this job?
Give reasons for your answers.

2 Lubricating oil is used to make engines run smoothly.
The oil reduces friction between moving parts.
Which properties make it useful for this job?
Explain why.

3 Bitumen is used to make the tarmac on roads.
Which properties make it useful for this job?
Give reasons for your answer.

■ Making long hydrocarbons more useful

We use more crude oil for fuel than for anything else. However, there are lots of long hydrocarbon molecules in crude oil and these are not very useful as **fuels**.

4 Write down <u>two</u> reasons why long hydrocarbon molecules do not make good fuels.

We can make long hydrocarbon molecules more useful if we split them up into smaller molecules. We call this **cracking**. We make most of our petrol this way.

5 Copy and complete the word equation

$$\text{decane} \xrightarrow{\text{cracking}} \underline{\hspace{2cm}} + \underline{\hspace{2cm}}$$

(10 carbon atoms   ___ carbon atoms   ___ carbon atoms)

A simpler way to write down this chemical reaction is to use the formula of each compound.

6 Copy and complete the formula equation

$$C_{10}H_{22} \xrightarrow{\text{cracking}} \underline{\hspace{2cm}} + \underline{\hspace{2cm}}$$

Cracking is another example of a thermal decomposition reaction.
We use a hot catalyst to speed up this reaction.

7 Explain why cracking is a thermal decomposition reaction.

REMEMBER

When thermal energy (heat) is used to break down or decompose a substance, we call the process **thermal decomposition**.

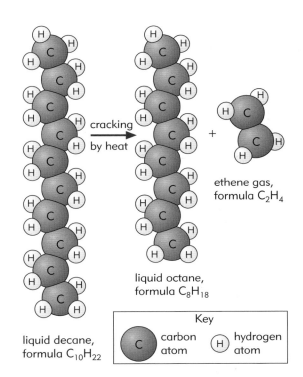

liquid decane,
formula $C_{10}H_{22}$

cracking by heat

ethene gas,
formula C_2H_4

liquid octane,
formula C_8H_{18}

Key: C carbon atom   H hydrogen atom

What you need to remember [Copy and complete using the **key words**]

Different hydrocarbons for different jobs

Small hydrocarbon molecules can:
- evaporate quickly (we say they are very _____)
- catch fire easily (we say they are very _____)
- pour easily (we say they are not very _____).

Larger hydrocarbons do <u>not</u> have these _____ and so they are not very good _____.

Large hydrocarbon molecules can be split up into smaller molecules that are more useful. We call this _____; it is a _____ _____ reaction.

These ideas are extended, for Higher Tier students, in Earth materials H1 on pages 94–95.

65

More about cracking hydrocarbons

■ Cracking hydrocarbons at a refinery

The diagram shows what happens in the part of a refinery where hydrocarbons are cracked.

1 Put the sentences in the right order to explain how we crack hydrocarbons.
The first sentence is in the correct place.

- ■ We heat the liquid containing the long hydrocarbon molecules.

- ■ The long molecules **split up** into a mixture of smaller ones.

- ■ We pass the vapour over a hot **catalyst**.

- ■ We separate the different small molecules.

- ■ The long hydrocarbons form a vapour. We say they **evaporate**.

2 Why do we use a catalyst in cracking?

REMEMBER

Large hydrocarbon molecules can be split up into smaller molecules.
We call this cracking.

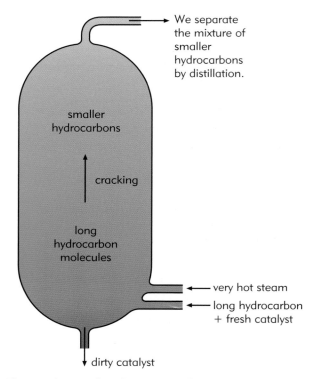

The catalyst makes the reaction happen
- ■ faster
- ■ at a lower temperature.

■ Cracking a hydrocarbon at school

Liquid paraffin is a hydrocarbon. It contains fairly large molecules. So it is not very runny.
The diagram shows how you can crack liquid paraffin.

3 Which <u>two</u> things show that you have cracked some of the liquid paraffin?

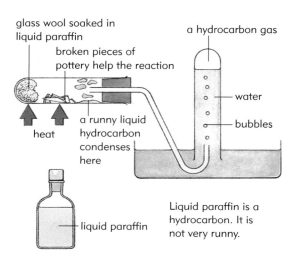

Liquid paraffin is a hydrocarbon. It is not very runny.

How we use the cracked hydrocarbons

Cracking produces the smaller molecules that we need as **fuels**. This is how we get most of the octane in petrol.

4 Look at the table.
   Why is octane better than decane for petrol?

Hydrocarbon	Formula	Boiling point (°C)
hexane	C_6H_{14}	70
octane	C_8H_{18}	126
decane	$C_{10}H_{22}$	175

Fuels with lower boiling points catch fire or ignite more easily.

We join up some of the small **molecules** to make new materials such as **plastics**. For example, we use ethene to make the plastic polyethene. 'Poly' means many. So polyethene means many ethenes. It is a very large molecule.

As well as plastics, many other large molecules are made of lots of small molecules joined together. We call them **polymers**.

5 What does the 'poly' in polymer mean?

6 Polypropene is a plastic. What smaller molecules is it made from? Explain your answer.

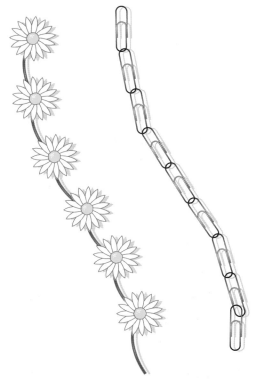

We make plastics by joining together lots of smaller molecules. It's a bit like joining lots of paper clips or daisies to form chains.

What you need to remember [Copy and complete using the **key words**]

More about cracking hydrocarbons

In a refinery, we heat large hydrocarbon molecules so that they _____.
We pass the vapours over a hot _____.
The large molecules _____ _____ to make smaller ones.
We use the small molecules as _____ and to make new materials such as _____.
We make plastics by joining lots of small _____ together.
We call these big molecules _____.

Plastics from oil

We can crack long hydrocarbon molecules to give smaller molecules. We can join up short hydrocarbon molecules to give larger molecules.
We call the large molecules polymers.

■ Using ethene to make a plastic

One of the small molecules we get by cracking hydrocarbon molecules is called ethene. If we join many ethene molecules together, we get a very long molecule that is a useful plastic.

1 (a) What is the name of the plastic made from ethene?

(b) Why does the plastic have this name?

People often call this plastic polythene.

■ What do we use polythene for?

The pictures show some of the things we can make using poly(ethene). The box shows some of the properties of poly(ethene).

> **Some properties of poly(ethene)**
>
> It is soft – you can scratch it easily and it wears away.
>
> It is tough – even if you drop it, it doesn't break.
>
> It isn't very clear – you cannot see clearly through it unless it is very thin.
>
> It is strong – it is hard to tear.
>
> It is flexible – you can bend it easily.
>
> It melts easily – but can stand boiling water.
>
> It is waterproof – liquids cannot soak through it.

2 Why wouldn't we use poly(ethene) to make these things?

(a) saucepans   (b) shoes   (c) car windscreen

■ More 'polys'

We can join up other hydrocarbon molecules to make polymers too. Different polymers have different properties. So we use them for different things.

3 Write down the name of the polymer made from propene.

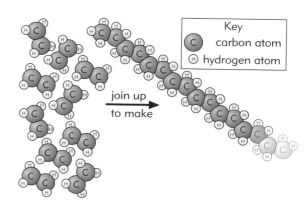

Lots of small ethene molecules join together to give a long molecule of **poly(ethene)**. 'Poly' means 'many'.

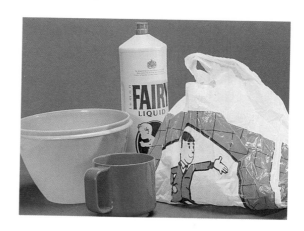

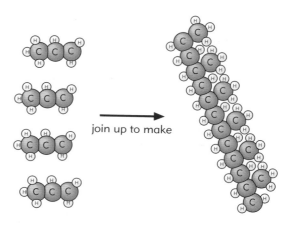

Lots of small propene molecules join up to form **poly(propene)**.

What do we use poly(propene) for?

We use poly(propene) to make milk crates and fibres for ropes and carpets. We used to make all ropes from natural fibres such as hemp. We often use poly(propene) and other man-made polymers now because they:

- are stronger
- are more hard-wearing
- do not shrink
- do not rot.

We choose different polymers for different jobs. For example, poly(propene) is a better polymer than poly(ethene) for making ropes because it doesn't stretch as easily.

4 Poly(propene) is also strong and hard-wearing. Explain why these two properties are important in a rope.

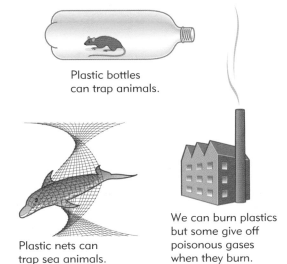

Plastic bottles can trap animals.

Plastic nets can trap sea animals.

We can burn plastics but some give off poisonous gases when they burn.

Plastics stay in the environment for a long time.

What happens to waste plastics?

Microorganisms break down natural fibres such as cotton and wool. So when we bury them in landfill sites, they rot. We say that they are **biodegradable**. Most plastics don't rot. They are not biodegradable.

5 What happens to plastics in landfill sites? Explain your answer.

6 Describe <u>two</u> other problems caused by plastics in the environment.

7 Scientists are developing some biodegradable plastics. Why do you think they are doing this?

8 Write down <u>one</u> problem of recycling plastics.

PE   HDPE   PET

We can recycle many plastics, but we have to sort them into their different kinds. Look out for recycling codes like these on plastics.

What you need to remember [Copy and complete using the key words]

Plastics from oil

Bottles can be made from a plastic called _____.

Crates and ropes can be made from a different plastic called _____.

Most plastics are not broken down by _____. We say that they are <u>not</u>

_____.

This means that waste plastics can be a problem in the environment.

[You should also be able to comment on the impact on the environment of plastic waste disposal.]

Burning fuels – where do they go?

We get gases, petrol and diesel from crude oil. When we burn these fuels, energy is released. New substances are also produced.

Look at the diagram.

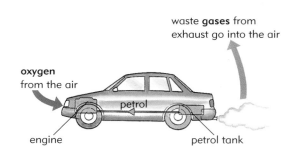

waste **gases** from exhaust go into the air

oxygen from the air

engine

petrol

petrol tank

1 What reacts with petrol to make it burn?

2 What happens to the new substances that are produced?

3 Copy and complete the word equation.

petrol + _____ ⟶ waste gases + ☼energy☼

All the fuels we get from crude oil produce the same new substances when they burn.

■ What new substances are made when fuels burn?

To find out what new substances are made when fuels burn, you need to trap them.

The diagram shows how you can do this.

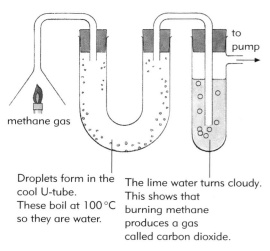

to pump

methane gas

Droplets form in the cool U-tube. These boil at 100 °C so they are water.

The lime water turns cloudy. This shows that burning methane produces a gas called carbon dioxide.

Trapping the new substances made when methane burns.

4 What <u>two</u> substances are made when methane burns?

5 Copy and complete the word equation

methane
+ ⟶ _____ + _____ + ☼energy☼
oxygen   _____

6 Write down <u>three</u> different ways of showing that the droplets of liquid are water.

7 How can you tell that the gas produced is carbon dioxide?

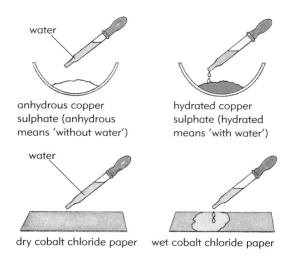

water

anhydrous copper sulphate (anhydrous means 'without water')

hydrated copper sulphate (hydrated means 'with water')

water

dry cobalt chloride paper

wet cobalt chloride paper

Two more tests for water.

■ What happens to molecules when methane burns?

The diagram shows what happens to a methane molecule when it burns.

8 Copy and complete the following sentences.

When methane burns

- the carbon atoms join with _____ atoms to make a molecule of _____ _____

- the hydrogen atoms join with _____ atoms to make a molecule of _____ .

When anything burns, its atoms join with oxygen atoms to make **oxides**. Water is hydrogen oxide.

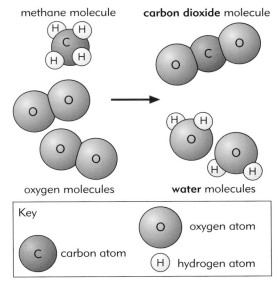

methane molecule   **carbon dioxide** molecule

oxygen molecules   **water** molecules

Key

O oxygen atom

C carbon atom

H hydrogen atom

We can write this: $CH_4 + 2O_2 \longrightarrow CO_2 + 2H_2O$

■ Burning other fuels

Fuels from crude oil are all hydrocarbons.
The diagrams show some hydrocarbon molecules.

9 Burning hydrocarbons always makes water and carbon dioxide. Why is this?

Many fuels contain sulphur as well as carbon compounds. When sulphur burns it makes a gas called **sulphur dioxide**. This gas is an important cause of acid rain.

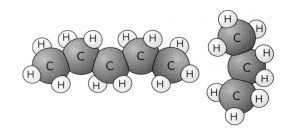

What you need to remember [Copy and complete using the **key words**]

Burning fuels – where do they go?

When fuels burn they react with _____ from the air.
The new substances that are produced are mainly _____ that escape into the air.
The atoms in fuels join up with oxygen atoms to form compounds called _____ .
When hydrocarbons burn:

- hydrogen atoms join up with oxygen atoms to make _____ molecules;
- carbon atoms join up with oxygen atoms to make _____ _____ molecules.

Sometimes fuels contain sulphur. Sulphur atoms join up with oxygen to form

_____ _____ .

It's raining acid

Acids are dangerous substances.
We know that they can 'eat away' at some things.

1 (a) What has happened to the statue in
the photograph?

   (b) What has caused this to happen to the statue?

Acid rain is a serious problem in many countries
including Britain. As well as damaging buildings, acid
rain can harm animals and plants.

2 Write down <u>two</u> ways acid rain can harm
living things.

We need to prevent acid rain from forming.
To do this we have to understand what causes it.

Acid rain can kill trees and the fish in lakes.

■ What turns our rain into acid?

When fuels burn they react with oxygen.
Atoms in the fuel join with oxygen atoms in the air.
New substances called oxides are made.

Most fuels contain carbon atoms.

3 What new substance do the carbon atoms make
when a fuel burns?

Many fuels also contain some sulphur atoms.

4 (a) What new substance do the sulphur atoms make
when the fuel burns?

   (b) Write down a word equation for this reaction.

Sulphur dioxide is a gas that can turn rain into acid.

carbon atom	oxygen molecule		carbon dioxide molecule

sulphur atom	oxygen molecule		sulphur dioxide molecule

We can also write these reactions like this:

$C(s) + O_2(g) \longrightarrow CO_2(g)$

$S(s) + O_2(g) \longrightarrow SO_2(g)$

(s) = solid, (g) = gas

How sulphur dioxide makes acid rain

5 Copy and complete the following sentences.

Some fuels contain sulphur.

When we burn these fuels we make a _____ called sulphur dioxide.

This goes into the _____.

The sulphur dioxide reacts with oxygen and then dissolves in droplets of _____.

This makes an acid called _____ _____.

Eventually the acidic droplets in the clouds fall as _____ _____.

Acid rain does not usually fall where it is made. Winds can blow the 'acid clouds' for hundreds of kilometres before they fall as rain.

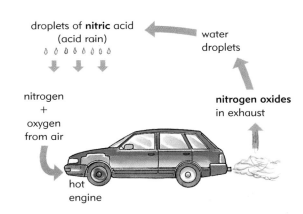

How rain turns into acid.

Don't just blame sulphur

It's not just the <u>sulphur</u> in fuels that causes acid rain. When we burn things at high temperatures the **nitrogen** in the air can join up with oxygen. This happens inside car engines.

6 What new substances are made when the nitrogen atoms join up with oxygen atoms?

7 What substance is produced when nitrogen oxides dissolve in droplets of water?

What you need to remember [Copy and complete using the **key words**]

It's raining acid

Acid rain can harm buildings and living things.
When we burn fuels that contain sulphur we make the gas called _____ _____.

This gas dissolves in water droplets to make _____ acid.
The heat from burning fuels makes oxygen and _____ from the air react together. This makes gases called _____ _____.
These gases dissolve in water to produce _____ acid.

The Earth's changing atmosphere

■ The atmosphere today

The Earth's atmosphere is a layer of gases above the surface. The air pressure gets lower and lower as you go up. At 150 km above the surface the pressure is so low that scientists sometimes call this the top of the atmosphere. The pie chart shows the main gases in the atmosphere. It has been like this for about 200 million years.

1 Copy and complete the following sentences.

The two main gases in the air are _____, about _____, and _____, about _____.

There is also a small amount of the _____ gases and an even smaller amount of _____ _____.

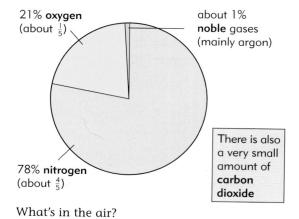

21% **oxygen**
(about $\frac{1}{5}$)

about 1%
noble gases
(mainly argon)

78% **nitrogen**
(about $\frac{4}{5}$)

There is also a very small amount of **carbon dioxide**

What's in the air?

■ From earliest times

The Earth was formed about 4600 million years ago. It was so hot that it was molten for millions of years. Then, as it cooled, a solid crust formed. There were lots of volcanoes. They poured out lava and a mixture of gases. These gases formed the Earth's atmosphere. It was a bit like the atmosphere on Venus.

2 Write down <u>two</u> differences between the Earth's early atmosphere and the atmosphere today.

3 The Earth's early atmosphere was not suitable for humans and other animals. Explain why.

The atmosphere 4000 million years ago
- little or no oxygen
- mainly **carbon dioxide**
- some **nitrogen** and **water** vapour
- small amounts of methane and ammonia

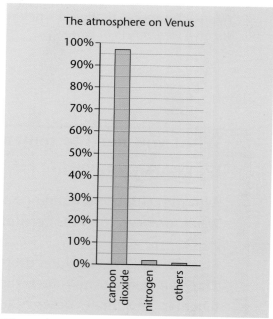

The atmosphere on Venus

We need oxygen, but carbon dioxide poisons us. So we can't live on Venus.

■ Changes soon began

The Earth continued to cool. Water vapour condensed and fell as rain. At first it was so hot that the water evaporated straight away. Later, parts of the surface were cool enough for some water to be liquid. By about 3800 million years ago, water was collecting in hollows on the surface. The first lakes and **oceans** were forming.

4 Write down the temperature at which water vapour can condense to form liquid water.

Carbon dioxide dissolves in water. So the amount of carbon dioxide in the atmosphere began to fall as the gas dissolved in the oceans and lakes.

■ Living things cause changes

Scientists are not sure about how life began or what it was like. The first living things were probably microorganisms that could use carbon dioxide in photosynthesis to produce food (carbohydrate), just like plants do.

carbon dioxide + water ⟶ carbohydrate + **oxygen**

These microorganisms took carbon dioxide from the atmosphere and released oxygen.

5 Look at the pictures. What is the evidence that photosynthesis has happened for millions of years?

6 Write down the name of the gas that photosynthesis adds to the atmosphere.

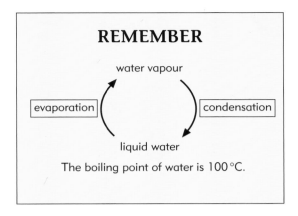

REMEMBER

water vapour

evaporation condensation

liquid water

The boiling point of water is 100 °C.

The atmosphere 3800 million years ago
■ most of the water vapour lost
■ carbon dioxide levels beginning to fall

These present-day stromatolites in Australia are built by plant-like microorganisms.

Fossil stromatolites are evidence that similar microorganisms lived about 3500 million years ago.

What you need to remember [Copy and complete using the **key words**]

The Earth's atmosphere now is about $\frac{4}{5}$ _____ and $\frac{1}{5}$ _____.
Other gases in it are _____ _____ and _____ gases.
The Earth's early atmosphere was made of gases that came out of volcanoes.
It was mainly _____ _____ with some _____ and _____
vapour. There were small amounts of methane.
Water vapour condensed to form the _____.
Microorganisms removed carbon dioxide from the atmosphere and added _____.

More oxygen, less carbon dioxide

The first bacteria and other microorganisms lived in an atmosphere that had little or no **oxygen**. But photosynthesis began to 'pollute' the atmosphere with oxygen. The oxygen was poisonous to some of the microorganisms. We say that they could not tolerate oxygen. So, gradually the number of habitats suitable for these microorganisms went down.

1 When the amount of oxygen increased, what do you think happened to the microorganisms that couldn't live where there was oxygen?

When oxygen was released, it reacted with the ammonia and methane in the atmosphere.
So the atmosphere changed even more.

> **methane** + oxygen $\longrightarrow$ carbon dioxide + water
>
> **ammonia** + oxygen $\longrightarrow$ nitrogen + water

2 Which gases took the place of methane and ammonia?

■ From the oceans to the land

As the atmosphere changed, tiny plants and then larger plants evolved. They all took in carbon dioxide and gave out oxygen. After millions of years, plants grew on the land too. Plants grew where there was light, water and a suitable temperature. So, the amount of oxygen in the atmosphere continued to increase.

3 (a) What was the percentage of oxygen in the atmosphere 400 million years ago?

   (b) Why was the amount of carbon dioxide going down?

By 200 million years ago, the amounts of oxygen and carbon dioxide in the atmosphere became steady. Microorganisms and animals were using oxygen and producing carbon dioxide at the same rate that plants were doing the opposite. The atmosphere had become nearly the same as it is today.

REMEMBER

In photosynthesis, plants:
- ■ remove carbon dioxide from air,
- ■ add oxygen to air.

The atmosphere 2200 million years ago
- ■ slow increase in oxygen levels
- ■ nitrogen level increasing
- ■ carbon dioxide level falling slowly

By 2200 million years ago, oxygen levels were high enough to oxidise iron; banded red ironstone rocks are evidence of this.

The atmosphere 1000 million years ago
- ■ increasing levels of carbon dioxide, nitrogen and oxygen
- ■ oxygen forms about 1% of the atmosphere

The atmosphere 400 million years ago
- ■ oxygen level rising to 2% of the atmosphere
- ■ carbon dioxide level falling

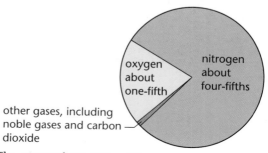

other gases, including noble gases and carbon dioxide

The atmosphere 200 million years ago.

Keeping carbon dioxide out of the atmosphere

Between 600 and 400 million years ago, many animals with shells evolved. The first ones were microscopic. Later, there were large animals such as corals and crinoids too. Most of these animals had hard parts made of calcium carbonate. When these animals died and sank to the bottom of the sea, their shells formed **carbonate** rocks such as limestone and chalk. These are sedimentary rocks and carbon can stay 'locked up' in them for millions of years.

The limestone is made from the remains of crinoids or sea lilies. These animals are related to starfish.

4 (a) Write down the name of one carbonate rock.

(b) What is the main carbon compound in this rock?

Plants and animals break down the carbon compounds that plants make in photosynthesis. They release carbon dioxide back into the air.

However, this doesn't always happen. Oil is the remains of microorganisms that were not broken down. So we call it a fossil fuel. The carbon compounds in oil and other **fossil fuels** have been 'locked up' for millions of years.

5 Look at the picture. Where does the carbon 'locked up' in coal come from?

The tropical forests of the Carboniferous period formed much of the world's coal.

What you need to remember [Copy and complete using the **key words**]

More oxygen, less carbon dioxide

Plants evolved and colonised most of the Earth's surface. They released _____ into the atmosphere. Oxygen reacted with _____ and _____, removing them from the air.

Most of the carbon from the carbon dioxide in the atmosphere became 'locked up' in sedimentary rocks as _____ _____ and _____ rocks.

These ideas are extended, for Higher Tier students, in Earth materials H2 on pages 96–97.

KS3B Ideas you need from Key Stage 3

The rock cycle

The Earth's crust formed when molten material cooled and became solid. New rocks still form like this today. We call them igneous rocks.

We call molten rock <u>magma</u>.

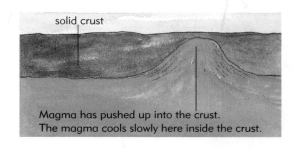

solid crust

Magma has pushed up into the crust.
The magma cools slowly here inside the crust.

■ Two kinds of igneous rock

Basalt forms from molten rock that cools down quickly outside the Earth's crust. The diagram shows how another igneous rock forms. This rock is granite, and it forms from molten rock that cools down slowly inside the Earth's crust.

Basalt is called an extrusive igneous rock because it forms <u>outside</u> the Earth's crust.

Granite is called an intrusive igneous rock because it forms <u>inside</u> the Earth's crust.

Granite has large crystals.

Basalt has small crystals.

Rocks under the microscope. You can see crystals of a variety of minerals.

1 Write down <u>two</u> differences in the ways that basalt and granite form.

2 Look at the pictures of thin slices of basalt and granite. Copy and complete the following sentences.

   Basalt and granite both contain crystals.
   The crystals in granite are _____.
   This is because the magma cooled _____ and the crystals had time to grow.

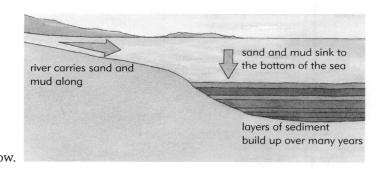

river carries sand and mud along

sand and mud sink to the bottom of the sea

layers of sediment build up over many years

■ New rocks from old

Old rocks break down and become the raw materials for making new rocks.

Rocks in the Earth's crust
↓ weathering
Bits of rock (e.g. sand and mud)
↓ erosion and deposition
Sediments
↓ cementing
Sedimentary rocks

Sandstone, mudstone and limestone are examples of sedimentary rocks.

3 Sand from a sandstone in a hillside can become a new sedimentary rock.
   Write a few sentences about how this happens.

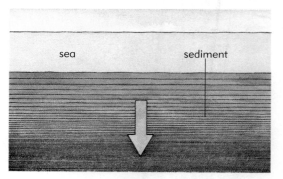

sea   sediment

The weight of the sediment layers presses down on the layers below. This squeezes out any water. Natural chemicals stick the bits of sand and mud together. We say they are cemented.

■ Changed rocks

Earth movements bury rocks deep inside the Earth's crust. These rocks get squeezed very hard and become very hot. The high pressure and high temperature can change rocks into new kinds of rocks called metamorphic rocks. This can happen to sedimentary, igneous and metamorphic rocks. Marble is a metamorphic rock. It has been changed from limestone.

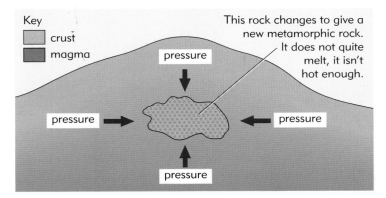

Key
- crust
- magma

This rock changes to give a new metamorphic rock. It does not quite melt, it isn't hot enough.

pressure

pressure ➡ ⬅ pressure

pressure

Limestone, a fairly soft rock that contains shells.

4 Copy and complete the following sentences.

When rocks change into metamorphic rocks, they become very hot but do not _____. If the rock did melt, it would cool to become an _____ rock.

■ The rock cycle

The materials that rocks are made from are being recycled all the time.

5 Copy and complete the diagram.

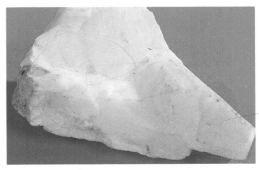

Marble, a hard rock made of crystals. Marble can be polished to give a shiny surface.

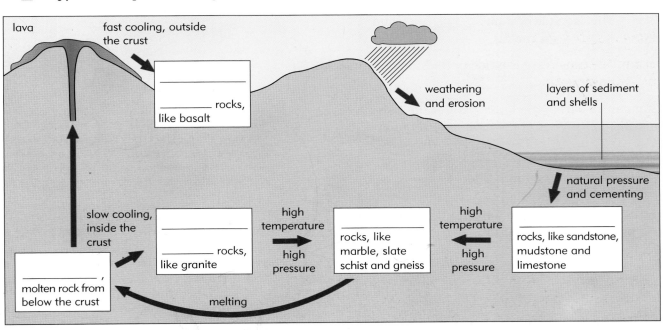

lava

fast cooling, outside the crust

_____ rocks, like basalt

weathering and erosion

layers of sediment and shells

natural pressure and cementing

slow cooling, inside the crust

_____ rocks, like granite

high temperature

high pressure

rocks, like marble, slate schist and gneiss

high temperature

high pressure

rocks, like sandstone, mudstone and limestone

_____, molten rock from below the crust

melting

79

The Earth

The Earth is nearly **spherical**. This means that it is round like a ball, although it is not perfectly round.

Look at the pictures.

1 Write down <u>two</u> things that mean the Earth is not perfectly round.

■ Inside the Earth

Even the deepest drill cannot make a hole through the Earth's **crust**. However, scientists think that the Earth is made of different layers. They have found out a bit about these layers by studying the way vibrations from explosions and earthquakes travel through the Earth. The diagram shows what these layers are probably like.

2 Imagine that you could drill a hole through the Earth to the centre.

Copy and complete the following sentences to say what you would find on the way through.

(a) First the drill would go through the solid rock in the Earth's _____.

(b) Next, the drill would reach the denser rocks of the _____. This has several layers.

(c) About halfway through to the centre of the Earth the drill would reach the outer _____.

This is made of liquid _____ and _____ metals.

(d) The inner core is made of the same two metals but they are _____.

Sometimes part of the lower crust or the outer mantle melts. We call the molten rock magma.

The Earth is much heavier than if it were only rock inside. We say that it has a higher density.

3 Why is the Earth much denser than the rocks that we find in the Earth's crust?

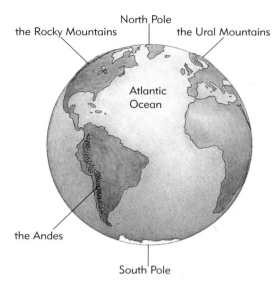

The surface of the Earth is bumpy. The Earth is slightly flattened at the North and South Poles.

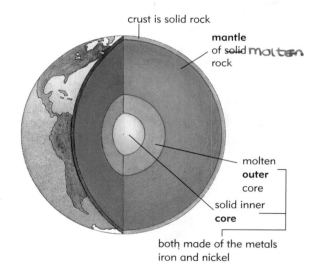

Nickel and **iron** are much heavier materials than rock. We say that they are **denser** than rock. The mantle is made of denser rock than the crust. This rock is solid, but the upper part is so near to its melting point that it is hot enough to **flow** very slowly.

Changes to the Earth's crust

The Earth's crust is changing all the time. Some of the changes happen quickly, but other changes are slow and can take millions of years. Look at the two diagrams and the two text boxes.

4 Write down <u>two</u> things that can change the Earth's crust quickly.

New rocks can form when things happen to the Earth's crust.

5 Copy the headings and complete the table.

What happens to the Earth's crust	Kind of rock formed

Some of the changes that happen to the Earth's crust wear away the hills and mountains.
Other changes help to form new hills and mountains.

6 Write down <u>two</u> changes that help to make new mountains.

When new mountains are made, rocks can be pushed up thousands of metres. This needs huge forces.

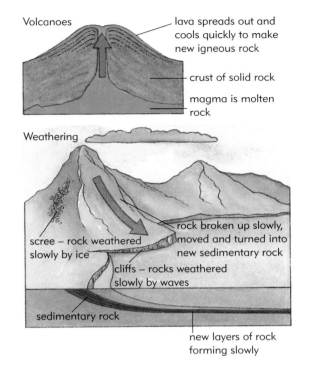

Volcanoes — lava spreads out and cools quickly to make new igneous rock — crust of solid rock — magma is molten rock

Weathering — scree – rock weathered slowly by ice — rock broken up slowly, moved and turned into new sedimentary rock — cliffs – rocks weathered slowly by waves — sedimentary rock — new layers of rock forming slowly

Earthquakes
The crust can suddenly move or break in an earthquake.

Rocks folding
Large forces can make rocks fold slowly. When rocks are folded upwards, they can form new hills and mountains. Some rocks can be changed into metamorphic rocks.

What you need to remember [Copy and complete using the **key words**]

The Earth

The Earth is shaped like a ball. We say it is nearly _____.

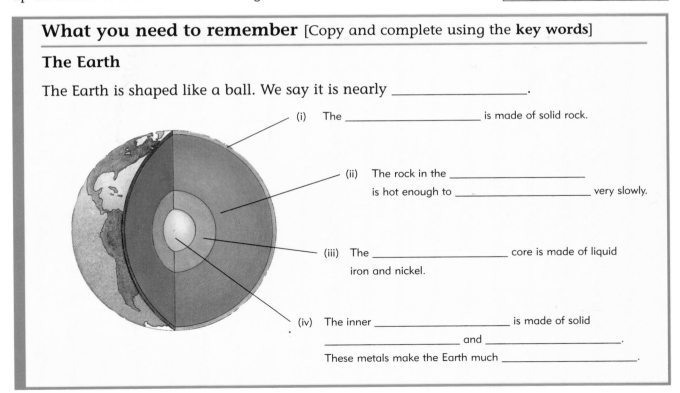

(i) The _____ is made of solid rock.

(ii) The rock in the _____ is hot enough to _____ very slowly.

(iii) The _____ core is made of liquid iron and nickel.

(iv) The inner _____ is made of solid _____ and _____.
These metals make the Earth much _____.

14 The present gives us clues to the past

> ## REMEMBER
> Sedimentary rocks are formed from layers of sediment containing sand, mud or shells. Another name for sediments is deposits.

We can see things now that give us clues to what happened millions of years ago. Look at the picture of the beach. Currents or waves made the **ripple marks** in the sand.

1 Look at the picture of the sandstone. What do the ripple marks tell you?

■ What forms the layers in sedimentary rocks?

Sometimes the kind of sediment changes. So a layer of different rock forms. Sometimes we see layers in rocks made from the <u>same</u> kind of sediment. This happens when sediments stop forming for a while and then start again. We say that there is a **break** in deposition. A new layer starts when sedimentation starts again.

2 What causes the layers in sedimentary rocks?

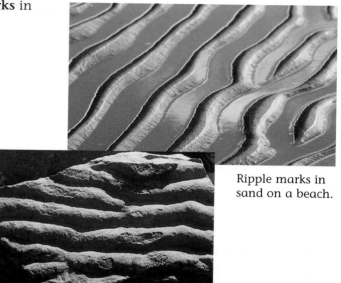

Ripple marks in sand on a beach.

Sandstone with ripple marks.

■ Why do layers vary in thickness?

Some layers in rocks are very thick. Others are thin. We find the thinnest layers in sediments from lakes that freeze. No sediments settle when the lake is frozen. A new layer forms each time it thaws. Each layer is the deposit of only one season and may be less than a millimetre thick.

Layers of limestone are often several metres thick. Each layer forms when tiny sea shells fall to the bottom of the sea continuously for hundreds or thousands of years.

3 The diagram shows thin layers of sandstone between layers of limestone. What you think happened to produce these layers?

Varves (very thin layers in rocks laid down in lakes which freeze seasonally). The rock formed shows many thin layers.

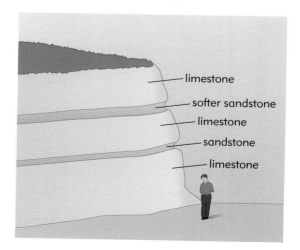

— limestone
— softer sandstone
— limestone
— sandstone
— limestone

■ Where are the oldest layers?

Rocks are very old compared to people.
But in rock age, 80 million years is really quite young.

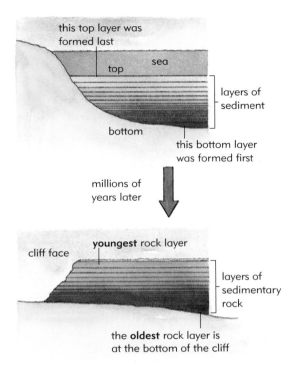

4 Look at the diagrams.
Copy and complete the following sentences.

The first layer of sediment is at the _____.

The last layer of sediment is at the _____.
This means that:

The oldest layer is at the _____.
The youngest layer of rock is at the _____.

Even if rocks have moved we can often tell which ones
are the oldest.

5 Look at the rock layers A, B, C, D.

(a) Which is the youngest rock?

(b) Which is the oldest rock?

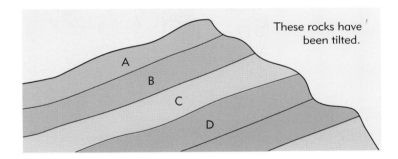

What you need to remember [Copy and complete using the **key words**]

The present gives us clues to the past

Often clues such as _____ _____ tell us about how rocks were formed.
A new layer in a sediment shows that there has been a _____ in deposition.
With sedimentary rock, normally:

■ the layer of rock at the bottom is the _____.

■ the layer of rock at the top is the _____.

This is usually true even when rocks have been moved.

15

Evidence for Earth movements

We often find layers of rock that have been tilted, folded and even broken or fractured. We call fractures in rocks <u>faults</u>.

Folds and faults are evidence that the Earth's crust moves.

It takes very large forces to fold and fracture rocks. Earthquakes happen when rocks move at a fault.

All these things are evidence that the Earth's crust is **unstable**.

1 Write down <u>three</u> different ways in which rocks can be moved.

> **REMEMBER**
>
> Sedimentary rocks are deposited in layers. The top layer of rock is usually the youngest.

■ Rocks that have moved

We can match the layers of rock that have been moved along a fault line or folded and partly worn away.

2 Find the rock on the right of the fault that is the same age as rock C.

3 Copy and complete the following sentences.

In the folded rocks:

Rock _____ is the same as rock A.

Rock _____ is the same as rock B.

These rocks have fractured. They have broken and slipped. We say that they have been **faulted**.

These rocks have been **folded**.
Then they have been partly worn away.

■ Upside down rocks

Sometimes layers of sedimentary rocks can get turned upside down by Earth movements. We know this has happened because of the ages of the fossils in the rocks.

How do we know when sediments are upside down?

In sedimentary rocks we often find **fossils**. These are the remains of plants and animals. Fossils tell us which kinds of plants and animals lived when the sediments were formed. Rocks that contain the same kinds of fossils are probably about the same age.

4 (a) Which kinds of rock contain fossils?

(b) Why don't you find fossils in igneous rocks?

5 How old are the following rocks?

(a) Rocks that contain dinosaur bones.

(b) Rocks that contain trilobites but not crinoids.

(c) Rocks that contain both sharks and crinoids.

6 Look at the diagram.

A friend says that these are sedimentary rocks so the oldest rocks must be at the bottom. Do you agree? Give a reason for your answer.

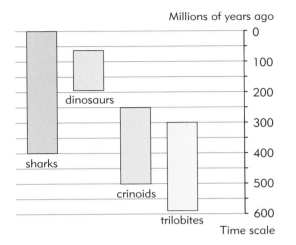

The bars show the ages of the fossils you might find.

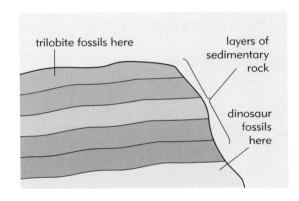

What you need to remember [Copy and complete using the **key words**]

Evidence for Earth movements

Large forces act on the Earth's crust.
So the crust is _____.
Sometimes layers of rock are tilted, _____ or _____.
Sometimes they are even turned upside down.

We can use _____ to tell us the age of each layer of rock.
Then we know whether or not the layers are the right way up.

Movements that make mountains

Movements of the **Earth's crust** can push up rocks for thousands of metres. We find rocks at the tops of mountains that formed from sediments in the sea. It takes a long time and huge forces for this to happen.

1 Look at the diagram. How do we know that rocks can be pushed up thousands of metres?

■ Some mountains are old, others are new

Different ranges of mountains were pushed up at different times during the Earth's history. As old mountains wore down in one place, new mountains were pushed up in others. The Scottish Highlands were part of a huge range of high mountains. They formed 450 to 550 million years ago. Since then, weathering and **erosion** have worn them down. Higher mountains such as the Alps are much younger. They formed 7 to 25 million years ago. The Andes and the Himalayas are even higher and they are still being pushed up.

2 Younger mountain ranges are usually higher than older mountain ranges. Explain why.

We call the Earth movements that build mountains **tectonic** activity. Where there is tectonic activity, there are volcanoes. So, we find igneous rocks as well as sedimentary rocks in mountains.

The movements in the Earth's crust during mountain-building produce high **temperatures** and **pressures**. So we find **metamorphic** rocks in places where mountains are forming. We also find metamorphic rocks where mountains formed in the past.

3 Why does mountain-building also result in the formation of metamorphic rocks?

This fossil came from an animal that lived in the sea millions of years ago.

> ### REMEMBER
>
> We call rocks that are altered by heat and pressure metamorphic rocks.

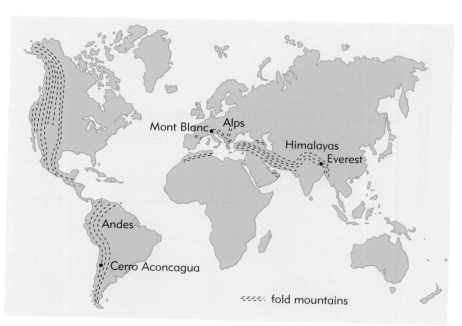

===== fold mountains

■ Earth movements cause earthquakes

Earthquakes happen when there is movement at faults. The most unstable parts of the Earth's crust are where the biggest earthquakes happen. Earthquakes sometimes kill thousands of people so finding out when one will happen is important. If scientists can predict when and where an earthquake will happen, people can move to a safer place.

■ The problem of predicting earthquakes

Scientists have set up seismic stations all round the world. These stations automatically record earthquakes. The scientists use the records to find out exactly where each Earth movement happened. They also look for patterns in the records to try to predict when and where earthquakes will happen. Another earthquake is expected in California soon. Unfortunately, scientists can't predict exactly where or when.

4 A lot of time and money is spent measuring earthquakes and trying to predict when they will happen.
Why do you think this is?

■ Predicting when a volcano will erupt

Predicting **volcanic eruptions** is also hard. Scientists also keep a close watch on volcanoes. They measure temperatures, pressures and the gases given off. This can be difficult and dangerous work. They can sometimes measure an increase in pressure and say that there will be an eruption in the next few months. But there are so many factors involved that, often, they cannot be more accurate.

5 Scientists cannot predict earthquakes and volcanic eruptions accurately. Write down a list of reasons for this.

Movement of rocks along the San Andreas fault caused the earthquake that destroyed this bridge in California.

Scientists predicted the eruption of Mount St. Helens and people were moved away from the upper slopes. But they were taken by surprise when the eruption caused all this damage.

What you need to remember [Copy and complete using the **key words**]

Movements that make mountains

Weathering and _____ wear mountains away.

Large-scale movements of the _____ _____ over millions of years cause new mountains to form.

Mountain-building involves high _____ and _____.

So _____ rocks form at the same time as new mountain belts.

Earthquakes and _____ _____ happen in places where there are Earth movements or _____ activity.

17 Why are some parts of the Earth's crust more unstable than others?

The Earth's crust and the upper part of the mantle are called the lithosphere.

The lithosphere is not made of one big piece of rock. Cracks split it into very large pieces called **tectonic plates**. The map shows some of them. The plates **move** all the time. They do not move very fast, just a few **centimetres** (cm) each year. But these small movements add up to big movements over a long time.

Did you know?

Tectonic plates move hardly any faster than your finger nails grow. They move at a slower rate than your hair grows.

This shows the way the plate is moving ➡

This shows the edges of the tectonic plates ——

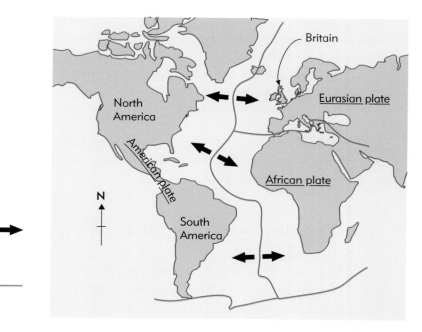

The lithosphere is most unstable in the places where two plates meet. These are the places that have earthquakes and volcanic eruptions.

1 Why do we have few earthquakes in Britain?

2 Copy and complete the following sentences.

Britain is on the _____ plate. North and South America are on the American _____.

3 (a) Which way is the American plate moving?

   (b) Which way is the Eurasian plate moving?

   (c) What is happening to the distance between America and Europe?

4 A plate moves about 5 cm each year.
   How far will the plate move in 1000 years?

The Earth today

The Earth millions of years ago

The **shapes** of South America and Africa fit together.

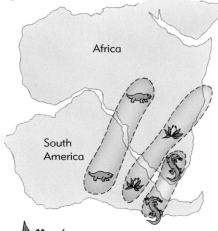

How do we know that plates move?

South America and Africa are on different plates. These plates have been moving away from each other for millions of years. Long ago, South America and Africa must have been together. Look at the diagrams.

5 The shapes of South America and West Africa tell us that they were once together. Explain why.

6 The rocks in South America and Africa also tell us that they were once joined together. Explain why.

Fossils of this fern have been found all over Africa and South America.

Fossils of this reptile have been found in Brazil and in Africa.

Fossils of this retile have been found in Argentina and in southern Africa.

How moving plates can make new mountains

Some of the plates of the Earth's crust are moving away from each other. Other plates are pushing into each other. When two plates move towards each other they can force rocks upwards to give new **mountains**.

7 Look at the diagram.

(a) Which <u>two</u> plates are pushing into each other?

(b) Which mountains have been formed by these moving plates?

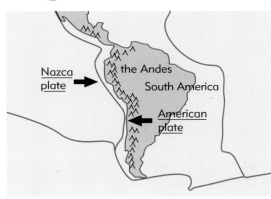

What you need to remember [Copy and complete using the **key words**]

Why are some parts of the Earth's crust more unstable than others?

The Earth's crust is cracked into large pieces. We call these _____ _____.

The plates _____ very slowly, just a few _____ each year.

Millions of years ago, South America and Africa were next to each other.

We know this because:

■ their _____ fit together well

■ they have rocks containing the same _____.

In some places, tectonic plates push together.

This forces some rocks upwards and makes new _____.

What keeps the Earth's crust moving?

Earthquake vibrations pass only through solids. So we know that the Earth's **mantle** is solid. But it is so close to its melting point that it can flow like a liquid. It flows very slowly. When there are movements in the mantle, the tectonic plates above also move.

■ What makes liquids move?

If a liquid gets hot, it moves around.
The diagrams show what happens.

1 Copy and complete the following sentences.

Water _____ around when you heat it. This is because hot water _____ and cold water moves _____ to take its place.

These movements are called **convection** currents.

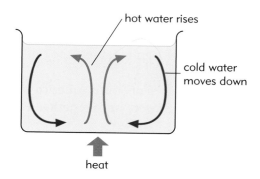

■ Convection currents inside the Earth

Heat produced inside the Earth causes slow convection currents in the mantle.

Look at the diagram.

2 Copy and complete the following sentences.

Convection currents in the mantle

■ make plates A and B move _____

■ make plates B and C move _____.

The plates can move because they 'float' on top of the _____. There are very slow _____ currents in the mantle.

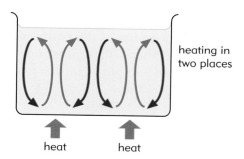

Movements of the mantle move the tectonic plates.

How does the inside of the Earth keep hot?

Something must be heating up the mantle or there wouldn't be any convection currents.

Radioactive substances inside the Earth produce the heat that is needed. The diagram shows how they do this.

3 Copy and complete the following sentences.

Uranium atoms _____ up into smaller atoms of _____ and _____. This change also releases some _____.

4 Radioactive substances will keep on heating up the inside of the Earth for a long time to come. Explain why.

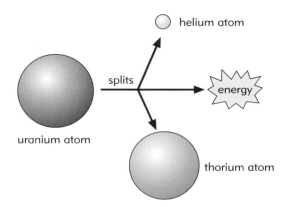

The Earth formed about 4.5 billion (4 500 000 000) years ago. Since then, about half of the uranium atoms have split up.

What happens when the tectonic plates move apart?

When tectonic plates push against each other, new mountains form.

The diagram shows what happens when plates move apart.

5 (a) What type of new rock spreads out through the cracks between plates?

(b) Why is this type of rock formed?

6 Look at the map. Write down the name of a country where basalt is forming.

The edges of the plates that are moving apart are usually under the sea.

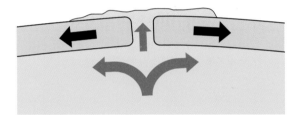

When two plates move apart, magma fills the gap. The magma quickly cools to form the igneous rock called basalt.

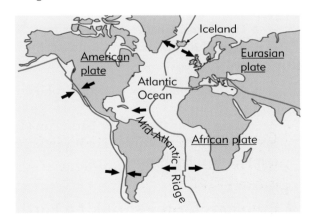

What you need to remember [Copy and complete using the **key words**]

What keeps the Earth's crust moving?

Tectonic plates move because of _____ currents in the _____ below the Earth's lithosphere.

The energy that produces the currents comes from _____ substances inside the Earth.

These ideas are extended, for Higher Tier students, in Earth materials H3 on pages 98–99.

19 Changing ideas about the Earth

Until about 200 ago, most people believed that the mountains, valleys and seas on the Earth had always been just like they are today. Many of these people thought the Earth was created only a few thousand years ago.

Then geologists started to study the rocks and to think about how they were formed. They realised that the Earth must be many millions of years old.

1 Why did they think that the Earth must be millions of years old?

2 What else did they then need to explain?

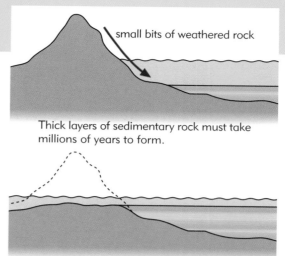

small bits of weathered rock

Thick layers of sedimentary rock must take millions of years to form.

Mountains would be completely worn away over millions of years. So geologists need to explain how new mountains are formed.

■ A cooling, shrinking Earth

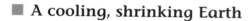

The diagrams show one theory about how new mountains are formed.

3 Write down the following sentences in the correct order.

- The molten core carries on cooling, but more and more slowly. It shrinks as it cools.

- The Earth began as a ball of hot, molten rock.

- The shrinking core makes the crust wrinkle. The high places become mountains, the low places become seas.

- As the molten rock cooled, a solid crust formed.

According to this theory, the Earth can't be more than about 400 million years old or it would be cool and completely solid by now.

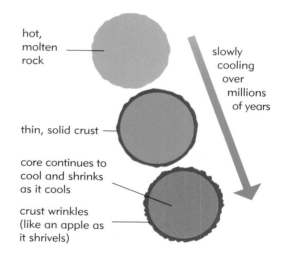

hot, molten rock

slowly cooling over millions of years

thin, solid crust

core continues to cool and shrinks as it cools

crust wrinkles (like an apple as it shrivels)

■ Problems for the shrinking Earth theory

We now know that the Earth is a lot older than 400 million years. We know this because the Earth contains quite a lot of radioactive elements such as uranium. The atoms of these elements gradually decay (break up). Heat is released as they do so.

4 What effect does this have on the Earth's core?

5 The oldest rocks on Earth are more than 3.5 billion years old. How do scientists know this?

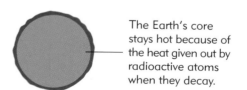

The Earth's core stays hot because of the heat given out by radioactive atoms when they decay.

Dating rocks

Scientists can measure

- the amounts of radioactive atoms in rocks

- the amounts of atoms produced when the radioactive atoms decay.

This tells them how old the rocks are.

The idea of a moving crust

Scientists now think that mountains are formed by the Earth's crust moving about. Alfred Wegener first suggested this idea during the early years of the twentieth century. But most scientists didn't agree for another 50 years. This idea was called the theory of continental drift.

6 Why was Wegener's theory of crustal movement called continental drift?

7 What evidence did scientists have for continental drift?

8 Why did many scientists not agree?

During the 1950s, scientists started to explore the rocks at the bottom of the oceans. The diagrams show what they found and how they explained it.

9 Copy and complete the following sentences.

Under the oceans are long _____ ridges.

These are made of rock that is quite _____.

The sea floor under the ocean is moving _____.

Magma from below the Earth's _____ moves up to make new rock.

The new evidence convinced scientists that the Earth's crust is made of a small number of separate sections called plates. Under the oceans these plates are moving apart. But in some places these plates are moving towards each other. This pushes rock upwards to make new mountains.

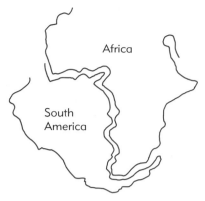

Some scientists suggested that South America and Africa must once have been together. Other scientists said that there was no way they could possibly have moved apart.

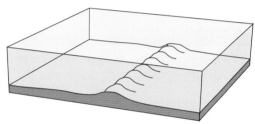

There are long mountain ridges underneath the ocean. They are made of young rocks.

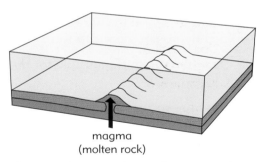

magma
(molten rock)

Sections of crust on the sea floor are moving apart. New rock forms to fill the gap.

What you need to remember

Changing ideas about the Earth

You should be able to:
- describe the 'shrinking Earth' model of how mountains are formed;
- explain why this model has been replaced by the idea of the Earth's crust being made up of moving plates;
- explain why the idea of moving continents was not accepted by most scientists until about 50 years after Wegener suggested it.

These ideas are extended, for Higher Tier students, in Earth materials H3 on pages 98–99.

H1   This extends *Earth materials* 6 for Higher Tier students

Two families of hydrocarbons

The strong bonds that hold atoms together in molecules of hydrocarbons are formed by shared pairs of electrons. We call them **covalent** bonds.
The diagrams show some hydrocarbon molecules.

Strong bonds hold the atoms together in the molecule, but there are only weak bonds <u>between</u> molecules. This means that many hydrocarbons are gases or liquids, or solids with low melting points.

Two families of hydrocarbons are **alkanes** and **alkenes**.

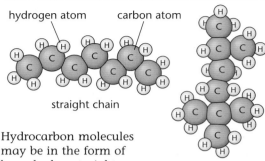

hydrogen atom   carbon atom

straight chain

Hydrocarbon molecules may be in the form of branched or straight chains, with carbon atoms forming the spine.

branched chain

The alkanes

Crude oil is a mixture of hydrocarbons, most of which are alkanes. The smallest alkane is methane: CH_4.

Sometimes it is useful to represent a substance with a structural formula. A structural formula shows how atoms are bonded in a molecule.

In all alkanes, the carbon atoms are joined by single bonds (that is, a single shared pair of electrons). Single bonds are shown as — in structural formulas. The structural formula for an alkane shows that:

- each carbon atom can form <u>four</u> bonds;
- each hydrogen atom can form <u>one</u> bond.

1 Draw the structural formula for the alkane butane, C_4H_{10}.

Alkanes are **saturated** hydrocarbons. This means that every carbon atom has used up all of its four bonds to link to other atoms.

The general formula for alkanes is C_nH_{2n+2}, where *n* is any number.

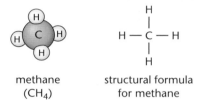

methane
(CH_4)

structural formula
for methane

Name of alkane	Molecular formula	Structural formula

ethane	C_2H_6	H H
		  | |
		H — C — C — H
		  | |
		H H

propane	C_3H_8	H H H
		  | | |
		H — C — C — C — H
		  | | |
		H H H

The alkenes

The alkenes are only found in small quantities in nature. Most are manufactured by cracking long chain alkanes.

Alkenes are not the same as alkanes. Alkenes have a double bond (that is, two shared pairs of electrons) between two of the carbon atoms in the chain.

2 Draw the structural formula for the alkene propene, C_3H_6.

3 What is the formula for the alkene that has <u>five</u> carbon atoms?

Alkanes are not very reactive because a lot of energy is needed to break C–H bonds. Reactions with other substances tend to be slow.

Structural formula for ethene (the simplest alkene).	 double bond

The general formula for alkenes is C_nH_{2n}.

The alkenes are much more reactive than the alkanes because the double carbon–carbon bonds can 'open up' to provide extra bonds. Extra atoms of other elements can be attached to these bonds. So we say that alkenes are **unsaturated**.

How do we test for alkenes?

Bromine is one of the elements that can join with the extra bonds formed when the double bonds in alkenes open up. Bromine water is yellow–brown. It becomes colourless as bromine reacts with ethene.
So we can use bromine water as a test for alkenes.

Alkanes do not react with bromine.

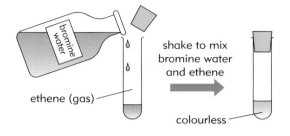

4 Write down what you would see when bromine water is shaken with
   (a) an alkene,
   (b) an alkane.

Alkenes joining together

Because of the double bond, alkene molecules can also react with each other. For example, when heated under pressure with a catalyst, ethene molecules will join together to form very long chain molecules.
The diagram shows what happens.

5 Copy and complete the sentence.

When unsaturated _____ molecules join together to produce a _____ and no other substance, it is called _____ polymerisation.

6 Copy and complete the following.

$$n \left(\begin{array}{c} H \quad H \\ | \quad\quad | \\ C = C \\ | \quad\quad | \\ H \quad Cl \end{array} \right) \longrightarrow$$

vinyl chloride monomers   poly(vinyl chloride) or PVC

Addition polymerisation

'Mono' means 'one'; 'poly' means 'many'.

many small molecules of ethene **(monomers)**	long chain molecule **(polymer)** called poly(ethene)

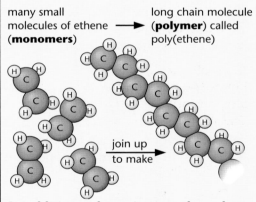

In addition polymerisation, the polymer is the only product. The reaction can be represented like this:

$$n \left(\begin{array}{c} H \quad H \\ | \quad\quad | \\ C = C \\ | \quad\quad | \\ H \quad H \end{array} \right) \longrightarrow \left(\begin{array}{c} H \quad H \\ | \quad\quad | \\ C - C \\ | \quad\quad | \\ H \quad H \end{array} \right)_n$$

monomer ethene   poly(ethene)
molecules
where n is a large number.

Using your knowledge

1 Explain why alkenes are more useful than alkanes.

2 The diagram represents the polymer poly(styrene). Draw a diagram to represent <u>one</u> molecule of the monomer from which the polymer was formed.

$$\left(\begin{array}{c} H \quad H \\ | \quad\quad | \\ C - C \\ | \quad\quad | \\ H \quad C_6H_5 \end{array} \right)_n$$

More about changes in the atmosphere

The amount of nitrogen increases

Today, about $\frac{4}{5}$ of the Earth's atmosphere today is nitrogen. The Earth's early atmosphere contained only small amounts of nitrogen. Some of the nitrogen was the element itself. The rest of it was in a compound called ammonia. Ammonia dissolves really well in water. So most of the ammonia in the early atmosphere dissolved in the rain and went into the seas. Some plants and bacteria used this ammonia. They released most of the nitrogen from ammonia.

1 Explain how ammonia got into the seas.

2 Describe a chemical reaction that releases nitrogen from ammonia.

3 Chemical reactions that release nitrogen also take place in living things. What kind of bacteria release nitrogen into the atmosphere?

The ozone layer forms

As the amount of oxygen increased, ozone formed. It collected in a layer in the upper atmosphere.

The **ozone** layer is important for living things. It filters out **ultra-violet radiation** from the Sun. This radiation can harm living things. Too much ultra-violet radiation can cause disorders such as skin cancer and cataract. Cataract is a clouding of the lens of the eye. This is why doctors say that it harms us to get sun-burned. Some scientists think that it was the ozone layer that let the first land plants evolve. Once plants managed to survive on the land, animals went there too.

4 Look at the diagram. Where is the ozone layer?

5 Write down <u>two</u> reasons why the ozone layer is important for living things.

REMEMBER

Photosynthesis adds oxygen to the atmosphere.

ammonia + oxygen → nitrogen + water

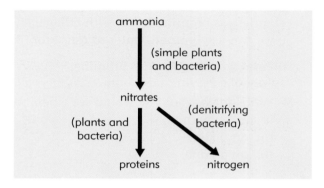

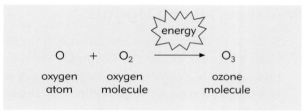

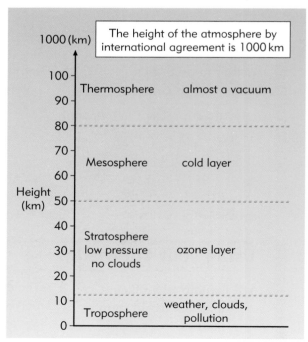

Layers of the atmosphere to show where the ozone layer is. Scientists usually call 150 km the top of the atmosphere.

■ 'Locked-up' carbon dioxide is released

The carbon in fossil fuels and carbonate rocks is not 'locked-up' forever. Sometimes Earth movements bury carbonate rocks so deeply in the Earth that they decompose and carbon dioxide is released. It gets back into the atmosphere through volcanoes.

$$\text{calcium carbonate} \xrightarrow{\text{heat}} \text{calcium oxide} + \text{carbon dioxide}$$

We add even more carbon dioxide to the atmosphere when we burn fossil fuels. Some of this carbon dioxide ends up in the sea as carbonates and hydrogen carbonates. Insoluble calcium carbonate and other carbonates form sediments. Hydrogen carbonates, mainly of calcium and magnesium, are soluble so they stay in the water.

Burning fuels releases carbon dioxide into the atmosphere.

6 Explain <u>two</u> ways that 'locked-up' carbon dioxide is released.

7 Write down the names of <u>two</u> groups of chemicals that form when carbon dioxide reacts with sea water.

■ A problem with carbon dioxide

Now, we burn so much fossil fuel that we are putting more carbon dioxide into the atmosphere than plants and the sea are taking out. This carbon dioxide acts like a blanket and makes the Earth warmer.

8 Write down <u>two</u> things that we can do to stop the amount of carbon dioxide in the atmosphere increasing further. Explain your answers.

Using your knowledge

1 The graph shows how the percentage of carbon dioxide in the Earth's atmosphere is believed to have changed over the past 4500 million years. Explain these changes as fully as you can.

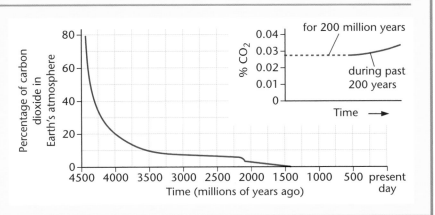

H3 This extends *Earth materials* 19 for Higher Tier students

More about tectonic plates

The Earth's lithosphere is cracked into a number of **tectonic plates**, which are slowly moving. Movement is caused by **convection currents** in the Earth's mantle.
Tectonic plates vary in thickness from 50 to 200 km.

The boundaries between the plates are called plate margins. At these plate margins, three different things can happen:

■ the plates can slide past each other;

■ the plates can move towards each other;

■ the plates can move apart.

1 Where on the map are the plates sliding past each other?

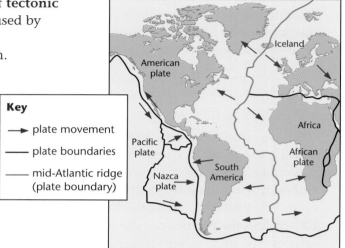

Key

→ plate movement

— plate boundaries

— mid-Atlantic ridge (plate boundary)

■ Plates sliding past each other

When two plates slide past each other, no crust is created or destroyed, but friction between the two plates leads to earthquakes.

San Francisco, in California, USA, sits on top of the San Andreas fault, where movement is about 5 cm per year. Small earthquakes happen often but Californians fear 'the big one'.

2 (a) What do we call the margin between two plates that slide past each other?

   (b) What effect do the sliding plates have?

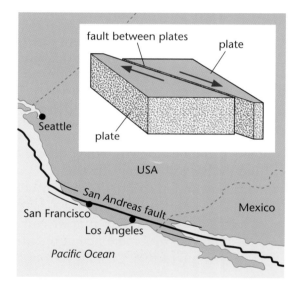

■ Plates moving towards each other

Oceanic crust is denser than continental crust. So when they are pushed against each other the oceanic crust is forced down or **subducted**. The huge forces crumple and push up the layers of rock in the oceanic crust to form a **fold mountain chain**. In places where the subducted crust melts, the magma rises and volcanoes form.

3 (a) Outline what happens when an oceanic and a continental plate move towards each other.

   (b) Where, on the map at the top of the page, are mountains being made in this way?

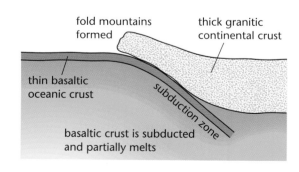

Plates moving apart

Where two plates are moving apart, the oceanic crust cracks. Magma rises to fill the cracks. It cools and solidifies forming new oceanic crust. New crust is added all the time as new cracks open.
This is **sea floor spreading**.

Sea floor spreading is happening in the middle of the Atlantic Ocean in a line between Europe and Africa and the Americas. We call it the mid-Atlantic ridge.

Occasionally the **oceanic ridge** rises above sea level to form volcanic islands. For example, the island of Surtsey rose out of the Atlantic Ocean in 1963 from a large submarine volcanic eruption.

4 Explain the positions of the rocks on Iceland and describe what is happening at this plate boundary.

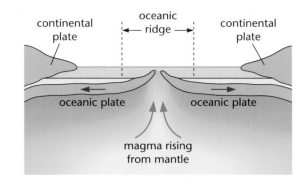

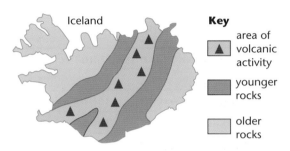

The island of Iceland sits astride an oceanic ridge called the mid-Atlantic ridge.

Scientists have found some interesting support for the theory of sea floor spreading. The Earth's magnetic field reverses from time to time. When magma solidifies, the iron-rich minerals in it line up with the magnetic field at the time.

Scientists looked at the magnetism of the rocks on either side of oceanic ridges. They found a pattern of magnetic stripes parallel to the ridges. This magnetic **reversal pattern** was the same on both sides of the ridges. In sea floor spreading, new rock moves away on both sides of a ridge, so the pattern was fairly symmetrical.

5 Describe the pattern of magnetic stripes found in rocks in certain places on the sea bed and explain how the stripes were formed.

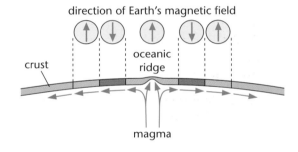

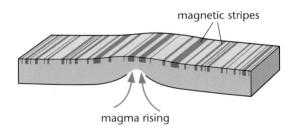

Using your knowledge

1 Explain why marine fossils are found high in the Andes mountains, on the west coast of South America.

2 Africa and South America are now about 5000 km apart. Assuming that plates move apart at an average speed of 2.5 cm per year, how long ago did they form one land mass?

How substances can change their state

Water is often a liquid. But it can also be a solid or a gas. Many other substances can also be a solid, liquid or gas. What state they are in depends on the temperature.

1 What do we call water

(a) when it is in the solid state?

(b) when it is in the gas state?

2 Copy and complete the table.

Change of state	What we call the change
solid into liquid	the solid has _____
liquid into solid	the liquid has _____
liquid into gas	the liquid has _____
gas into liquid	the gas has _____

Scientists use the idea of particles to explain changes of state.

■ Why do solids melt?

If we heat up a solid we give the particles more <u>energy</u>. They can move from side to side more quickly. When they get enough energy the particles break away from their fixed positions. They are then free to move around each other.

3 Look at the diagrams below, then copy and complete the following sentences.

If we make a solid hot enough then all of the _____ break away from their fixed positions, and can _____ around each other.

The solid turns into a _____.

REMEMBER

■ Substances can be solids, liquids or gases. We call these the three states of matter.

■ All substances are made of very small particles.

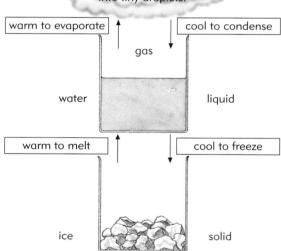

water vapour

You <u>can't</u> see water vapour unless it has already condensed into tiny droplets.

warm to evaporate   cool to condense

gas

water   liquid

warm to melt   cool to freeze

ice   solid

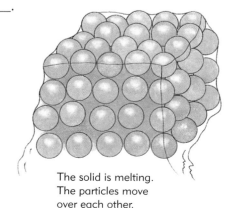

Solid. Particles in fixed positions.

The solid is melting. The particles move over each other.

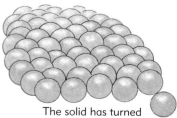

The solid has turned into a liquid.

The temperature at which a solid melts is called the <u>melting point</u> of that solid.

4 What is the melting point of

(a) ice?

(b) gold?

■ Why do liquids evaporate?

Liquids can evaporate even when they are quite cool. If you spill petrol on to a garage floor it 'dries up' quickly. The petrol <u>evaporates</u>.

We can make liquids evaporate more <u>quickly</u> if we heat them up.

5 Look at the diagram.

(a) What happens to the particles in a liquid if we heat them up?

(b) What happens to the particles in a liquid when they gain enough energy?

(c) What do the escaped particles form?

■ What happens when a liquid boils?

If we heat a liquid its temperature will rise. If we keep on heating it, the liquid will <u>boil</u>. When it is boiling the temperature of the liquid stays the same. This temperature is called the boiling point.

6 A kettle is switched on to make a pot of tea. The graph shows the temperature of the water inside the kettle. Copy and complete the following sentences.

The kettle boiled at _____ °C.
It took _____ seconds for the water to boil.

7 The diagram shows what happens when a liquid boils.

(a) How can you <u>see</u> when a liquid is boiling?

(b) Where have the bubbles of gas come from?

When a liquid is boiling, <u>all</u> the energy we supply is used to change the liquid into gas. So the temperature stays the same.

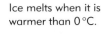

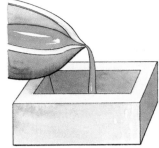

Ice melts when it is warmer than 0 °C.

Gold melts if it is hotter than 1064 °C.

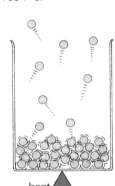

If we heat up a liquid the particles move more quickly.

If the particles have enough energy they escape. The particles now form a gas.

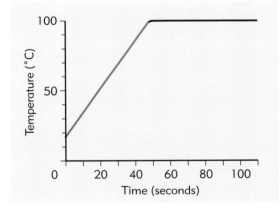

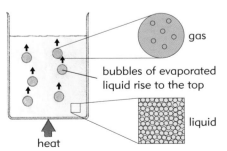

gas

bubbles of evaporated liquid rise to the top

liquid

heat

A boiling liquid

Elements and compounds

All chemical substances are made from tiny **atoms**.
There are about 100 different kinds of atoms in nature.
If a substance is made from just one kind of atom, we
call it an **element**.

1 How many elements do you think there are?
Give a reason for your answer.

Carbon is an element.
It contains only carbon
atoms.

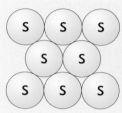

Sulphur is an element.
It contains only sulphur
atoms.

■ **Using letters to stand for elements**

Kenneth Gill's briefcase.

We can save time and space by using our initials instead
of writing our full name.
In science we often use the initials of an element instead
of the whole word. We call these letters the **symbols** of
the elements.

The table shows some of these symbols.

2 What is the symbol for

(a) carbon?

(b) sulphur?

3 (a) What are the symbols for calcium and
for silicon?

(b) Why do you think these elements need to have a
second, smaller letter in their symbol?

Some of the symbols we use come from the old names of
the elements.

4 Copy and complete the following table.

Element	Old name	Symbol
	cuprum	
sodium		

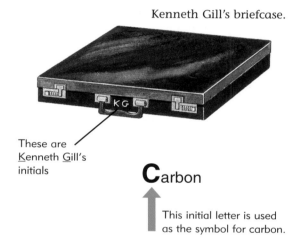

These are
Kenneth Gill's
initials

Carbon

This initial letter is used
as the symbol for carbon.

Element	Symbol we use	
carbon	C	
calcium	Ca	
copper	Cu	from *cuprum*, the old name
nitrogen	N	
neon	Ne	
sulphur	S	
silicon	Si	
sodium	Na	from *natrium*, the old name

What are compounds?

When atoms of different elements join together we get substances called **compounds**.
Most substances are compounds.

The diagrams show some compounds. Each compound has its own **formula**. The formula of a compound tells us two things:

- it tells us which elements are in the compound

- it tells us how many atoms of each element there are in the compound.

5 Copy the table. Then complete it to include all of the compounds shown on this page.

Name of compound	Formula	Atoms in the compound
carbon dioxide	CO_2	1 carbon atom, 2 oxygen atoms
water		
ammonia		
calcium oxide		
copper sulphate		
calcium hydroxide		

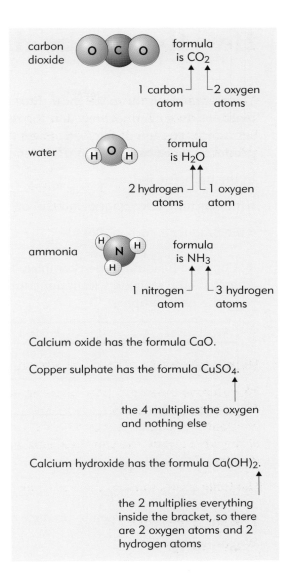

carbon dioxide — formula is CO_2 — 1 carbon atom — 2 oxygen atoms

water — formula is H_2O — 2 hydrogen atoms — 1 oxygen atom

ammonia — formula is NH_3 — 1 nitrogen atom — 3 hydrogen atoms

Calcium oxide has the formula CaO.

Copper sulphate has the formula $CuSO_4$.

the 4 multiplies the oxygen and nothing else

Calcium hydroxide has the formula $Ca(OH)_2$.

the 2 multiplies everything inside the bracket, so there are 2 oxygen atoms and 2 hydrogen atoms

---

What you need to remember [Copy and complete using the **key words**]

Elements and compounds

All substances are made from tiny _____.
If the substance has atoms that are all of one type, we call it an _____.
Substances made from atoms of different elements joined together are called

_____.

We use letters to stand for elements. We call these _____.
The _____ of a compound tells us which atoms are in the compound.

[If you are given the formula of a compound, you should be able to say how many atoms there are of each element in the compound.]

How to describe chemical reactions

The diagrams on this page show three different chemical reactions. In a chemical reaction the **reactants** are the substances you use at the start. These turn into **products**, the substances left at the end.

In the barbecue reaction:

- the reactants are oxygen and carbon

- the product is carbon dioxide

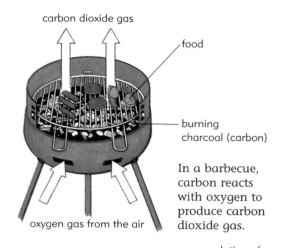

In a barbecue, carbon reacts with oxygen to produce carbon dioxide gas.

1 Copy the headings. Then complete the table to include the reaction with magnesium ribbon shown in the photographs.

Reactant(s)	Product(s)
carbon oxygen	carbon dioxide

Writing word equations

In the barbecue reaction:

carbon reacts with oxygen to produce carbon dioxide

We can write this:

carbon + oxygen $\longrightarrow$ carbon dioxide

We call this a **word equation**.

2 Write down a word equation for the reaction between zinc and copper sulphate shown in the photographs.

Understanding symbol equations

There is another way to write down what happens in a chemical reaction. We can replace the <u>name</u> of each reactant and product with a **formula**.

For the barbecue reaction the two kinds of equation look like this:

carbon + oxygen $\longrightarrow$ carbon dioxide

C + O_2 $\longrightarrow$ CO_2

Magnesium reacts with dilute hydrochloric acid to produce hydrogen gas and a solution of magnesium chloride.

Zinc reacts with copper sulphate solution to produce zinc sulphate solution and copper metal.

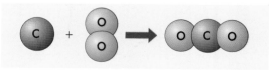

Carbon reacts with oxygen to produce carbon dioxide.

We call the second one a **symbol equation**.

The box shows the symbol equations for the other two reactions shown on the last page.

3 Copy each of the symbol equations from the box. Write the name of each reactant and product underneath the right formula.

The atoms of elements that are gases often go round in pairs.

4 Write down the names of <u>three</u> gases, besides oxygen, with atoms that go round in pairs.

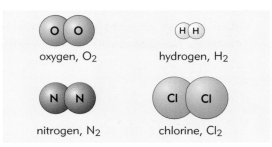

Mg + 2HCl ⟶ MgCl₂ + H₂
Zn + CuSO₄ ⟶ ZnSO₄ + Cu

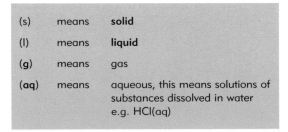

oxygen, O₂   hydrogen, H₂

nitrogen, N₂   chlorine, Cl₂

Oxygen is a gas. Oxygen atoms go round in pairs. The atoms of some other gases also go round in pairs.

Adding state symbols

Reactants and products can be solids, liquids or gases, or can be dissolved in water.
We can show this by using state symbols.

In the barbecue reaction:

carbon is a solid

oxygen and carbon dioxide are both gases

We can now write the equation like this:

C(s) + O₂(g) ⟶ CO₂(g)

5 Add state symbols to the symbol equations for the other two reactions. Remember that solutions need the state symbol (aq).

(s)	means	solid
(l)	means	liquid
(g)	means	gas
(aq)	means	aqueous, this means solutions of substances dissolved in water e.g. HCl(aq)

What state symbols mean.

What you need to remember [Copy and complete using the **key words**]

How to describe chemical reactions

We can describe a chemical reaction using a **word** _____.
The substances that react are the _____.
The new substances that are produced are the _____.
We can replace the names of each reactant and product by writing its _____.
The equation for the reaction is now called a _____ **equation**.
In a symbol equation, (s) stands for _____, (l) stands for _____, _____ stands for gas, _____ stands for aqueous solution.

[You should now be able to:
■ write word equations for reactions you know about
■ explain what a symbol equation means in words.]

Where did the idea of atoms come from?

The most important theory in chemistry is the atomic theory. An Englishman called John Dalton put forward this theory about 200 years ago. His idea was that there is a small number of different types of atoms. These atoms can join together in different ways to produce millions of new substances.

■ Earlier ideas about atoms

The idea of everything being made of small particles is actually a very old idea. It was first thought of 2000 years ago by the ancient Greeks (see Box). Much later, in the seventeenth century, Robert Boyle used the idea to explain why you can squeeze air and other gases into a smaller space. Dalton had read about Boyle's work and realised that he could use the idea of particles to explain discoveries that chemists had made during the eighteenth century. One of these discoveries was that there is a small number of simple substances, or elements, from which all other substances are made.

1 (a) When and where was the idea of atoms first used?

  (b) What does the word 'atom' mean?

  (c) Where did Dalton meet the idea of particles?

John Dalton (1766–1844)

Where the word *atom* comes from

The Greek word *atomos* means 'can't be cut'.

■ The idea of elements

The idea of everything being made from a small number of elements also dates back to the ancient Greeks. But their idea of what these elements were – air, earth, fire and water – was completely wrong. But alchemists believed in this idea for nearly 2000 years. This is why they kept on trying to do impossible things such as changing lead into gold.

2 Why did alchemists think that they should be able to change lead into gold?

The alchemist's quest

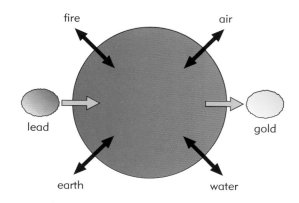

By getting just the right mix of the four elements you could turn lead into gold.

How chemists discovered elements

During the eighteenth century, chemists realised that there were some substances that they couldn't split up into anything simpler. So they decided that these substances must be the simplest possible substances. In other words these substances were <u>elements</u>.

The diagrams show the kinds of observations that chemists made to find out which substances were elements.

3 (a) Is the white powder an element?
Give a reason for your answer.

(b) Is the yellow powder an element?
Give a reason for your answer.

(c) Is the shiny bead of metal an element?
Give a reason for your answer.

The following word equations describe the reactions shown in the diagrams:

lead carbonate → lead oxide + carbon dioxide

lead oxide + carbon → lead + carbon dioxide

4 (a) What is the white powder?

(b) What is the yellow powder?

(c) What is the shiny metal?

So, by the end of the eighteenth century, chemists had the idea of an element based on their experiments. An element was a substance that could not be split up into simpler substances (see Box). All other substances were compounds made from two, or more, different elements. By using chemical reactions, you could split up compounds into the elements they were made from.

5 By the end of the eighteenth century, chemists knew that it was impossible to turn lead into gold. Explain why they knew this.

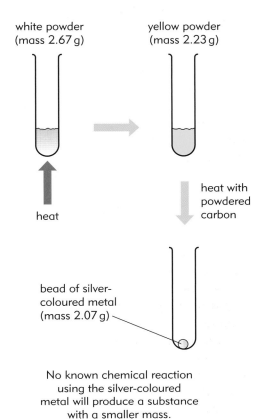

white powder (mass 2.67 g)   yellow powder (mass 2.23 g)

heat

heat with powdered carbon

bead of silver-coloured metal (mass 2.07 g)

No known chemical reaction using the silver-coloured metal will produce a substance with a smaller mass.

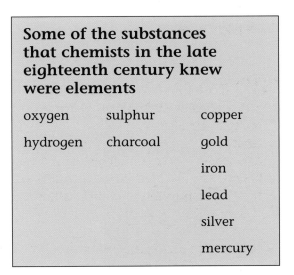

Some of the substances that chemists in the late eighteenth century knew were elements

oxygen	sulphur	copper
hydrogen	charcoal	gold
		iron
		lead
		silver
		mercury

This topic continues on the next page.

Where did the idea of atoms come from? *continued*

■ Dalton's atomic theory

Dalton explained <u>why</u> there are different elements by using these ideas:

- ■ elements are made up of small, indestructible particles which can be called atoms;

- ■ the atoms of a particular element are identical, for example in size and weight (mass);

- ■ the atoms of different elements are different;

- ■ compounds are formed by atoms of different elements joining together.

6 How would Dalton explain why it is impossible to change lead into gold?

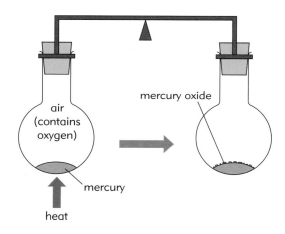

lead is made of indestructible lead atoms

changing lead into gold is impossible

gold is made of indestructible gold atoms

Dalton's ideas also explained another important discovery that chemists had made during the eighteenth century. They had found that when a chemical reaction happens inside a closed container there is never any change in mass.

7 Use Dalton's atomic theory to explain:

(a) why there is no change in mass when mercury reacts with oxygen inside a closed container;

(b) why there is a change in mass when mercury reacts with oxygen in the open.

A chemical reaction in a sealed container. There is no change in mass.

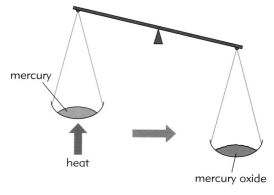

When the reaction occurs in the open there is an increase in mass.

What makes Dalton's theory scientific?

The problem with the ancient Greeks' idea of atoms was not that it was wrong but that they had no way of testing it. It was <u>just</u> an idea. There was no way of finding out whether it was right or wrong. So it wasn't really a scientific theory.

But Dalton's idea of atoms was not just an idea. It was a <u>scientific theory</u> which explained many observations and measurements that scientists had made. As scientists made lots more observations and measurements the theory explained all of them too. So scientists became more and more sure that the theory was correct.

8 Explain why:

   (a) Dalton's atomic theory is a genuine <u>scientific</u> theory;

   (b) most other chemists at the time quickly accepted Dalton's theory;

   (c) Dalton's theory is now very firmly established.

How the news about Dalton's theory spread

Dalton earned his living as a schoolteacher and private tutor. He had to use his spare time to study science and to do scientific experiments. He spoke in public about his scientific ideas at the Manchester Literary and Philosophical Society. These talks were then published in print so many other people, including other scientists, soon knew about his new atomic theory.

9 How did other chemists very quickly find out about Dalton's atomic theory?

For Higher Tier students only

Dalton's theory succeeds again

By the end of the eighteenth century, chemists had also discovered that each particular chemical compound always contains the same elements in exactly the same proportions by weight (mass).

Water, for example, is always made up of 8 grams of oxygen combined with 1 gram of hydrogen.

Dalton explained this by suggesting that the atoms of different elements in a particular compound always join together in the same proportions. In some compounds there might be equal numbers of atoms of each element. In other compounds there might be two atoms of one element for each atom of another element.

In water, for example, Dalton thought that there was probably an equal number of oxygen and hydrogen atoms:

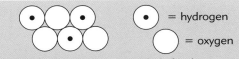

These are Dalton's own symbols for the atoms.

We now know that in water there are in fact two hydrogen atoms for every oxygen atom.

10 How many times heavier is an oxygen atom than a hydrogen atom:

   (a) for Dalton?

   (b) for modern chemists?

What you need to remember

Where did the idea of atoms come from?

You do not need to <u>remember</u> any information from this topic.
You need to be able to <u>interpret</u> information you are given in the same sort of way.

Two families of elements

■ A table of elements

During the nineteenth century, chemists discovered how to compare the weights of different atoms.
In other words, they found the **relative atomic mass** of each element.

Mendeleev then produced a **Periodic Table**:

■ by listing the elements in order starting with the element that had the lightest atoms;

■ by arranging the list of elements in rows as shown on this page.

Each column in the table contains similar elements. These columns are called **Groups**.

[You will find more about how chemists developed the Periodic Table on pages 116–117.]

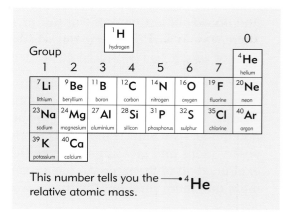

Periodic Table showing the first 20 elements.

1 Write down the names of the first three elements:

(a) in Group 1;

(b) in Group 0.

2 Potassium atoms have a <u>smaller</u> mass than argon atoms. But potassium was placed <u>after</u> argon in the Periodic Table. Explain why.

Note
Potassium atoms actually have a smaller relative atomic mass than argon atoms.
But we still put potassium <u>after</u> argon in the Periodic Table.
We do this because potassium is similar to the elements in Group 1 and argon is similar to the elements in Group 0.

■ Group 1 elements – the alkali metals

The elements in Group 1 of the Periodic Table are all metals. They are good conductors of heat and electricity. They can also be bent or hammered into shape without breaking. But they are softer than most other metals and have lower melting points and boiling points.

The diagram shows what happens when an alkaline metal reacts with water.

3 How do we know that the colourless solution is alkaline?

4 Sodium gives an alkali with water. What is the name of this alkali?

All alkali metals react with water to give **alkaline** solutions. This is why we call these metals the **alkali metals**.

The sodium moves about on top of the water, making it fizz. A colourless solution of sodium **hydroxide** is produced.

dropper containing universal indicator

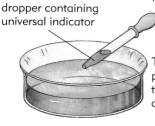

The indicator turns purple, which shows that the solution is alkaline.

Group 0 elements – the noble gases

The elements in Group 0 aren't very interesting. They are colourless gases so you cannot see them. You cannot use them to make new substances, because they are **unreactive**. This is why we call them **noble gases**.

Because they are so unreactive, or <u>inert</u>, noble gases have some important uses.

5 Copy and complete the table.

Name of noble gas	How we use the noble gas	Why we can use the gas like this
helium	used to fill balloons and airships	helium is lighter than air and does not burn

The diagrams below show another difference between noble gases and other elements that are gases at room temperature (20°C).

Atoms of noble gases go around by themselves. We say that they are **mon**atomic. [mon = 1]

Atoms of other gases join in pairs to form **molecules**. We say they are diatomic. [di = 2]

6 (a) How do atoms of noble gases go around?

(b) How is this different from the atoms of other elements that are gases?

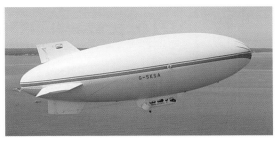

Helium is lighter than air. It is safe in balloons and airships because it is non-flammable (does not burn).

A tube filled with neon glows red when electricity is passed through it.

Argon won't react with the metal filament in a lamp, even when it is white hot.

What you need to remember [Copy and complete using the **key words**]

Two families of elements

Elements can be listed in order of the mass of their atoms (their _____ **atomic mass.**)

This list can then be arranged in rows to make a _____ **Table.**

In this table, elements with similar properties are all in the same _____.

The elements in Group 1 of the Periodic Table are called _____ _____

They all react with water to produce an _____ solution of the metal _____.

The elements in Group 0 of the Periodic Table are called _____ _____

They are _____. This makes _____ a safe gas to use in balloons and airships, and _____ a suitable gas to fill the bulbs of filament lamps.

The atoms of noble gases do not pair up to form _____.

So we say noble gases are _____atomic.

The halogens – another chemical family

We have already learnt about one family of elements, the alkali metals. The alkali metals are all in Group 1 of the Periodic Table of the elements.

In **Group 7** there is another family of elements. We call this family of elements the **halogens**.

1 Write down the names of <u>four</u> elements in the halogen family.

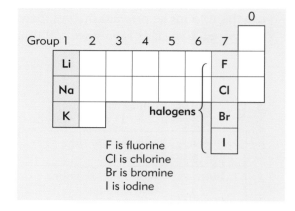

F is fluorine
Cl is chlorine
Br is bromine
I is iodine

■ What are the halogens like?

The halogens are non-metals. The diagrams show what some of the halogens look like at room temperature.

2 At room temperature:

(a) which halogen is a solid?

(b) which <u>two</u> halogens are gases?

(c) which halogen is a liquid that gives off a gas?

The halogens are all coloured when they are gases. Other elements that are gases have no colour, so we say they are colourless. An example is oxygen gas.

3 Copy and complete the table. The first row has been filled in for you.

Name of the halogen	Colour of gas
fluorine	pale yellow

Fluorine.

Bromine.

Chlorine.

Iodine crystals.

heat

Iodine crystals produce iodine gas when you heat them.

4 Look at the diagram. Copy and complete the following sentence.

Halogen _____ contain pairs of halogen atoms.

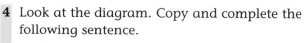

fluorine   chlorine   bromine   iodine

Halogen atoms are joined together in pairs. We call these pairs **molecules**.

Halogens can react with metals

Halogens react with metals to form compounds called **halides**. Halides are part of a family of compounds called **salts**. The word 'halogen' means 'salt maker'. The diagram shows how you can make ordinary salt, the kind you can put on your food.

5 What is the chemical name for ordinary salt?

6 Which two elements are in ordinary salt?

7 Write down a word equation for the reaction to make salt.

The other alkali metals react with halogens in the same kind of way. The box shows how we name the salts.

8 What do we call the salt made from:

   (a) potassium and iodine?

   (b) lithium and bromine?

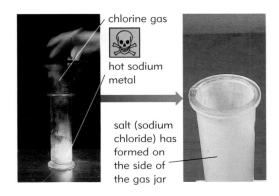

chlorine gas

hot sodium metal

salt (sodium chloride) has formed on the side of the gas jar

$$2Na(s) + Cl_2(g) \longrightarrow 2NaCl(s)$$

The names we give to salts from the halogens

fluorine gives salts called fluorides

chlorine gives salts called chlorides

bromine gives salts called bromides

iodine gives salts called iodides

Halogens can react with other non-metals

Halogen atoms can join up with atoms of other **non-metals** such as hydrogen and carbon. The diagrams show some of the new compounds that can be made.

9 Write down the name and the formula of a halogen compound that we use to make a plastic.

10 (a) Draw a molecule that contains <u>two</u> different halogens.

   (b) For what was this compound once used?

   (c) Why don't we use this compound any more?

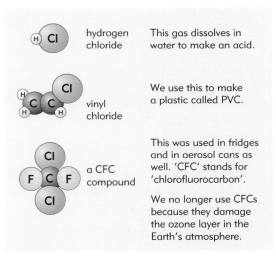

hydrogen chloride — This gas dissolves in water to make an acid.

vinyl chloride — We use this to make a plastic called PVC.

a CFC compound — This was used in fridges and in aerosol cans as well. 'CFC' stands for 'chlorofluorocarbon'.

We no longer use CFCs because they damage the ozone layer in the Earth's atmosphere.

Some compounds of the halogens with other non-metals.

What you need to remember [Copy and complete using the **key words**]

The halogens – another chemical family

The elements that are 'salt makers' are called _____.

These elements are all in **Group** _____ of the Periodic Table.

Atoms of the halogens join up in pairs. We call these pairs _____.

Halogens react with metals to form compounds we call _____.

These compounds are part of a family of compounds called _____.

Halogens also react with other _____-_____ such as hydrogen and carbon.

Differences between elements in the same Group

Elements in the same Group of the Periodic Table are similar to each other, but they are not exactly the same.

■ Differences between alkali metals

Alkali metals all react with water to produce the same kinds of products. Even so, there are some differences in how they each react.

Look at the pictures of three alkali metals reacting with water.

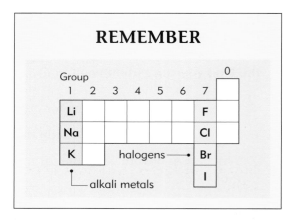

REMEMBER

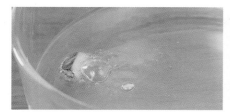

Lithium floats and bubbles.
Hydrogen gas forms.
The water becomes alkaline.

Sodium floats and gets so hot it melts.
Hydrogen gas forms rapidly.
The water becomes alkaline.

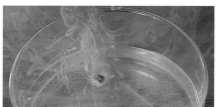

Potassium floats. It reacts violently.
The hydrogen gas burns.
The water becomes alkaline.

1 Write down <u>two</u> ways in which all these reactions are the same.

2 Write down <u>one</u> way in which they are different.

3 Put the three metals in order to show how reactive they are. Start with the one that reacts most quickly.

We say that there is a pattern, or trend, in the way the alkali metals react. The further down Group 1 you go, the more **reactive** the metals are.

The information table shows the **melting points** and **boiling points** of some elements.

4 Copy and complete this table for the alkali metals, using the figures from the information table shown opposite.

Element	Melting point in °C	Boiling point in °C
lithium		
sodium		
potassium		

5 What is the trend in melting points and boiling points as you go further down Group 1?

Element	Melting point in °C	Boiling point in °C
bromine	−7	59
calcium	840	1484
chlorine	−101	−35
copper	1084	2570
iodine	114	184
lithium	180	1340
magnesium	650	1110
potassium	63	760
sodium	98	880
zinc	420	907

Trends in the halogens

The halogens are the elements in Group 7 of the Periodic Table. The halogens also show trends as you go **down** the Group.

Element	Melting point in °C	Boiling point in °C
chlorine		
bromine		
iodine		

6 Copy and complete the table.

7 What happens to the melting points and boiling points as you go down Group 7?

Some halogens are more reactive than others

One halogen can sometimes push a different halogen out of its compound. Here is an example.

chlorine + potassium iodide ⟶ iodine + potassium chloride

We say that in this reaction chlorine **displaces** iodine. Chlorine pushes iodine out of its compound, potassium iodide. This happens because chlorine is more **reactive** than iodine.

The diagrams show two more displacement reactions.

8 Write down the word equation for each reaction.

9 Copy and complete the following sentences.

The reactions show that:

- _____ is more reactive than bromine

- bromine is more reactive than _____ .

As you go down Group 7, the halogens become _____ reactive.

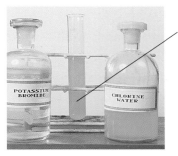

bromine + solution of potassium chloride

Chlorine displaces bromine from a solution of potassium bromide. The solution goes yellow.

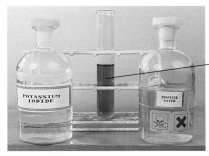

iodine + solution of potassium bromide

Bromine displaces iodine from a solution of potassium iodide. The solution goes brown.

most reactive

chlorine

bromine

iodine

least reactive

What we learn from displacement reactions.

What you need to remember [Copy and complete using the **key words**]

Differences between elements in the same Group

The further down Group 1 you go:
- the lower the _____ **points** and the _____ **points** are, and
- the more _____ the metals are.

The further _____ Group 7 you go:
- the higher the melting points and boiling points are, and
- the halogens become less _____ .

A more reactive halogen _____ a less reactive halogen from its compounds.

These ideas, together with those from Structure and bonding 11, are extended, for Higher Tier students, in Structure and bonding H1 on pages 138–139.

How the Periodic Table was discovered

The story of the Periodic Table tells us a lot about how scientists find things out.

By 1850, scientists knew:

- that everything is made from the atoms of a small number of elements;

- how heavy the atoms of different elements are compared to each other (we call this their relative atomic mass);

- that there are families of elements that have similar properties (see Box).

1 Write down the names of <u>two</u> families of elements that scientists knew about in 1850.

2 Scientists put the elements calcium and magnesium into the same family. Explain why.

> Scientists in 1850 knew about:
>
> - the family of elements that we call alkali metals [including lithium, sodium and potassium];
>
> - the family of elements that we call halogens [including chlorine, bromine and iodine].

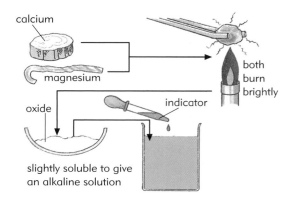

slightly soluble to give an alkaline solution

■ The first Periodic Table

In 1864, an English scientist called John Newlands wrote down the elements in order, starting with the lightest atoms. He only wrote down the elements he knew about at the time.

He noticed that if you count along seven from any element you reach another similar element.
So he wrote down the elements in rows of seven.

This was the first Periodic Table.

3 (a) Write down <u>three</u> differences between Newlands' Periodic Table and the Periodic Table that we use today (for the first twenty elements only).

(b) Why do you think Newlands' table did not include the noble gases?

■ Improving the idea

Newlands' way of making a Periodic Table worked fine for the lighter elements. But it didn't work for heavier elements. At the time, most other scientists regarded Newlands' table as nothing more than a 'curiosity'.

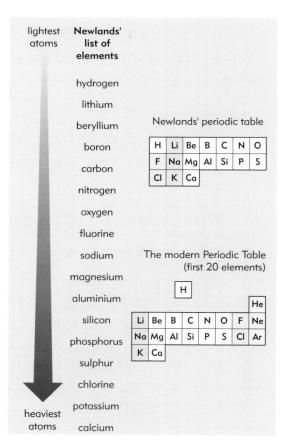

A Russian scientist called Dmitri Mendeleev found a way to include all the elements he knew about. He did this:

- by putting any elements that didn't fit the table into a 'dustbin' column (he put many of the elements we call transition metals into this column);

- by putting each element into the Group where it fitted best, even when this meant leaving some blank spaces in his table.

Mendeleev didn't worry about the blank spaces. He just said that there must be some elements which hadn't been discovered yet.

4 Look at the diagram.

   (a) Where was there an element missing in Mendeleev's Periodic Table?

   (b) What did Mendeleev expect this element to be like?

   (c) Was Mendeleev right about this element?

Mendeleev's Periodic Table helped scientists to discover many new elements. So most scientists then realised that the Periodic Table was a very useful tool.

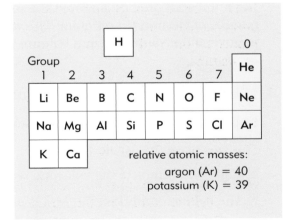

Group 4

| carbon |
| silicon |
| unknown element |
| tin |

What Mendeleev said the unknown element would be like (in 1869)

- a grey metal
- its oxide would be white
- its chloride:
   would boil at less than 100 °C
   each cm³ would have mass 1.9 g

The element germanium (discovered 27 years later)

- a grey metal
- a white oxide
- its chloride:
   boils at 86.5 °C
   each cm³ has mass 1.8 g

■ A problem with a noble gas

When some new elements called noble gases were discovered, it was very easy to add a new Group to the Periodic Table. But the mass of argon atoms meant that it wasn't in quite the right place.

5 Where <u>should</u> argon have gone in the Periodic Table?

   Give a reason for your answer.

Many years later, scientists discovered a better way of arranging the elements in order. Argon then came <u>before</u> potassium, where it fits best in the Periodic Table.

		H					0
Group							He
1	2	3	4	5	6	7	
Li	Be	B	C	N	O	F	Ne
Na	Mg	Al	Si	P	S	Cl	Ar
K	Ca						

relative atomic masses:
   argon (Ar) = 40
   potassium (K) = 39

What you need to remember

How the Periodic Table was discovered

You don't need to <u>remember</u> the information on these pages.

You need to be able to <u>interpret</u> information you may be given about earlier versions of the Periodic Table just like you have on these pages.

You also need to be able to compare earlier tables with the modern Periodic Table.

8

What are atoms made of?

■ Looking inside atoms

The diagram shows what is inside a helium atom. In the centre of the atom is the **nucleus**.
Electrons move in the space around the nucleus.

1   (a) What <u>two</u> sorts of particles do you find in the nucleus of an atom?

(b) What is the same about these two particles?

(c) What is different?

2   Copy and complete the table.

Name of particle	Mass	Electrical charge
proton	1	+1
neutron		
electron		

3   The complete helium atom has no electrical charge overall. Why is this?

The number of protons is always the same as the number of electrons in an atom. This means that the positive and negative charges balance in an atom.

■ The symbols that show what atoms contain

This diagram tells you everything you need to know about a helium atom.

4   Copy and complete the following sentences.

The helium atom has _____ protons.

So it must also have _____ electrons.

The helium atom has a mass number of _____.

So it must contain two _____ in its nucleus.

The proton number of an atom tells us what element the atom is. So an atom with 2 protons must be a helium atom.

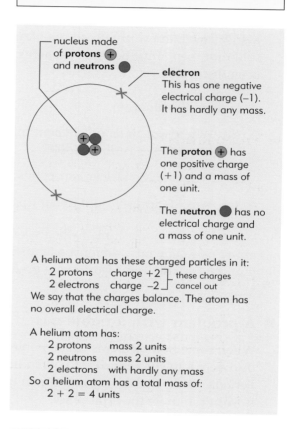

nucleus made of **protons** ⊕ and **neutrons** ●

electron
This has one negative electrical charge (–1). It has hardly any mass.

The **proton** ⊕ has one positive charge (+1) and a mass of one unit.

The **neutron** ● has no electrical charge and a mass of one unit.

A helium atom has these charged particles in it:
  2 protons   charge +2 ⎤ these charges
  2 electrons   charge –2 ⎦ cancel out
We say that the charges balance. The atom has no overall electrical charge.

A helium atom has:
  2 protons   mass 2 units
  2 neutrons   mass 2 units
  2 electrons   with hardly any mass
So a helium atom has a total mass of:
  2 + 2 = 4 units

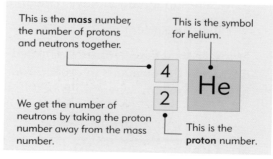

This is the **mass** number, the number of protons and neutrons together.

This is the symbol for helium.

We get the number of neutrons by taking the proton number away from the mass number.

This is the **proton** number.

4

2

He

The diagrams show a hydrogen atom and a lithium atom.

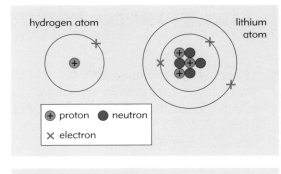

5 Write down the following symbols. Add the mass number and the proton number for each one.

(a) H   (b) Li

6 Copy and complete the following sentence.

A sodium atom has _____ protons

and _____ electrons

and _____ neutrons.

$$^{23}_{11}\text{Na}$$ a sodium atom

■ **Three kinds of carbon**

All carbon atoms contain 6 protons, so they have a proton number of 6.

Carbon atoms can have different numbers of neutrons. This gives the atoms different masses. Atoms of the same element that have different masses are called **isotopes**.

7 Copy and complete the table. The first row has been filled in for you.

Mass number of carbon isotope	Number of protons	Number of neutrons
12	6	6

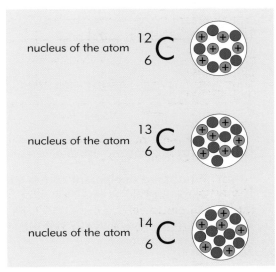

Three isotopes of the element carbon.

What you need to remember [Copy and complete using the **key words**]

What are atoms made of?

The centre of an atom is called the _____.
This can contain two kinds of particle:
■ particles with a positive charge called _____
■ particles with no charge called _____
Atoms of the same element always have the same number of protons.
So every element has its own special _____ number.
The total number of protons and neutrons is called the _____ number.
Atoms of the same element that have different numbers of neutrons are called

_____.

Around the nucleus there are particles with a negative charge called _____.

The modern Periodic Table

We now put the elements into the Periodic Table in the order of their **proton numbers**. The proton number also tells you the number of **electrons** in each atom. The number of electrons is what gives an element its **properties**.

1 Why is it better to list the elements in order of their proton numbers than in order of their mass numbers?

REMEMBER

this is the mass number → $^{40}_{18}\mathrm{Ar}$ $^{39}_{19}\mathrm{K}$
this is the proton number →

So argon has a higher mass number than **potassium** but it has a lower proton number.

Looking for patterns in a list of elements

The diagram below shows the first 20 elements in the order of their proton numbers.

1H 2He 3Li 4Be 5B 6C 7N 8O 9F 10Ne 11Na 12Mg 13Al 14Si 15P 16S 17Cl 18Ar 19K 20Ca
halogen
alkali metal
noble gas

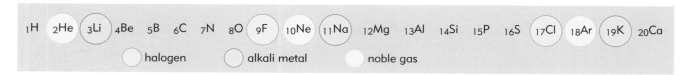

2 Look carefully at the list of elements.

(a) What kind of element comes straight after each noble gas?

(b) What kind of element usually comes just before each noble gas?

(c) How would the list be different if the elements were listed in order of relative atomic masses (mass numbers)?

Making the list of elements into a Periodic Table

To make the list of elements into the Periodic Table:

- you place hydrogen and helium as shown opposite;
- you start a new row of the table every time you reach an element that is an alkali metal.

3 Copy and complete the table.

Group	What we call elements in the Group
1	
	halogens
0	

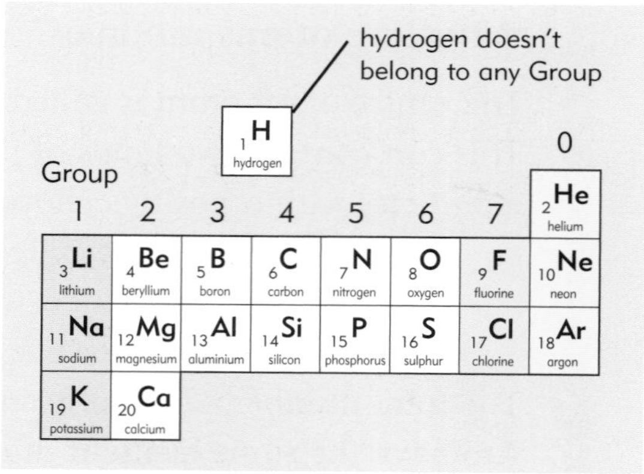

hydrogen doesn't belong to any Group
1 H hydrogen
Group
1 2 3 4 5 6 7 0
2 He helium
3 Li lithium
4 Be beryllium
5 B boron
6 C carbon
7 N nitrogen
8 O oxygen
9 F fluorine
10 Ne neon
11 Na sodium
12 Mg magnesium
13 Al aluminium
14 Si silicon
15 P phosphorus
16 S sulphur
17 Cl chlorine
18 Ar argon
19 K potassium
20 Ca calcium

The first 20 elements in the modern Periodic Table.

Completing the Periodic Table

The complete Periodic Table shows all the elements that we know about. This makes it look more complicated.

4 There are lots of elements that are not placed in Groups 0 to 7. What do we call these elements?

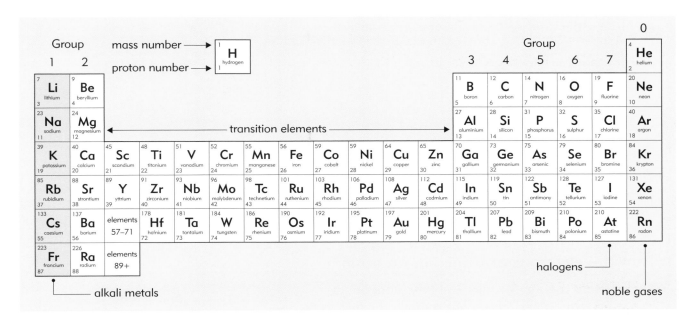

Using the Periodic Table

The Periodic Table is very useful. You can use it to make good guesses about elements you have never seen. This is because there are patterns we can understand in the table. For example, elements in the same Group are very much alike.

The complete Periodic Table usually shows us the mass number and the proton number of each atom. If you know how to use them, these numbers tell you a lot about the structure of each atom (see pages 122–123).

5 (a) In which Group is the element krypton (Kr)?

(b) What do you already know about the elements in this Group?

(c) What can you work out from this about krypton?

6 (a) What is the mass number of phosphorus?

(b) What is the proton number of nitrogen?

What you need to remember [Copy and complete using the **key words**]

The modern Periodic Table

In the modern Periodic Table, elements are listed in order of their _____ _____.

This number also tells you the number of _____ in each atom.

This is what gives an element its particular _____.

Argon then comes before _____, where it fits best.

Why are there families of elements?

What elements are like and the way they react depends on the electrons in their atoms. The proton number of an atom tells you how many protons there are in the nucleus. It also tells you how many electrons there are around the nucleus, because the number of protons in an atom is the same as the number of electrons.

1 How many electrons are there in:

(a) a lithium atom

(b) a sodium atom

(c) a potassium atom?

These alkali metals have different numbers of electrons, but the metals still react in a similar way. This is because the electrons are arranged in a similar way.

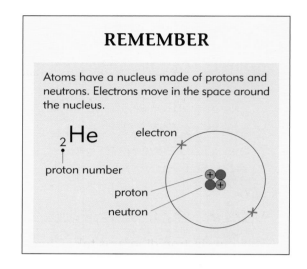

REMEMBER

Atoms have a nucleus made of protons and neutrons. Electrons move in the space around the nucleus.

$_2$He — electron

proton number

proton

neutron

| Lithium | Sodium | Potassium |
| $_3$Li | $_{11}$Na | $_{19}$K |

Some alkali metals.

How are electrons arranged in an atom?

The electrons around the nucleus of an atom are in certain **energy levels**. The diagram shows the first three energy levels for electrons.

2 Copy and complete this table.

Energy level	Number of electrons that can fit into this level
first (lowest energy)	
second	
third	

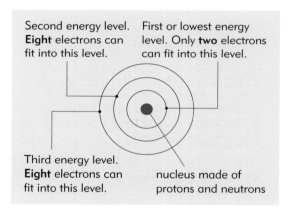

Second energy level. **Eight** electrons can fit into this level.

First or lowest energy level. Only **two** electrons can fit into this level.

Third energy level. **Eight** electrons can fit into this level.

nucleus made of protons and neutrons

How electrons fill up the energy levels

The first energy level is the **lowest**. The electrons start to fill up this level first. When the first energy level is full, electrons start to fill up the second level.

The diagrams show where the electrons are in the first three elements.

3 Draw the same kind of diagram for:

(a) a carbon atom $_6$C

(b) an oxygen atom $_8$O

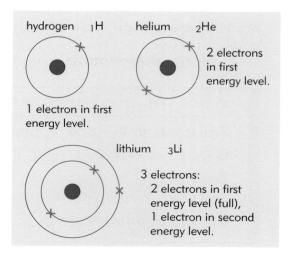

hydrogen $_1$H

1 electron in first energy level.

helium $_2$He

2 electrons in first energy level.

lithium $_3$Li

3 electrons: 2 electrons in first energy level (full), 1 electron in second energy level.

Why alkali metals are in the same family

Lithium, sodium and potassium are very similar elements. We call them alkali metals and put them in Group 1 of the Periodic Table.

The diagrams show why these elements are similar. The **top** energy level is the one on the outside of the atom.

4 Copy and complete the following sentences.

   The elements in Group 1 are similar to each other. This is because they all have just _____ electron in their top energy level.

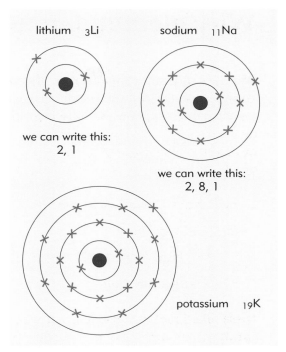

lithium   3Li   sodium   11Na

we can write this:
2, 1

we can write this:
2, 8, 1

potassium   19K

These show the arrangement of electrons in the alkali metals of Group 1.

A simple way to show electrons

Drawing electron diagrams takes time. Here is a quicker way to show how electrons are arranged in atoms.

sodium   11Na is   2,   8,   1

two electrons in lowest   eight electrons in second   one electron in
energy level which is full   level which is full   top energy level

5 Write down the electron arrangement for potassium.

Other families of elements

Elements in the same Group always have the same number of electrons in their top energy levels.

6 Look at the diagram. Copy and complete the table.

Family	Group in the Periodic Table	Number of electrons in top energy level
alkali metals		
halogens		

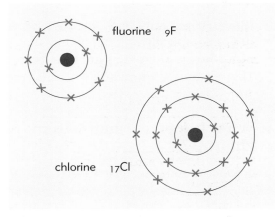

fluorine   9F

chlorine   17Cl

Electrons in Group 7 (halogen) atoms.

What you need to remember [Copy and complete using the **key words**]

Why are there families of elements?

In atoms the electrons are arranged in certain _____ **levels**. The first level has the _____ energy. The lowest level can take up to _____ electrons. The second and third energy levels can each take up to _____ electrons. Elements in the same Group have the same number of electrons in their _____ energy level. This number is the same as the Group number, e.g. Group **7** elements have ____ electrons in their top energy level.

[You should be able to show how the electrons are arranged in the first 20 elements of the Periodic Table.]

Why elements react to form compounds

Atoms of different elements react together to form compounds. For example, sodium reacts with chlorine to produce the compound sodium chloride.

Elements react because of the electrons in their atoms. The diagrams show the electrons in a sodium atom and in a chlorine atom.

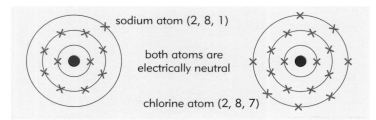

1 How many electrons are there in the top energy level of

(a) a sodium atom?

(b) a chlorine atom?

Atoms like to have each energy level either completely full or completely empty just like they are in the **noble** gases. The atoms are then more stable. This is why sodium reacts with chlorine.

■ **What happens when sodium reacts with chlorine?**

A sodium atom has just 1 electron in the top energy level. The easiest way to become stable is to lose this single electron. The next energy level is now the top one, and is completely full.

A chlorine atom has 7 electrons in its top energy level. The easiest way to become stable is to find 1 more electron. This makes the top energy level completely full.

The diagrams show what happens when sodium reacts with chlorine.

2 Copy and complete the following sentences.

The sodium atom gives the _____ in its top energy level to the _____ atom.

Both atoms now have an electrical _____.

We call Na⁺ a sodium _____.
We call Cl⁻ a _____ ion.

> **REMEMBER**
>
> Atoms have electrons in different energy levels around the nucleus. The top energy level is the level on the outside of an atom. There is room for:
>
> 2 electrons in the first energy level
>
> 8 electrons in the second energy level
>
> 8 electrons in the third energy level
>
> The number of electrons in an atom is the same as the number of protons. The proton number tells us how many protons are in the nucleus.
>
> Electrons have a charge of −1.
>
> Protons have a charge of +1.
>
> Atoms have no charge overall because there are equal numbers of protons and electrons in each atom.

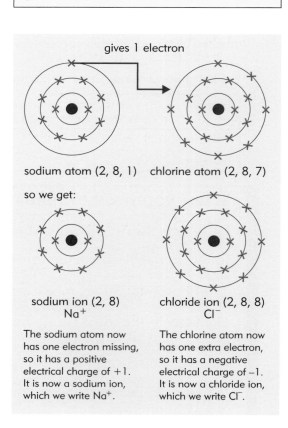

The sodium atom now has one electron missing, so it has a positive electrical charge of +1. It is now a sodium ion, which we write Na⁺.

The chlorine atom now has one extra electron, so it has a negative electrical charge of −1. It is now a chloride ion, which we write Cl⁻.

3 Copy the diagram of a lithium atom and a fluorine atom. Then add an arrow to show how the electron moves when they react together.

Substances made from **ions** are called **ionic** substances.

Some more ionic substances

When a metal reacts with a non-metal we get an ionic substance. The metal atoms give away **electrons**. They form **positive** ions. The non-metals take electrons. They form **negative** ions. The diagrams show two examples.

4 Copy the table. Complete it for all the ions shown in the diagrams. The first one is done for you.

Name of ion	Symbol for the ion
magnesium	Mg^{2+}

5 Draw diagrams to show how sodium oxide is formed.

The formula of an ionic substance

Sodium chloride has 1 chloride ion for each sodium ion. We write its formula as NaCl. In calcium chloride there are 2 chloride ions for each calcium ion. We write its formula as $CaCl_2$.

6 Write down the formula for magnesium oxide.

7 Sodium oxide has two Na^+ ions for every one O^{2-} ion. Write down the formula of sodium oxide.

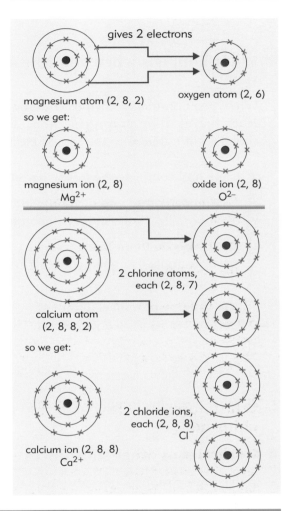

fluorine atom (2, 7)
F

lithium atom (2, 1)
Li

gives 2 electrons

magnesium atom (2, 8, 2)   oxygen atom (2, 6)

so we get:

magnesium ion (2, 8)   oxide ion (2, 8)
Mg^{2+} O^{2-}

calcium atom (2, 8, 8, 2)

2 chlorine atoms, each (2, 8, 7)

so we get:

2 chloride ions, each (2, 8, 8)
Cl^-

calcium ion (2, 8, 8)
Ca^{2+}

What you need to remember [Copy and complete using the **key words**]

Why elements react to form compounds

When a metal reacts with a non-metal, the metal atoms always give away _____. They form ions that have a _____ charge.
The non-metal atoms take electrons. They form _____ that have a _____ charge. Both ions then have electron structures like _____ gases.
The substances produced when metals react with non-metals are called _____ substances.

[You should be able to show the arrangements of electrons in the ions for sodium chloride, magnesium oxide and calcium chloride.]

These ideas are extended, for Higher Tier students, in Structures and bonding H1 on pages 138–139.

How atoms of non-metals can join together

A non-metal such as chlorine can react with a metal such as sodium. This produces an ionic compound called sodium chloride. Chlorine can also react with another non-metal such as hydrogen.

■ What happens when chlorine and hydrogen react?

When two non-metals such as chlorine and hydrogen react, they do it by **sharing** electrons. The diagram shows what happens to the shared electrons.

1   Copy and complete the following sentences.

A hydrogen atom and a chlorine atom share one pair of _____. Each atom is then more stable.

The hydrogen atom has a total of _____ electrons in its first energy level. This level is now _____.

The chlorine atom has a total of _____ electrons in its third energy level. This level is also _____.

This makes a _____ of hydrogen chloride.

2   Write down the formula of hydrogen chloride.

■ Molecules of other substances

Molecular substances are substances that are made of molecules, like hydrogen chloride. Atoms of different non-metals can join together to make molecules. Atoms of the <u>same</u> non-metal element can also share electrons to make molecules.

The diagrams show some molecules of each type.

REMEMBER

We say atoms are stable when each energy level is either completely full of electrons or completely empty.

Atoms with partly full or partly empty energy levels can become more stable if they join up with other atoms.

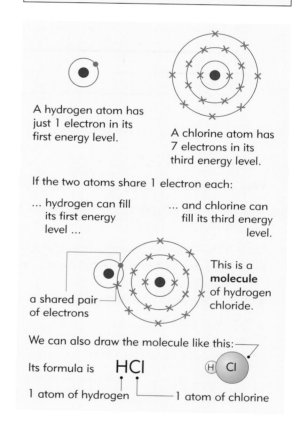

A hydrogen atom has just 1 electron in its first energy level.

A chlorine atom has 7 electrons in its third energy level.

If the two atoms share 1 electron each:

... hydrogen can fill its first energy level ...

... and chlorine can fill its third energy level.

a shared pair of electrons

This is a **molecule** of hydrogen chloride.

We can also draw the molecule like this:

Its formula is   HCl

1 atom of hydrogen ———— 1 atom of chlorine

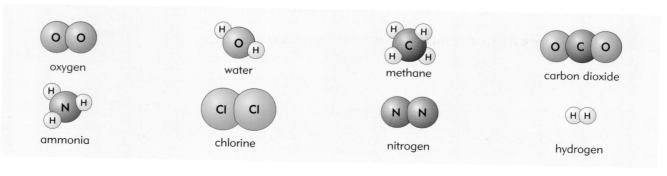

oxygen   water   methane   carbon dioxide

ammonia   chlorine   nitrogen   hydrogen

3 Copy and complete these two tables. The box shows the formula for each molecule in the diagram at the bottom of page 126.

The first row in each table has been filled in for you.

(a)

Name of element	Formula of molecule
oxygen	O_2

(b)

Name of compound	Formula of molecule
water	H_2O

You can also use a formula to show the atoms in a molecule

CH_4 Cl_2 CO_2

H_2 H_2O

N_2 NH_3 O_2

▪ Atoms that don't join together

Atoms of the noble gases don't usually join with atoms of other elements. Noble gas atoms don't even join up with each other to make molecules.

Look at the way the electrons are arranged in helium, neon and argon atoms. They are all noble gases.

4 Why don't these noble gas atoms give, take or share electrons?

The atoms of noble gases are very stable.

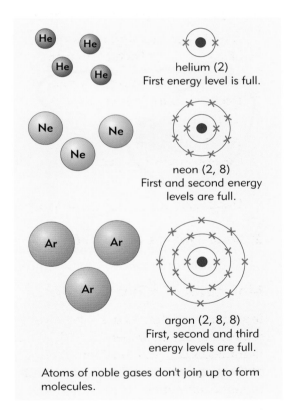

helium (2)
First energy level is full.

neon (2, 8)
First and second energy levels are full.

argon (2, 8, 8)
First, second and third energy levels are full.

Atoms of noble gases don't join up to form molecules.

What you need to remember [Copy and complete using the **key words**]

How atoms of non-metals can join together

Atoms of non-metal elements can join by _____ electrons.

When atoms join together in this way they form a _____ .

Substances made of molecules are called _____ substances.

[You should know the formula of each molecule shown on these pages.]

13 Why different types of substances have different properties

■ Differences between ionic and molecular substances

The table shows some of the properties of ionic and molecular substances. The diagram shows some tests we can do.

		Melting point in °C	Boiling point in °C
ionic substances	sodium chloride	801	1413
	calcium chloride	782	1600
	magnesium oxide	2852	3600
molecular substances	methane	−182	−161
	ammonia	−77	−34
	water	0	100

REMEMBER

Metal atoms give electrons to non-metal atoms. This makes new substances that are made of <u>ions</u>. We call them <u>ionic</u> substances.

Non-metal atoms can share electrons with each other. This makes new substances that are made of <u>molecules</u>. We call them <u>molecular</u> substances.

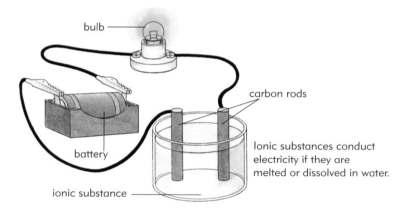

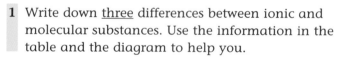

bulb

carbon rods

battery

Ionic substances conduct electricity if they are melted or dissolved in water.

ionic substance

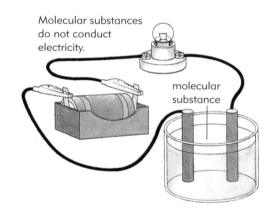

Molecular substances do not conduct electricity.

molecular substance

1 Write down <u>three</u> differences between ionic and molecular substances. Use the information in the table and the diagram to help you.

■ Why do ionic compounds have high melting points and high boiling points?

Sodium chloride is an ionic compound. There are strong forces of **attraction** between Na⁺ and Cl⁻ ions. Each Na⁺ ion is surrounded by six Cl⁻ ions in a **giant** structure. So ionic structures have **high** melting points and high boiling points.

2 Explain the following properties of sodium chloride.

(a) Crystals of sodium chloride have a regular shape.

(b) Sodium chloride has a high melting point (801 °C) and a high boiling point (1413 °C).

Molecular substances are made of separate **molecules**. These are easily pulled apart so molecular structures have **low** melting points and low boiling points.

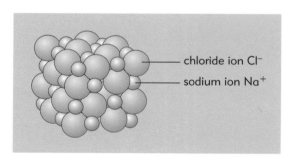

chloride ion Cl⁻

sodium ion Na⁺

The ions in sodium chloride make a regular giant ionic lattice.

Sodium chloride crystals.

■ Why do ionic substances conduct electricity?

Ionic substances are made up of ions. These are particles with electrical charges. An ionic substance will only conduct electricity if its charged particles can **move** about (see diagram).

3 Why must we melt or dissolve an ionic substance before it will conduct electricity?

4 Why can't molecular substances conduct electricity?

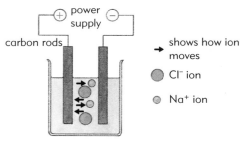

→ shows how ion moves

⬤ Cl⁻ ion

• Na⁺ ion

The ions can only move if we **melt** the substance or **dissolve** it in water. Molecules do not have electrical charges.

■ Explaining the properties of metals

Metals allow electric currents and heat (thermal energy) to pass through them easily. We say that they are good conductors of electricity and heat. Metals can also be hammered or bent into shape without breaking.

The diagrams show why metals have these properties.

Electrons in the metal that are free to move:

■ can carry an electric current through the metal;
■ can carry heat (thermal energy) through the metal.

5 Copy and complete the sentences.

Electrons move through the structure of metals. They hold the _____ together in a regular structure.

Metals bend easily because the _____ can slide over each other.

The free electrons allow metals to be good conductors of _____ and _____.

In a piece of metal, electrons from the highest energy level of each atom are free to move anywhere in the metal. These electrons bind all of the metal atoms together into a single giant structure.

The metal atoms can slide over each other but are still held together by the free electrons.

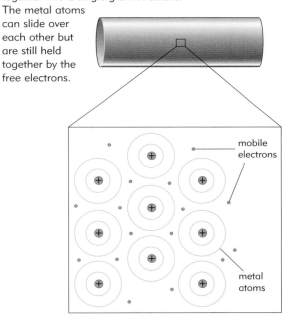

mobile electrons

metal atoms

What you need to remember [Copy and complete using the **key words**]

Why different types of substances have different properties

Molecular substances have _____ melting points and boiling points.
This is because they are made of individual _____ that are easy to separate from each other.
Ionic substances form _____ structures of ions that are held together by strong forces of _____ between ions of opposite charges.
This is why they have _____ melting points and boiling points.
Ionic compounds will conduct electricity if the ions are free to _____.
This can happen if we _____ the compounds in water or _____ them.

These ideas are extended, for Higher Tier students, in Structure and bonding H2, H3 & H4 on pages 141–143.

Salt – a very useful substance

Ordinary salt is a very important chemical.
We use salt for lots of things, and we can make other
useful substances from salt.

on food

on icy roads

to preserve food

to make soap

for margarine and plastics

You can get salt by letting seawater evaporate.

1 Write down <u>three</u> different ways to use salt.

2 Write down <u>three</u> materials we can make from salt.

■ Where do we get the salt we need?

There is a lot of salt dissolved in the **sea**. In some places
there are large amounts of salt **underground**. Salt is a
cheap raw material because it is easy to collect.

3 How can you get salt from sea water?

4 (a) Where did the underground salt come from?

   (b) How do we usually get salt from under
        the ground?

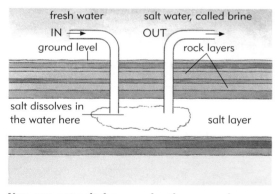

You can get salt from under the ground.

■ What are the elements in ordinary salt?

The chemical name for ordinary salt is
sodium chloride.

5 What are the <u>two</u> elements in salt?

6 The two elements by themselves are very different
   from salt. Write down <u>three</u> differences between salt
   and the elements sodium and chlorine.

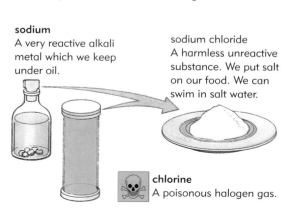

sodium
A very reactive alkali
metal which we keep
under oil.

sodium chloride
A harmless unreactive
substance. We put salt
on our food. We can
swim in salt water.

chlorine
A poisonous halogen gas.

What kind of substance is salt?

The diagram shows the arrangement of the particles in sodium chloride.

7 Copy and complete the following sentences.

Sodium chloride is an _____ substance.
It is made of sodium _____
      and chloride _____.

When we dissolve salt in water, the sodium ions and chloride ions can move about and conduct electricity.

How can we turn salt into other substances?

The diagram shows how we can make other chemicals from salt. We dissolve salt in water to give a solution called **brine**. Next we pass an electric current through the brine. We call this **electrolysis**.

The electrolysis of brine produces three useful substances:

- **chlorine** gas   ■ **hydrogen** gas
- a solution of the alkali **sodium hydroxide**

8 Copy and complete the table.

Gas	Which electrode produces the gas?	How can you test the gas?
hydrogen		
chlorine		

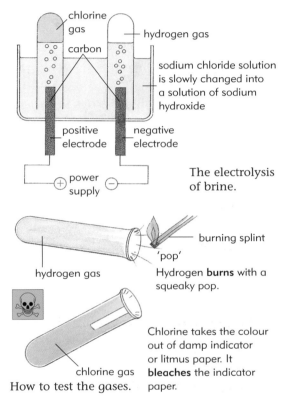

Sodium chloride is an ionic compound.
  Na^+ is a sodium ion,
  Cl^- is a chloride ion.
The ions are arranged in a regular pattern.

chloride ion Cl^-
sodium ion Na^+

chlorine gas — hydrogen gas
carbon
sodium chloride solution is slowly changed into a solution of sodium hydroxide
positive electrode   negative electrode
power supply

The electrolysis of brine.

burning splint
'pop'
hydrogen gas

Hydrogen **burns** with a squeaky pop.

chlorine gas
How to test the gases.

Chlorine takes the colour out of damp indicator or litmus paper. It **bleaches** the indicator paper.

What you need to remember [Copy and complete using the **key words**]

Salt – a very useful substance

The chemical name for salt is _____ _____.
It contains the alkali metal _____ and the halogen _____.
We find salt dissolved in the _____ and buried _____.
A solution of salt in water is called _____.
_____ of brine produces useful new substances.
At the positive electrode we get _____, which _____ damp indicator paper.
At the negative electrode we get _____, which _____ with a squeaky pop.
The solution left at the end contains _____ _____.

15 Using the chemicals we make from salt

How do we use chlorine?

Chlorine is one of the three useful materials we produce from salt water. Chlorine is a poisonous gas.
This is useful when we want to kill harmful **bacteria**, but it can also be dangerous.

1 Write down <u>two</u> places where we can kill bacteria with the help of chlorine.

We can use chlorine to make a plastic called **PVC**.

2 (a) Write down <u>two</u> ways in which we can use PVC.

(b) What do the letters PVC stand for?

You can also make **bleach** from chlorine.

3 (a) What is bleach used for?

(b) Why is it a bad idea to use bleach with brightly coloured clothes?

How do we use hydrogen?

Hydrogen is also made from salt water by electrolysis. Hydrogen is the lightest gas of all, and many years ago airships were filled with hydrogen.

4 Airships filled with hydrogen were very dangerous. Explain why.

We can use hydrogen to make **ammonia**.

5 (a) Which element do we react with hydrogen to make ammonia?

(b) What useful material is made from ammonia?

Margarine is made using hydrogen.

6 What do you react the hydrogen with to make margarine?

Very small amounts of chlorine in water kill dangerous bacteria.

Disinfectants are made from chlorine. They can kill bacteria.

Bleach can be made from chlorine. Bleach removes stains from cloth and makes colours fade.

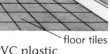

window frame   floor tiles

PVC plastic contains chlorine. PVC is short for poly(vinyl chloride).

Hydrogen gas is flammable. It catches fire very easily.

Ammonia is made from hydrogen and nitrogen. Ammonia is turned into fertiliser to grow more crops.

How do we use sodium hydroxide?

The third material made from salt water is
sodium hydroxide.

7 (a) Write down <u>one</u> use of sodium hydroxide
       in the home.

   (b) Why should we use safety glasses and gloves
        when handling sodium hydroxide?

8 Sodium hydroxide is used to make some other
   useful products. Write down <u>three</u> examples.

Making hydrochloric acid

When **hydrogen chloride** gas dissolves in water, we get
a solution of hydrochloric **acid**. The equation shows how
we can make hydrogen chloride gas. This is a dangerous
reaction, which we do not carry out in school.

9 Write down a word equation for this reaction.

10 How can you show that a solution of hydrogen
    chloride is an acid?

Solutions of hydrogen fluoride, hydrogen bromide and
hydrogen iodide are also acidic. Because these
compounds are all made from hydrogen and the
halogen elements they are called hydrogen **halides**.

Sodium hydroxide is
used in oven cleaner.
It is corrosive.

Sodium hydroxide
attacks and destroys
skin and eyes.

Sodium
hydroxide:
■ helps turn
  woodpulp
  into paper;
■ is used in
  making
  ceramics
  (pottery).

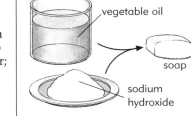
vegetable oil
soap
sodium
hydroxide

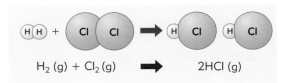

$$H_2 (g) + Cl_2 (g) \rightarrow 2HCl (g)$$

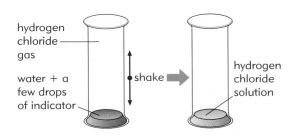

hydrogen
chloride
gas

water + a
few drops
of indicator

shake

hydrogen
chloride
solution

What you need to remember [Copy and complete using the **key words**]

Using the chemicals we make from salt

The three useful materials made by passing electricity through salt water are
_____, _____ and sodium hydroxide.

Chlorine is used:
■ in substances that kill _____
■ to make a plastic called _____
■ to make _____, which removes stains and fades colours.

Hydrogen is used:
■ to make _____, which can be turned into fertiliser
■ to change vegetable oils into _____.

Paper, ceramics and soap are all made using _____ _____.

Hydrogen reacts with chlorine to make _____ _____.

This dissolves in water to make hydrochloric _____.

Other compounds of hydrogen and halogens (hydrogen _____)
also dissolve in water to make acidic solutions.

The chemicals we use to make photographs

We need special chemicals that react to light to make photographs. These chemicals are placed in layers on a film (or paper) that can be used in a camera. The simplest kind of film produces black and white photographs.

Colour photographs use the same basic chemical reactions, but use lots of other reactions too.

> ### REMEMBER
> Halogens react with metals to form compounds called halides.

This photograph was made using chemicals that are changed by light.

Chemicals that react to light

One of the chemicals we can use to make photographs is silver chloride.
The diagram shows how we can make silver chloride.
It also shows what happens when light shines on silver chloride.

1 Complete the word equation for this reaction.

_____ + sodium chloride ⟶ _____ + sodium nitrate

2 (a) What colour is freshly prepared silver chloride?

(b) How does this colour change in the light?

3 Copy and complete the following sentence.

The light changes the white specks of silver chloride into _____ specks of _____ metal.

We say that the light **reduces** the silver chloride to **silver metal**. The same kind of change happens when the other silver **halides** react to light.

4 Write down the names of <u>two</u> other silver halides.

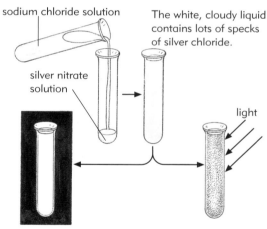

sodium chloride solution

silver nitrate solution

The white, cloudy liquid contains lots of specks of silver chloride.

light

In the dark, the white specks of silver chloride stay white.

In the light, the white specks of silver chloride turn into black specks of silver metal.

What is photographic film?

The diagram shows what photographic **film** is made from.

5 Copy and complete the following sentence.

Photographic film is made from specks of silver _____ on a _____ plastic sheet.

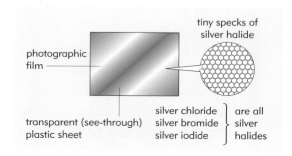

photographic film

tiny specks of silver halide

transparent (see-through) plastic sheet

silver chloride
silver bromide
silver iodide
} are all silver halides

How does photographic film work?

The diagrams show what happens if you take a photograph of a black cross.

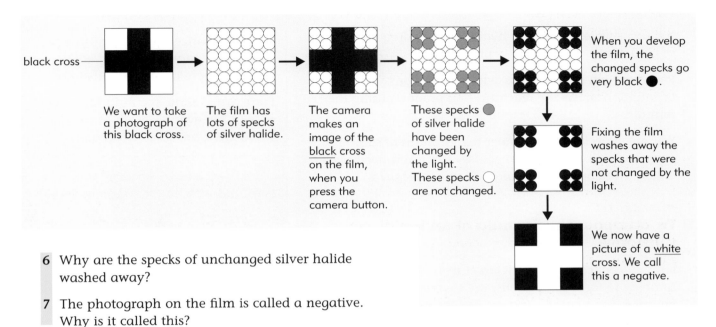

black cross

We want to take a photograph of this black cross.

The film has lots of specks of silver halide.

The camera makes an image of the <u>black cross</u> on the film, when you press the camera button.

These specks ● of silver halide have been changed by the light. These specks ○ are not changed.

When you develop the film, the changed specks go very black ●.

Fixing the film washes away the specks that were not changed by the light.

We now have a picture of a <u>white</u> cross. We call this a negative.

6 Why are the specks of unchanged silver halide washed away?

7 The photograph on the film is called a negative. Why is it called this?

Photographic paper works in the same way.

What else can change silver halides?

X-rays and the radiation from **radioactive** materials will also reduce silver halides.

8 How can X-rays make a photograph of bones inside your body?

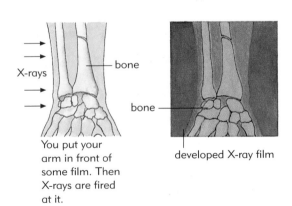

X-rays — bone

You put your arm in front of some film. Then X-rays are fired at it.

bone — developed X-ray film

What you need to remember [Copy and complete using the **key words**]

The chemicals we use to make photographs

Silver chloride, silver bromide and silver iodide are all silver _____ .

Light can change silver halides into _____ **metal.**

We say that light _____ silver halides to silver metal.

Silver halides are also reduced by _____-_____ and the radiation from _____ substances.

We use silver halides to make photographic _____ and photographic paper.

135

How to write balanced symbol equations

A word equation shows the reactants and products in a chemical reaction. For example:

sodium + water → sodium hydroxide + hydrogen
<u>reactants</u>   <u>products</u>

Reactions can be written as <u>symbol equations</u>. This type of equation shows the reactants and products using their formulas.

You are expected to remember the formulas of some common molecular substances (see Box). You need to be able to work out the formulas of ionic substances.

■ Working out the formula of an ionic substance

Ionic substances form giant structures. When ions combine to form compounds, the electrical charges must **balance**. For example, if there are two positive charges, there must also be two negative charges. Look at the examples in the box.

1 Write down the formula for each of these:

  (a) potassium bromide   (d) calcium hydroxide

  (b) magnesium sulphide   (e) sodium hydroxide

  (c) aluminium chloride   (f) aluminium oxide

■ Why symbol equations need to be balanced

Atoms don't just disappear during chemical reactions. So there must be exactly the same number of each type of atom in the products as there was in the reactants. In other words, symbol equations must be <u>balanced</u>.

2 Copy the symbol equation below. Then show that it is balanced.

   $Mg + 2HCl \rightarrow MgCl_2 + H_2$

REMEMBER

Each substance has a formula which shows how many atoms of each element there are in the substance.

For example, the formula for water is H_2O: for every 1 atom of oxygen there are 2 atoms of hydrogen.

Formulas for some common molecules

oxygen	O_2	methane	CH_4
hydrogen	H_2	ammonia	NH_3
nitrogen	N_2	carbon dioxide	CO_2
chlorine	Cl_2	carbon monoxide	CO
water	H_2O	hydrogen chloride	HCl

Na^+ balances Cl^- to give the formula $NaCl$

Ca^{2+} balances $\begin{cases} Cl^- \\ Cl^- \end{cases}$ to give the formula $CaCl_2$

Mg^{2+} balances O^{2-} to give the formula MgO

Mg^{2+} balances $\begin{cases} OH^- \\ OH^- \end{cases}$ to give the formula $Mg(OH)_2$

Some common ions

sodium	Na^+	chloride	Cl^-
potassium	K^+	bromide	Br^-
calcium	Ca^{2+}	hydroxide	OH^-
magnesium	Mg^{2+}	oxide	O^{2-}
aluminium	Al^{3+}	sulphide	S^{2-}

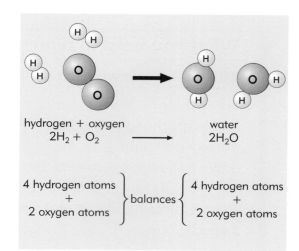

hydrogen + oxygen   water
$2H_2 + O_2$ ⟶ $2H_2O$

4 hydrogen atoms   4 hydrogen atoms
+   balances   +
2 oxygen atoms   2 oxygen atoms

How to write a balanced symbol equation

Step 1. Write down the word equation for the reaction.

Step 2. Write down the formulas for the reactants and products.

Step 3. Check to see if the equation is balanced. Count the atoms on both sides of the equation.

[You do not need to write this down.]

If the equation is not balanced, you need to go on to Step 4.

Step 4. Balance the equation. This is done by writing a number in front of one or more of the formulas. This number increases the numbers of all of the atoms in the formula.

Check that the equation is now balanced.

3 (a) Write down the word equation and the unbalanced symbol equation for the following reaction:

calcium + water → calcium + hydrogen
hydroxide

$$Ca + H_2O \rightarrow Ca(OH)_2 + H_2$$

(b) Balance the symbol equation.

(c) Add state symbols to your equation (see Box).

4 Write balanced symbol equations for these reactions. [Show all the steps.]

(a) potassium + chlorine → potassium chloride

(b) copper + hydrogen → copper + water
oxide

Example: The reaction between sodium metal and water

sodium + water → sodium hydroxide + hydrogen

$$Na + H_2O \rightarrow NaOH + H_2$$

Reactants		Products
1	sodium atoms	1
2	hydrogen atoms	3
1	oxygen atoms	1

The equation is <u>not</u> balanced because the number of hydrogen atoms is not the same on each side.

We can balance the hydrogen atoms by doubling up the water + sodium hydroxide.

$$2Na + 2H_2O \rightarrow 2NaOH + H_2$$

2NaOH means 2 Na atoms, 2 O atoms and 2 H atoms.

This means 4 H atoms and 2 O atoms

So the O atoms also balance (two on each side).

This 2 is then needed so that there are 2 Na atoms on each side.

Check

Reactants		Products
2	sodium atoms	2
4	hydrogen atoms	4
2	oxygen atoms	2

The equation now balances. There are the same numbers of each type of atom on each side.

Adding state symbols

When you have balanced an equation, you should then add state symbols. For example:

$$2Na(s) + 2H_2O(l) \rightarrow 2NaOH(aq) + H_2(g)$$

Remember: (s) = solid, (l) = liquid, (g) = gas, (aq) = in solution in water

---

What you need to remember

How to write symbol equations

You need to remember the formulas of the molecules shown on page 213.

You need to be able to work out the formulas of ionic compounds.

You need to be able to write balanced symbol equations as on this page.

These ideas are extended, for Higher Tier students, in Structure and bonding H5 on page 143.   137

H1 This extends *Structure and bonding* 6 and 11 for Higher Tier students

Explaining trends in reactivity within Groups

REMEMBER

Elements in the same Group have similar properties.

In Group 1, metals lower in the Group are <u>more</u> reactive.

In Group 7, non-metals lower in the Group are <u>less</u> reactive.

Atoms give, take or share electrons so that they have full outer shells of electrons. They are then stable like atoms of noble gases (Group 0).

Group								
1	2	3	4	5	6	7	0
Li							F	
Na							Cl	
K							Br	

alkali metals   halogens

The way that elements react depends largely on the number of electrons in their highest energy level (outer shell).

■ Elements in Group 1

1 Copy and complete the sentences.

Elements in Group 1 have similar properties because they have the same number of _____ in the _____ energy level (outer shell). For example, they all react with water to produce a _____ and _____.

2 Write down a word equation for the reaction of lithium with water.

Reactivity increases further <u>down</u> the Group because potassium loses its outer electron more easily than sodium does, and sodium more easily than lithium.

3 Look at the diagrams, then copy and complete the sentences.

The higher the atomic number and the _____ the atomic radius, the further the outer electron is from the positive nucleus. So for elements further down Group 1, the force of attraction between the nucleus and this electron is _____ so the electron is more easily _____.
Reactivity therefore _____ from lithium to sodium to potassium.

Electron arrangement in atoms of Group 1 elements

lithium Li	2, <u>1</u>
sodium Na	2, 8, <u>1</u>
potassium K	2, 8, 8, <u>1</u>

Group <u>1</u> elements all have <u>one</u> electron in the highest energy level (outer shell).

All the metals in Group 1 <u>lose</u> the outer electron easily to form a positive ion, so they are all very reactive and react in the same way. For example:

sodium + water → sodium hydroxide + hydrogen

potassium + water → potassium hydroxide + hydrogen

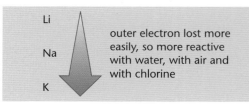

Li
Na
K
outer electron lost more easily, so more reactive with water, with air and with chlorine

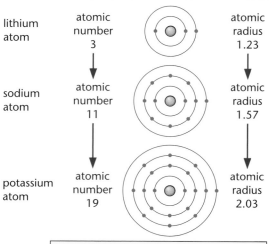

lithium atom	atomic number 3		atomic radius 1.23
sodium atom	atomic number 11		atomic radius 1.57
potassium atom	atomic number 19		atomic radius 2.03

○ positively charged nucleus
(attracts negatively charged electrons)

Elements in Group 7

The elements in Group 7 all react with metals to form compounds called **halides**.

4 Copy and complete the sentences.

Elements in Group 7 have similar properties because they have the same number of _____ in the _____ energy level (outer shell). For example, they all react with metals to produce metal _____.

5 Write down a word equation for the reaction between fluorine and sodium.

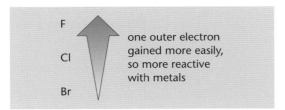

one outer electron gained more easily, so more reactive with metals

Reactivity increases further <u>up</u> the Group because fluorine gains an electron more easily than chlorine does, and chlorine more easily than bromine.

6 Look at the diagrams, then copy and complete the sentences.

The lower the atomic number and the _____ the atomic radius, the closer an outer electron is to the nucleus. So for elements further up Group 7, the force of attraction for the outer electrons is _____ and this means that an extra electron is _____ more easily. Reactivity, therefore, _____ from bromine to chlorine to fluorine.

Halogens can also react with hydrogen. They do this by sharing electrons and forming covalent compounds.

7 How do the reactivities of the halogens with hydrogen compare with their reactivities with metals?

Electron arrangement in atoms of Group 7 elements

fluorine F   2, <u>7</u>
chlorine Cl   2, 8, <u>7</u>
bromine Br   2, 8, 18, <u>7</u>

Group <u>7</u> elements all have <u>seven</u> electrons in the highest energy level (outer shell).

All the halogens in Group 7 react with metals by <u>gaining</u> an electron to form a negative ion.
For example:

chlorine + iron → iron chloride
bromine + iron → iron bromide

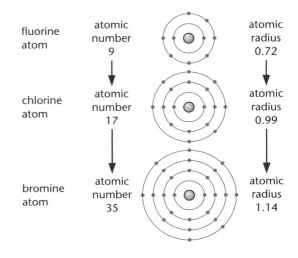

fluorine atom	atomic number 9	atomic radius 0.72
chlorine atom	atomic number 17	atomic radius 0.99
bromine atom	atomic number 35	atomic radius 1.14

How halogens react with hydrogen

Fluorine: reacts explosively in dark conditions.
Chlorine: reacts in dim light, but explosively in sunlight.
Bromine: no reaction in sunlight, but reacts if heated to 200°C.

Using your knowledge

1 Beryllium, magnesium and calcium are three metal elements in Group 2 of the Periodic Table. Their electronic structures are:

Be (2, 2) Mg (2, 8, 2) Ca (2, 8, 8, 2)

(a) Would you expect these elements to have similar properties? Explain your answer.

(b) Arrange the three elements in order of reactivity and give reasons for your order.

Explaining the properties of molecular substances

In molecular substances atoms join together by sharing electrons from the highest energy level (outer shell). These shared pairs of electrons are called **covalent bonds**.

The diagrams below show two molecules which are held together in this way.

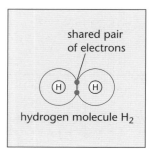

shared pair of electrons

hydrogen molecule H_2

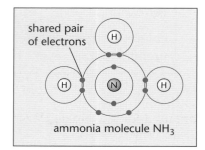

shared pair of electrons

ammonia molecule NH_3

Molecular substances have low melting points and low boiling points. They do not conduct electricity.

The diagrams opposite explain why a molecular substance has these properties.

1 Copy and complete the sentences.

Molecular substances are made of _____ in which atoms are held together because they share pairs of _____. The strong bonds between atoms are called _____ bonds. The forces between the separate molecules are _____.

2 Why do molecular substances:

(a) have a low melting point;
(b) have a low boiling point?

3 Explain why molecular substances do not conduct electricity.

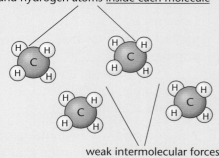

strong covalent bonds between carbon and hydrogen atoms inside each molecule

weak intermolecular forces

Because there are only weak forces <u>between the molecules</u>, melting and boiling points are low.
The molecules do not carry an overall electric charge, so molecular substances do not conduct electricity.

This molecular solid is melting. The molecules do not need much energy to be able to move over each other.

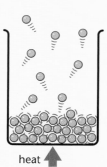

This molecular liquid is boiling.
The molecules do not need much energy to be able to escape from the surface of the liquid into the air.

heat

Using your knowledge

1 Substance A is a liquid at room temperature. It will not conduct an electric current.

Explain as fully as you can why substance A probably has a molecular structure.

Give reasons for your answer.

2 Draw the electron structure and label a shared pair of electrons
(a) for a water (H_2O) molecule
(b) for a methane (CH_4) molecule

carbon atom C

oxygen atom O

These ideas are extended, together with those on Structure and bonding H3, for Higher Tier students, in Structure and bonding H5 on page 143.

H3   This extends *Structure and bonding* 13 for Higher Tier students

Graphite and diamond – giant structures

Graphite and diamond are two very different forms of the element carbon. Even though carbon atoms form covalent bonds with each other, these two forms have a <u>giant</u> structure rather than a molecular structure.

1 Diamond has a melting point of 3550 °C. It is used in cutting and drilling tools.
Explain its properties by reference to its structure.

Graphite is unusual as a non-metal, because it will conduct an electric current. It is used for electrodes in electric furnaces and for 'brushes' in electric motors.

Each carbon atom has <u>four</u> outer-shell electrons, but in graphite layers only <u>three</u> of these electrons are used for bonding with other carbon atoms. So the other electron is free to move. These free electrons in the graphite structure can carry an electric current, which is a flow of electrons.

2 Graphite is used as a lubricant and as the 'lead' in soft pencils. Explain why graphite flakes easily.

3 Explain why graphite is an electrical conductor.

In graphite, bonds between carbon atoms in the layers are strong covalent bonds. But the bonds between layers of carbon atoms are weak, so the layers slide over each other. This makes the surface flaky and soft. Graphite has a high melting point.

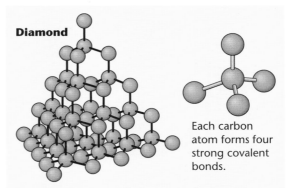

Diamond

Each carbon atom forms four strong covalent bonds.

Diamond has a rigid giant covalent structure of atoms (a lattice of atoms).
All the bonds are strong bonds, so this is a strong 3D structure with no weak links.

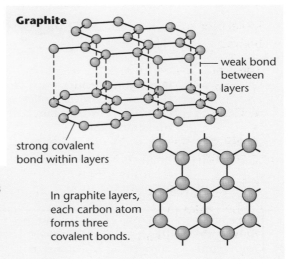

Graphite

weak bond between layers

strong covalent bond within layers

In graphite layers, each carbon atom forms three covalent bonds.

Using your knowledge

1 (a) Describe two major differences in the properties of diamond and graphite.

(b) Explain these differences in terms of their atomic structure.

2 Which properties of silicon dioxide (silica) suggest that it has a giant covalent structure?

Silica, the compound silicon dioxide (SiO_2), is used on the surface of sandpaper. It is very hard. Its melting point is 1610°C.

These ideas are extended, for Higher Tier students, in Structure and bonding H5 on page 143.

H4 This extends *Structure and bonding* 13, H2 and H3 for Higher Tier students

Comparing giant structures

Three different types of substance each consist of giant structures.

Each type of substance has its own particular type of giant structure.

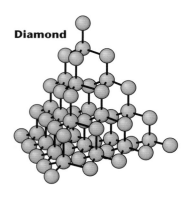

Diamond

In **giant molecules**, each atom shares electrons with several other atoms. So there is a network of covalent bonds throughout the whole structure.

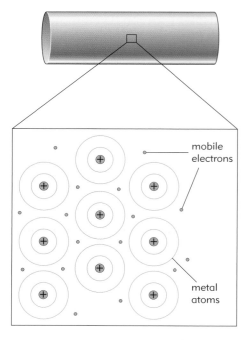

mobile electrons

metal atoms

In **metals**, atoms lose outer electrons to become ions. The positively charged ions are held together by a 'sea' of negatively charged free electrons.

1 Copy and complete the table.

Type of substance with giant structure	Example of this type of substance	Is substance made of atoms or ions?	What holds the atoms/ions together?

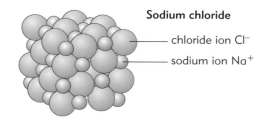

Sodium chloride

chloride ion Cl⁻

sodium ion Na⁺

In **ionic compounds**, each ion is surrounded by, and strongly attracted to, oppositely charged ions.

Using your knowledge

1 Most substances with a giant structure are solids with a high, or fairly high, melting point. Explain why.

2 Which type of solid giant structures

(a) always conduct electricity?

(b) never conduct electricity?

3 Which solid giant molecular substance conducts electricity, and why?

[Refer back to page 141 if you need to.]

Writing chemical equations for electrolysis reactions

When ionic compounds are dissolved in water or melted, they conduct electricity. Chemical changes occur when an electric current is passed through them. This is <u>electrolysis</u>.

At the negative electrode, positively charged ions gain electrons from the electrode to produce neutral atoms or molecules.

At the positive electrode, negatively charged ions lose electrons to the electrode to produce neutral atoms or molecules.

The diagram shows the electrolysis of copper chloride solution. The information below the diagram shows how the change at each electrode can be represented by a **half-equation**.

You may be given some information about a half-equation, then asked to balance it. The example in the box shows you how to do this.

1   Copy and then balance these half-equations for the electrolysis of sodium bromide.

   (a) $Br^- - e^- \rightarrow Br_2$ [bromine molecule]

   (b) $Na^+ \qquad \rightarrow Na$ [sodium atom]

Example

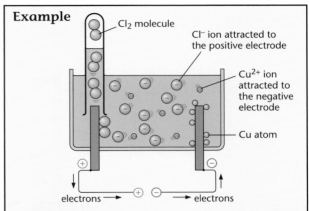

In the electrolysis of copper chloride solution:

- copper atoms are released at the negative electrode;

- chlorine molecules are released at the positive electrode.

At the negative electrode copper ions gain electrons to become copper atoms:
$$Cu^{2+} \quad + \quad e^- \quad \rightarrow \quad Cu$$

When balanced, this half-equation is:
$$Cu^{2+} \quad + \quad 2e^- \quad \rightarrow \quad Cu$$
copper ion   two electrons from   copper atom
               the electrode   (neutral)

At the positive electrode chloride ions lose electrons and form chlorine molecules:
$$Cl^- \quad - \quad 2e^- \quad \rightarrow \quad Cl_2$$

When balanced, this half-equation is:
$$2Cl^- \quad - \quad 2e^- \quad \rightarrow \quad Cl_2$$
two chloride   two electrons   one chlorine
ions   to the electrode   molecule (neutral)

Using your knowledge

1   Complete and balance these half-equations which occur during the extraction of aluminium from aluminium oxide.

(a) $Al^{3+} + e^- \rightarrow Al$

(b) $O^{2-} - \quad \rightarrow O_2$

Using heat to speed things up

Some chemical reactions are very fast, others are slow.
The reactions go at different speeds or **rates**.

The explosion takes a fraction of a second.

The tablet reacts with water in about a minute.

The nail takes a few hours to start rusting. It takes many months to rust completely.

1 Describe <u>one</u> example each of a chemical reaction that is

(a) very slow, which takes hours or days,

(b) very fast, which takes seconds or less,

(c) medium speed, which takes one minute or so.

■ Speeding up reactions in the kitchen

When we cook food there are chemical reactions going on. How fast the food cooks depends on how hot we make it.

2 Look at the pictures.

(a) Which is faster, cooking in boiling water or in cooking oil?

(b) Why do you think this is?

boiling water at 100 °C

potato pieces

The pieces of potato take about 20 minutes to cook.

cooking oil at 130 °C, a **higher** temperature than water

potato pieces

The potatoes take less than 10 minutes to cook.

How much difference does temperature make?

Look at the colour change reaction.

3 Copy and complete the following sentences.

The higher the temperature the _____ the time the reaction takes.
This means that the rate of reaction is _____.

4 How long do you think the reaction will take at temperatures of

(a) 60 °C   (b) 10 °C?

Using temperatures to control reactions

If you increase the temperature by 10°C, chemical reactions go about twice as fast. To **slow down** a chemical reaction you must reduce the temperature.

5 Where can you put milk to slow down the chemical reactions that make it go bad?

6 About how long will it take the milk to go sour in the fridge?

7 (a) How many times faster do the potatoes cook in the pressure cooker?

(b) What does this tell you about the temperature of the water inside the pressure cooker?

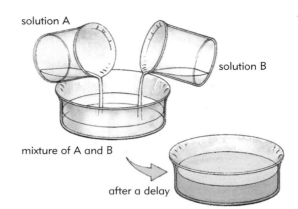

solution A

solution B

mixture of A and B

after a delay

A colour change reaction. The table shows how long it takes for the mixture to change colour.

Temperature (°C)	20	30	40	50
Time taken to go blue (seconds)	400	200	100	50

Chemical reactions make food go bad.

Inside a fridge, the milk takes many days to go sour.

Outside, the milk goes sour in two days.

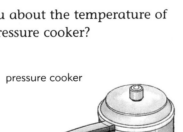

water boiling at 100 °C

pressure cooker

The potatoes take about 24 minutes to cook.

The potatoes take about 6 minutes to cook.

What you need to remember [Copy and complete using the **key words**]

Using heat to speed things up

Chemical reactions go at different speeds or _____.
Chemical reactions go faster at _____ temperatures.
At low temperatures, chemical reactions _____ _____.

2

Making solutions react faster

Some substances will dissolve in water to make a **solution**. You can use solutions for many chemical reactions. The speed of these chemical reactions depends on how strong the solutions are.

1 What is the chemical solution in a car battery?

■ 'Strong' and 'weak' solutions

Your friend likes her tea to taste sweet, but not too sweet.

one spoonful — sugar — not sweet enough — sugar solution is too weak

two spoonfuls — just right

three spoonfuls — too sweet — sugar solution is too strong

2 Look at the diagrams. Copy and complete the table.

Spoonfuls of sugar	What your friend's tea tasted like	Strength of sugar solution
1		
2		perfect
3		

3 A mug of tea is 1.5 times bigger than one of the cups shown above.
How many spoonfuls of sugar should your friend put into a mug of tea? Give a reason for your answer.

■ Dilute to taste

We call a 'strong' solution a **concentrated** solution.
To make a solution 'weaker', we **dilute** it with water.

4 Look at the diagrams.
Copy and complete the following sentences.

The orange drink in the bottle is _____.
To make it good to drink you need to _____ it.

REMEMBER

A reaction that takes a short time has a high speed or rate.

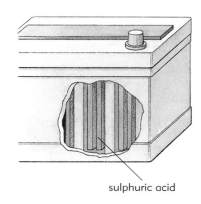

sulphuric acid

The chemical reactions in a car battery need sulphuric acid of just the right strength.

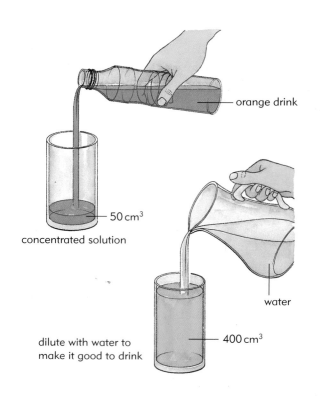

orange drink

50 cm³
concentrated solution

water

dilute with water to make it good to drink

400 cm³

How does concentration affect the speed of a chemical reaction?

Look at the pictures of the reaction between a chemical we call thio and an acid.

5 Copy and complete the following sentences.

The most concentrated solution contains _____ spatulas of thio crystals.

The reaction with the most concentrated thio solution takes the _____ time.

This means that this reaction has the _____ rate.

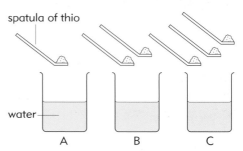

spatula of thio

water

A   B   C

Some students make 3 different strengths of thio solution.

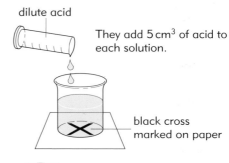

dilute acid

They add 5 cm³ of acid to each solution.

black cross marked on paper

The solution gradually goes cloudy.

Eventually you can't see the cross when looking down through the solution.

Results.

Solution	Time for cross to disappear
A	8 minutes
B	4 minutes
C	2.5 minutes

Making gases react faster

Some gases will react together to make new substances. For example, you can make ammonia gas by reacting together a mixture of nitrogen and hydrogen gases.

You can squeeze gases into a smaller space. This is like making a more concentrated solution. The gases will then react together faster. A **high** pressure gas is like a very concentrated solution.

6 A chemical factory makes ammonia gas. They already make the hydrogen and nitrogen as hot as they can. What else should they do to make the reaction go faster?

What you need to remember [Copy and complete using the **key words**]

Making solutions react faster

When you dissolve a substance in water you get a _____.

A solution that contains a lot of dissolved substance is a _____ solution.

To make a concentrated solution react more slowly, you can _____ it.

To make gases react faster, you need a _____ pressure.

3

Making solids react faster

The diagrams show a chemical reaction between a solid and a solution.

1 Write down

(a) the name of the solid in the reaction

(b) the name of the solution used

(c) the name of the gas produced.

2 Copy and complete the word equation for this reaction.

bubbles of carbon dioxide gas

dilute hydrochloric acid

limestone

During the reaction.

$$\underline{\hspace{2cm}} + \underline{\hspace{2cm}}\,\text{acid} \longrightarrow \underline{\hspace{2cm}}\,\text{dioxide} + \underline{\hspace{2cm}}$$

solution of calcium chloride

limestone (now smaller)

When all the acid has been used up, the reaction stops.

■ Making the reaction faster

One way to make the reaction faster is by using more concentrated acid. But how fast the limestone reacts also depends on how big the pieces of limestone are.

3 Look at the diagrams.

Copy and complete the table.

Size of solid pieces	Time taken to react	Speed of reaction
one large piece		
several small pieces		
lots of very small pieces		

4 Copy and complete the following sentence.

The smaller the bits of limestone, the _____ they react with the acid.

With one large piece of limestone, the gas bubbles continue for 10 minutes.

50 cm³ acid

50 cm³ acid

With smaller pieces, the gas bubbles continue for 1 minute. The bubbling is faster.

50 cm³ acid

With very small pieces, the gas bubbles continue for a few seconds. The bubbling is very fast.

Do you suck or crush sweets?

Think about eating a hard sweet. If you suck the sweet in one piece it lasts quite a long time. If you crush the sweet into little pieces it doesn't last so long.

5 Why does the crushed sweet dissolve faster? Explain your answer as fully as you can.

Sucking your sweet. Your saliva can only get at the outside **surface** of the sweet.

one large piece

Crushing your sweet. Your saliva can get at more of the sweet at once.

many small pieces

Why small bits react faster

The same amount of limestone in smaller bits reacts **faster**. The acid can get at smaller bits better. This is because they have more **surface area**.

6 Look at the large cube of limestone.

   (a) How many little squares are there on one face of the large cube?

   (b) How many faces are there on the cube?

   (c) What is the total number of small squares on the surface of the cube? This is the surface area of the cube.

7 Now look at the large cube broken up into smaller cubes.

   (a) What is the surface area of each small cube?

   (b) What is the total surface area of all the small cubes added together?

   (c) How many times more surface area do the small cubes have than the large cube?

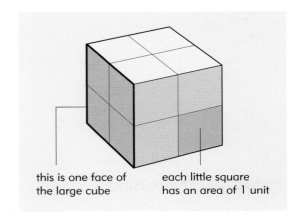

this is one face of the large cube

each little square has an area of 1 unit

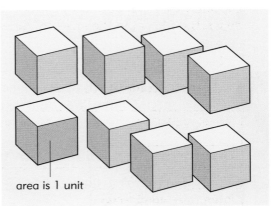

area is 1 unit

What you need to remember [Copy and complete using the **key words**]

Making solids react faster

A solid can react with a liquid only where they touch. The reaction is on the
_____ of the solid.
If we break up the solid, we increase the total _____ _____.
This means that smaller pieces react _____.

149

Substances that speed up reactions

People use hydrogen peroxide to bleach hair. It does this by releasing oxygen. The oxygen turns the hair a very pale blonde colour.

1 Copy and complete the word equation for this reaction

hydrogen peroxide ⟶ _____ + _____

In the bottle, the hydrogen peroxide very slowly splits up into oxygen gas and water.

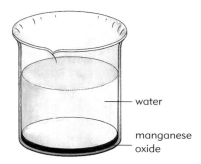

hydrogen peroxide solution

The hydrogen peroxide starts to bubble very fast. It splits up.

When all the hydrogen peroxide has split up, the manganese oxide is still there.

2 Look at the diagrams. What happens if you put a tiny amount of manganese oxide into some hydrogen peroxide?

A substance which speeds up a chemical reaction in this way has a special name. We call it a **catalyst**.

You can use the same manganese oxide **over** and **over** again. First filter the water and manganese oxide.

Put the manganese oxide into some fresh hydrogen peroxide.

It starts to bubble quickly.

■ Why don't you need much of the catalyst?

3 Copy and complete the following sentences using the diagrams to help you.

The _____ _____ is not used up in the chemical reaction. It is still there at the end. You can use it over and over again to split up more _____ _____.

4 How could you collect the catalyst so that you could use it again?

5 How does this experiment show that a catalyst is not used up in the reaction?

You can show that the catalyst is not one of the ordinary chemicals that react, by writing your equation like this.

$$\text{hydrogen peroxide} \xrightarrow{\text{manganese oxide}} \text{oxygen} + \text{water}$$

We write the name of the catalyst above the arrow.

Sunflower oil is a vegetable oil. This oil can be reacted with hydrogen to make margarine, using nickel as a catalyst.

■ What can we make using catalysts?

We can make lots of useful materials using catalysts. These materials **cost** less to make when you use a catalyst. Usually each chemical reaction needs its own **special** catalyst.

6 What is the catalyst we use to make margarine?

7 What substance do we make using a catalyst called vanadium oxide?

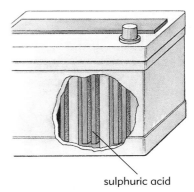

sulphuric acid

■ Why do cars have catalytic converters?

Look at the diagrams.

Car batteries contain sulphuric acid. We make this acid using a catalyst called vanadium oxide.

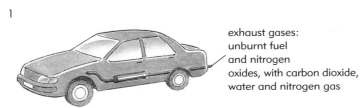

1

exhaust gases:
unburnt fuel
and nitrogen
oxides, with carbon dioxide,
water and nitrogen gas

2

exhaust gases:
carbon dioxide,
water and
nitrogen gas

catalytic converter

The catalytic converter changes harmful gases into safer gases. The catalyst is not **used up** in the reactions.

8 Why do we fit cars with catalytic converters?

9 You often have to fill up a car's fuel tank.
You don't have to add more catalyst to the converter.
Why is this?

What you need to remember [Copy and complete using the **key words**]

Substances that speed up reactions

A substance that speeds up a chemical reaction is called a _____.

The catalyst increases the rate of reaction but is not _____ _____.

You can use catalysts _____ and _____ again.

Each chemical reaction needs its own _____ catalyst.

Useful materials such as margarine and sulphuric acid _____ less to make when we use catalysts.

Investigating the speed of reactions

■ Looking and timing

All you need to measure the speed of many chemical reactions is a clock. You can then watch the reaction carefully to see how it changes.

You need to look out for different things in different reactions.

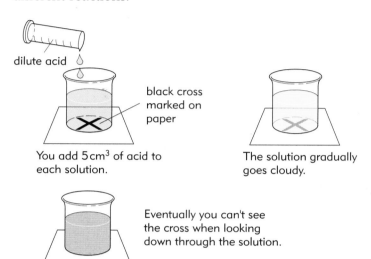

dilute acid

black cross marked on paper

You add 5 cm³ of acid to each solution.

The solution gradually goes cloudy.

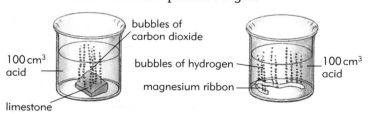

Eventually you can't see the cross when looking down through the solution.

1 Write down <u>three</u> different things you might look for when you are timing a chemical reaction.

■ How much gas is produced?

Some chemical reactions produce a gas.

bubbles of carbon dioxide

100 cm³ acid

bubbles of hydrogen

magnesium ribbon

100 cm³ acid

limestone

2 Write down the name of the gas produced when

(a) limestone reacts with acid

(b) magnesium reacts with acid.

You can collect the gas and measure how much there is. Then you can use your results to draw a graph.

3 How can you collect and measure a gas produced during a reaction?

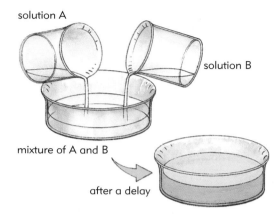

solution A

solution B

mixture of A and B

after a delay

bubbles of carbon dioxide gas

dilute hydrochloric acid

limestone

During the reaction.

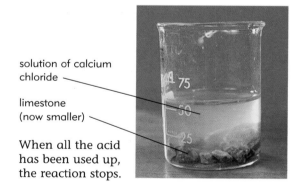

solution of calcium chloride

limestone (now smaller)

When all the acid has been used up, the reaction stops.

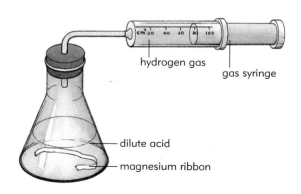

hydrogen gas

gas syringe

dilute acid

magnesium ribbon

Look at the graph. It shows the results of the experiment of magnesium reacting with acid.
A gas syringe was used to collect the gas.

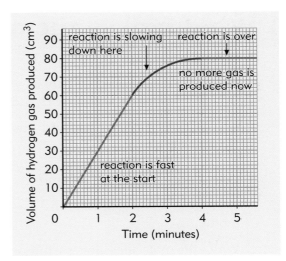

4 Copy and complete the following sentences.

During the first two minutes the reaction is

_____.

Then for the next two minutes the reaction is

_____ _____.

After four minutes the reaction is _____, and no more _____ is produced.

How does the mass change?

You can also measure the rate of reaction by weighing. If a gas escapes into the air during a reaction, the mass of what is left goes down.

The graphs show some students' results for this experiment.

5 Look at the graphs.

(a) Which reaction takes longer to finish?

(b) Which reaction has the faster rate?

(c) How much carbon dioxide gas is produced in each reaction?

6 Why is there a cotton wool plug in the neck of the flask?

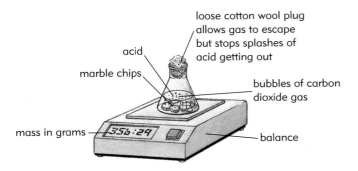

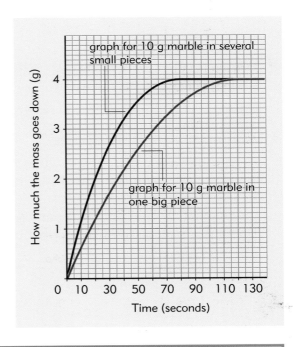

What you need to remember

Investigating the speed of reactions

You may be given some similar information to the examples given above.
You must be able to explain what the information tells you about the rate of reactions.

What makes chemical reactions happen?

Chemical reactions can only happen when the particles of different substances **collide** with each other.

The diagram shows what happens when carbon burns in oxygen.

1 Copy and complete the sentences.

A molecule of oxygen contains _____ oxygen atoms.

When the molecule collides with some hot carbon, the oxygen atoms join with a _____ atom to make a molecule of _____ _____.

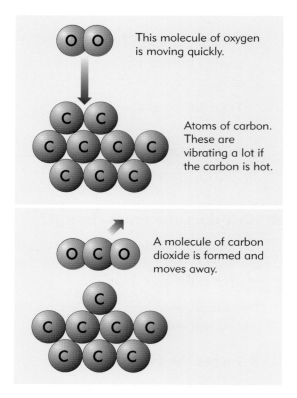

This molecule of oxygen is moving quickly.

Atoms of carbon. These are vibrating a lot if the carbon is hot.

A molecule of carbon dioxide is formed and moves away.

Why do reactions speed up when you increase the temperature?

The higher the temperature, the **faster** the oxygen molecules move.

2 Write down <u>two</u> reasons why faster-moving oxygen molecules react more easily with carbon.

The smallest amount of energy particles must have for a reaction to occur is called the **activation** energy.

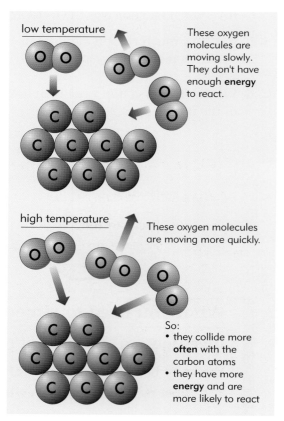

low temperature

These oxygen molecules are moving slowly. They don't have enough **energy** to react.

high temperature

These oxygen molecules are moving more quickly.

So:
• they collide more **often** with the carbon atoms
• they have more **energy** and are more likely to react

Why does breaking up a solid make it react faster?

A lump of iron doesn't react very quickly with oxygen, even if it is very hot. But the tiny specks of iron in a sparkler burn quite easily.

3 Why do tiny specks of iron react more easily than a big lump of iron?

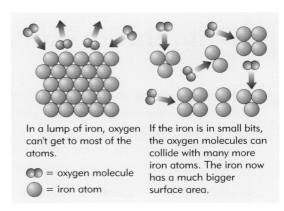

In a lump of iron, oxygen can't get to most of the atoms.

If the iron is in small bits, the oxygen molecules can collide with many more iron atoms. The iron now has a much bigger surface area.

⬤⬤ = oxygen molecule

⬤ = iron atom

Why do strong solutions react faster?

Magnesium metal reacts with acid.

The reaction is faster if the acid is made more concentrated.

4 Explain why the reaction is faster in more concentrated acid.

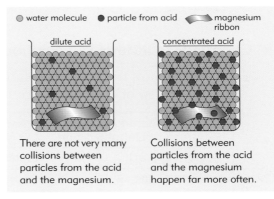

○ water molecule   ● particle from acid   ⬭ magnesium ribbon

dilute acid

concentrated acid

There are not very many collisions between particles from the acid and the magnesium.

Collisions between particles from the acid and the magnesium happen far more often.

Another way to make gases react faster

Gases react faster if they are hot.

The diagrams show another way to make gases react faster.

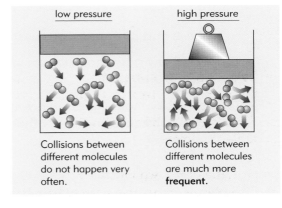

low pressure

high pressure

Collisions between different molecules do not happen very often.

Collisions between different molecules are much more **frequent**.

What you need to remember [Copy and complete using the **key words**]

What makes chemical reactions happen?

For substances to react:

■ their particles must _____;

■ the particles must have enough _____ when they do this.

The smallest amount of energy they need is called the _____ energy.

If you increase the temperature, reactions happen faster. This is because the particles collide more _____ and with more _____.

Breaking solids into smaller pieces, making solutions more concentrated and increasing the pressure of gases all make reactions _____.

All these things make the collisions between particles more _____.

Living things can do our chemistry for us

Lots of people think that chemistry happens only in laboratories. They imagine that chemicals react in strange bits of glass – a bit like in a horror film! But chemistry happens wherever we change the substances we start with into new substances.

So, there are lots of places where chemical reactions happen. One of these places is inside your body.

■ Chemical reactions in your body

1 Lots of chemical reactions take place in your body all the time. A few of them are shown in the table.

Part of body	Starting material in chemical reaction	New material made in chemical reaction
mouth	starch	maltose (a sugar)
muscles	glucose	carbon dioxide + water
gut	maltose	glucose

(a) Which part of your body turns starch into maltose?

(b) What new substances do your muscles change glucose into?

(c) Your body makes glucose in your gut. What substance do you eat that your gut makes into glucose?

Yeast cells are used to make bread.

■ Chemical reactions in other living cells

Chemical reactions take place in the cells of all living things. We can use **living cells** to make chemicals for us.

2 Look at the photographs.

Copy the table below. Then fill it in using the information in the photographs. The first one is done for you.

Type of living cells	What the living cells help us to make
yeast	bread

Yeast cells help us to make beer.

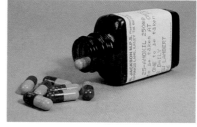

The drug penicillin is made by **moulds**.

Bacteria help us to make yogurt.

Using yeast to make wine

Yeasts are very useful living things. Yeast cells make the chemical called **alcohol** in wine and beer.

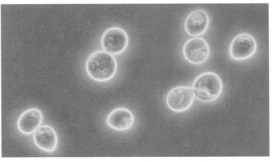

These are yeast cells. When they have plenty of food (**sugar**) they can grow and divide quickly. They turn the sugar into alcohol and the gas carbon dioxide.

3 Look at the photograph of yeast cells under the microscope.

   Copy and complete the word equation.

   sugar $\xrightarrow{\text{yeast}}$ _____ + _____ _____

We call this reaction **fermentation**.

4 Look at the picture of wine being made.

   How can you tell that the grape juice is fermenting?

Using yeast to make bread

The **carbon dioxide** that the yeast makes is useful too. This gas helps to make bread rise. When you slice through bread you can see lots of tiny holes.

5 What do you think causes these holes?

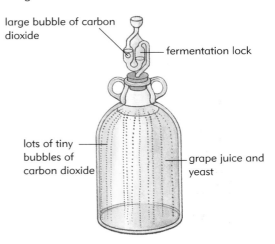

large bubble of carbon dioxide

fermentation lock

lots of tiny bubbles of carbon dioxide

grape juice and yeast

Making wine. The sugar for the reaction comes from the grape juice.

6 Look at the diagram on the right. Copy and complete the following sentence.

   You can tell that yeast makes carbon dioxide gas because this gas makes _____ _____ turn milky.

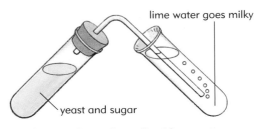

lime water goes milky

yeast and sugar

A simple test for carbon dioxide.

What you need to remember [Copy and complete using the **key words**]

Living things can do our chemistry for us

We can use _____ _____ to help us make new substances.

Examples of living things we can use in this way are _____ and _____.

When we make wine and beer, we use yeast cells to turn _____ into _____ . We call this reaction _____.

Yeast also makes the gas called _____ _____.

The bubbles of this gas help bread to rise.

More cells that will work for us

Bacteria are living cells. Some bacteria can be harmful to us. Other bacteria are very helpful.

1 Look at the photos.

Write down (a) <u>one</u> example of harmful bacteria

(b) <u>one</u> example of helpful bacteria.

■ Making yogurt

The diagram shows how you can make yogurt.

2 Copy and complete the following sentences.

To turn milk into _____ we need living cells called _____.

They feed on the _____ in the milk and turn it into _____ _____.

3 Where do the bacteria come from to make the next batch of yogurt?

■ Just the right temperature

Living cells make new substances fastest if they are at just the right temperature. If the cells are too cold then the reactions only happen slowly. If cells are too hot, they can be damaged.

4 Copy and complete the following sentence.

The best temperature for making yogurt is _____.

■ Why are living things such good chemists?

Living things contain **enzymes**, which help them to make new materials. Enzymes do this by speeding up chemical reactions. Because of enzymes, reactions in cells are quite fast, even though the cells are not very hot.

There are thousands of different enzymes, just as there are thousands of chemical reactions that happen in living things.

> **REMEMBER**
>
> Living cells can make chemicals that are very useful to us.

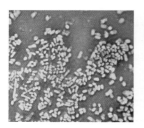

Harmful bacteria that cause the disease cholera.

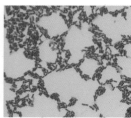

Helpful bacteria that we use to make yogurt.

yogurt bacteria

milk

Milk contains a **sugar** called lactose.

Yogurt bacteria use up the sugar and make **lactic acid**.

keep in a warm place (about 40 °C) for 12 hours

there are now many more bacteria, so we can use a little of this yogurt to start the next batch

yogurt

The milk turns into yogurt.

5 What do we call substances (like enzymes) that speed up chemical reactions?

6 Copy and complete the following sentence.

Because of _____, reactions in living cells are quite fast, even though the temperature isn't very _____.

■ Why mustn't enzymes be made too hot?

Enzymes are made from **protein**. They are big molecules and they have special shapes that help them to work.

There are proteins in the white of an egg. If you put an egg in hot water the protein **changes**, and you can't change it back again.

A raw egg.

An egg after it has been heated.

7 Why do you think heat damages or destroys enzymes?

8 Look at the pictures about making bread.

(a) What makes the dough rise?

(b) Why must the dough be left in a warm place for this to happen?

(c) What happens to the live yeast in the hot oven?

Make the dough.

(flour + water + sugar + yeast + salt)

Put dough in the tin.

Leave in a warm place. (25 to 30 °C)

bubbles of carbon dioxide make the dough rise

Bake in a hot oven. (230 °C)

What you need to remember [Copy and complete using the **key words**]

More cells that will work for us

The type of living cells that make yogurt are called _____.
They feed on the _____ in the milk and turn it into _____
_____.

To speed up their chemical reactions, living cells contain _____.
These need to be warm to work well, but must not get too hot as they are made from _____.

Protein _____ when it is heated and cannot be changed back again.

159

Not too hot and not too cold

■ What makes food go bad?

Food will not stay fresh for ever, sooner or later it starts to break down or go bad.

This is because the **living cells** of moulds, yeasts and bacteria start to feed on it. They use enzymes to break down the food. Then they take the food into their cells. They use it to grow and to reproduce.

So in a warm room, living cells like moulds and bacteria grow and multiply quite fast.

1 Why can moulds and bacteria break down food quickly in a warm room?

2 The temperature in our bodies is 37 °C. This temperature is ideal for any bacteria that get inside us. Explain why.

■ Keeping food fresh

To stop food from going bad we often keep it in a **fridge** or a **freezer**. The diagrams tell you why this works.

3 Copy and complete the table.

	Temperature	How well enzymes work	How long food stays fresh
fridge			
freezer			

REMEMBER

Living cells use enzymes to speed up their chemical reactions.

Most enzymes work best at **35 to 40 °C**.

This rotting orange is covered in mould.

 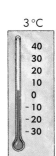

In the fridge, living cells can only break down food slowly. Their **enzymes** do not work well at this **low** temperature. Food stays fresh for several days.

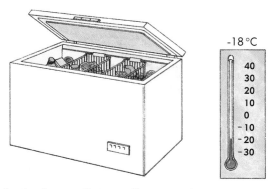

In the freezer, living cells cannot break down food at all. Their enzymes do not work at this very low temperature. Food stays fresh for weeks or even months.

Nice and warm

We need to keep living things warm when we use their enzymes to make things for us. So when we use yeast to make wine, we must keep it at the right temperature.

4   Joe set up three identical fermenting bottles to make strawberry wine. He put one in the kitchen, one in the bedroom and one in the garage.

Five days later he looked at the bottles.
The table shows what he saw.

(a) In which bottle was the yeast working most quickly?

(b) Why do you think the yeast in the other two bottles was working more slowly?

(c) Which gas were the bubbles made from?

(d) After 10 days, no more bubbles were made by the bottle in the kitchen. Why not?

The right pH

The **pH** affects how well enzymes work. Different enzymes work best in different conditions.

5   The diagram shows some enzymes in your digestive system. Write down the name of an enzyme that works best in (a) acid conditions and (b) alkaline conditions.

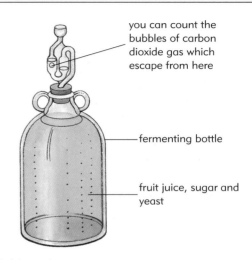

<table>
<tr><td>REMEMBER</td></tr>
<tr><td>sugar $\xrightarrow{\text{yeast}}$ alcohol + carbon dioxide</td></tr>
</table>

you can count the bubbles of carbon dioxide gas which escape from here

fermenting bottle

fruit juice, sugar and yeast

Making wine.

Where Joe put the fermenting bottles	Number of bubbles per minute on day 5
bedroom (15 °C)	15
kitchen (25 °C)	30
garage (10 °C)	10

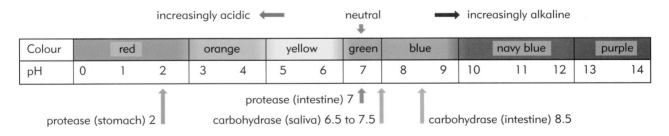

increasingly acidic ⟵   neutral   ⟶ increasingly alkaline

Colour	red		orange		yellow		green	blue		navy blue		purple	
pH	0	1	2	3	4	5	6	7	8	9	10	11	12	13	14

protease (stomach) 2

protease (intestine) 7
carbohydrase (saliva) 6.5 to 7.5

carbohydrase (intestine) 8.5

What you need to remember [Copy and complete using the **key words**]

Not too hot and not too cold

Food goes bad when _____ _____ feed on it.

We can keep food fresh for longer by keeping it in a _____ or a

_____. This is because living cells use _____ to speed up

their reactions. These work slowly if the temperature is _____.

Useful living cells like yeast work best at temperatures around _____.

Different enzymes work best at different _____ values.

10

More uses of enzymes

■ Where do the enzymes come from?

Most of the enzymes that we use come from
microorganisms. For some jobs we extract the enzymes
from the microorganisms. For other jobs, we use the
whole microorganism.

■ Enzymes that we use at home

Lots of washing powders contain enzymes that come
from bacteria. They are the enzymes that the bacteria use
to digest proteins and fats. So we can use them to digest
stains like egg, blood and gravy because those things
contain proteins and fats. The enzymes break down the
large molecules into much smaller ones that will rinse
out.

1 We call washing powders that contain enzymes
   biological washing powders. Why is this?

2 Copy and complete the sentences.

   Biological washing powders contain _____
   for breaking down the proteins in stains. They also
   contain _____ for breaking down the fats.

REMEMBER
■ **Enzymes** in the cells of bacteria and fungi do some of our chemistry for us.
■ Temperatures above 45 °C damage most enzymes.
■ Examples of enzymes: **Proteases** digest proteins. **Lipases** digest fats (lipids).

Biological powders work at lower temperatures
than ordinary powders. So less energy is used
to heat water.

3 Look at the table.

   (a) At which temperature is 'Cleeno' best at
       removing blood stains? Why is this?

   (b) 'Cleeno' can't remove blood stains at all at 55 °C.
       Why not?

Biological powders are good at removing certain stains.
But they can cause problems. Your skin is made of
protein. So you shouldn't use biological powders for
washing clothes by hand. Also, some people get rashes
because they are allergic to the enzymes.

4 The enzymes in biological washing powders work best
   at fairly low temperatures.
   Write down <u>one</u> benefit and <u>one</u> problem of using
   biological washing powders.

Temperature of wash in °C	What happened to blood stain
15	
25	
35	
45	
55	

Enzymes that we use in industry

In the chemical industry many processes need high **temperatures** and **pressures**. So they need expensive equipment as well as expensive energy. Sometimes chemists choose enzymes to carry out a process because this is much cheaper. Enzyme reactions happen at **normal** temperatures and pressures.

5 Many industrial processes are expensive. Write down <u>two</u> reasons for this.

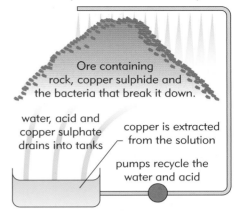

A sprinkler system sprays water and sulphuric acid onto the heap.

Ore containing rock, copper sulphide and the bacteria that break it down.

water, acid and copper sulphate drains into tanks

copper is extracted from the solution

pumps recycle the water and acid

Extracting copper

Some ores have only a small percentage of copper in them. We call them low-grade ores. Often we don't use low-grade ores because it costs too much to get the copper out. We say that it is uneconomic.

Now scientists have found a new, cheap way of getting the copper out of low-grade ores. They use the enzymes in bacteria. The bacteria change insoluble copper sulphide to soluble copper sulphate.

Few plants can grow on land contaminated with copper. So it is hard to reclaim land around copper mines.

$$\text{copper sulphide} + \text{oxygen} + \text{water} \xrightarrow[\text{bacteria}]{\text{enzymes in}} \text{copper sulphate} + \text{sulphuric acid} + \text{energy}$$

Scientists also use this method to clean up waste tips at copper mines.

6 Look at the diagram and the word equation. What change do the bacteria make to the copper compound in the ore?

7 How do bacteria that use copper sulphide help the environment?

What you need to remember [Copy and complete using the **key words**]

More uses of enzymes

It is important to use biological washing powders at low temperatures because high temperatures damage the _____ in them. The washing powders contain _____ to digest proteins and _____ to digest fats.

Some industries use high _____ and _____. This is expensive.

Enzymes carry out reactions at _____ temperatures and pressures.

[You may be given similar information about using an enzyme to bring about a chemical reaction. You should be able to explain the advantages and disadvantages of using the enzyme.]

These ideas, together with those from Patterns of chemical change 11, are extended, for Higher Tier students, in Patterns of chemical change H1 on pages 184–185.

Enzymes in the food industry

Our food comes from plants and animals. A lot of the food we buy now is changed. We say that it is processed. We call the people who work out how to do this processing food technologists. Often food technologists change cheap raw materials into expensive products. We say that they add value to the raw materials.

> ## REMEMBER
>
> We use the enzymes in cells such as yeast. We use enzymes extracted from cells too.

■ Making sugar syrups

One example of added value is the sugar syrup in sweets, cakes and many other foods. Food technologists make these syrups by digesting cheap starch. They used to digest the starch using acid. Then they found that it was cheaper to use enzymes.

1 Look at the label. Write down the names of <u>two</u> sugar syrups.

2 (a) Copy and complete the word equations to show <u>two</u> ways of digesting starch to make glucose syrup.

starch $\xrightarrow{\rule{2cm}{0pt}}$ glucose

starch $\xrightarrow{\rule{2cm}{0pt}}$ glucose

   (b) Which of these ways is used most? Explain why.

   (c) Write down <u>two</u> plants that we get the cheap starch from.

■ Which enzymes digest starch?

Each enzyme only does one job. So the enzymes that food technologists use to digest starch are not the same as the ones they use to digest proteins.

Starch is a carbohydrate. **Carbohydrases** are the only enzymes that digest carbohydrates. Food technologists get these enzymes from microorganisms. The fungi and bacteria that they use have to be the kind that don't cause disease.

3 Write down the name of the group of enzymes that we can use to change starch to glucose.

INGREDIENTS
Pear Slices, Water, Syrup, Glucose Syrup, Corn Syrup, Citric Acid.

NUTRITION INFORMATION

Average values per 100g of product	
Energy:	281KJ
	66kcal
Protein:	0.5g
Carbohydrate:	16.0g
of which sugars:	16.0g
Fat:	Trace
of which saturates:	Trace
Fibre:	1.5g
Sodium:	Trace

A label from tinned pears.

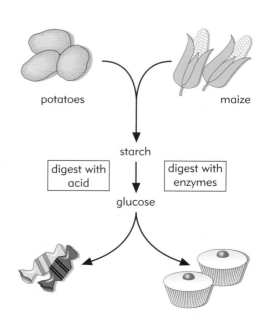

Making an even sweeter syrup

Food technologists often use fructose syrup in slimming foods. It is more expensive than glucose, but it is sweeter too. This means that they use only small amounts. So the foods contain less energy.

They make fructose syrup using enzymes too.

$$\text{glucose} \xrightarrow{\text{isomerase}} \text{fructose}$$

4 Write down the name of an enzyme that we use to change glucose to fructose.

5 We use fructose to sweeten foods for slimmers and diabetics. Explain why.

Enzymes for tenderising meat

We can also use enzymes to make meat tender. Meat tenderisers contain **proteases** that digest some of the protein. This makes the meat softer.
South American Indians have used an enzyme called papain to tenderise meat for centuries. The enzyme is in papaya fruits and in the papaya leaves that they wrap their meat in before they cook it.

6 Is papain a carbohydrase, an isomerase or a protease? Explain your answer.

We use proteases in the food industry. Proteases make cheap cuts of meat tender and cooking times shorter. The proteins in beans are not very easy to digest. So we use proteases to pre-digest some bean products. Babies don't digest some protein foods very easily. So baby foods are mashed up and sometimes partly digested too.

7 Why is the protein in baby foods often pre-digested?

INGREDIENTS
Fructose Syrup, Cocoa Mass, Maltitol, Sorbitol, Cocoa Butter, Glycerine, Flavouring, Emulsifier (Soya Lecithin)

NUTRITIONAL INFORMATION
Typical Values Grams per 100g

Energy Value:	1432kj (344kcal)
Protein:	2.3g
Carbohydrate:	66.8g
of which Sugars:	1.1g
Fructose:	15.6g
of which Polyols:	50.1g
of which Starch:	1.0g
Total Fat:	16.3g
of which Saturates:	9.9g
Fibre:	4.4g
Sodium:	0g

People with diabetes have to limit the amount of sugars and other carbohydrates that they eat. This is a label from a diabetic food.

Ingredients

Rice, Vegetables (4%) in variable proportion (Red Pepper, Green Pepper, Mushrooms), Mushroom Extract, Flavourings, Hydrogenated Vegetable Oil, Salt, Hydrolysed Vegetable Protein, Vegetable Bouillon, Parsley, Garlic.

CONTAINS MILK, WHEAT AND SOYA.

You can find out if a food contains pre-digested proteins by looking at the label. It will say 'extract of protein' or 'hydrolysed protein'. Both these mean digested protein. This savoury rice mix contains hydrolysed protein.

What you need to remember [Copy and complete using the **key words**]

Enzymes in the food industry

Job	Enzyme(s)
break down starch into glucose	
change glucose to a sweeter sugar called fructose	
to 'pre-digest' the proteins in some baby foods	

These ideas are extended, for Higher Tier students, in Patterns of chemical change H1 on pages 184–185.

Getting energy out of chemicals

On a barbecue you **burn** charcoal to cook the food.
Burning charcoal releases **energy** in the form of **heat**.
Burning charcoal is an example of a chemical reaction.

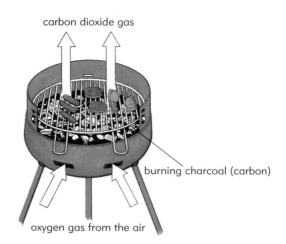

carbon dioxide gas

burning charcoal (carbon)

oxygen gas from the air

1 Copy and complete the word equation for the
   chemical reaction.

   _____ + carbon ⟶ _____ + ⚡energy⚡

Substances that we burn to release energy are
called **fuels**.

■ Are all fuels the same?

All fuels release energy as they burn. Different fuels give
different waste gases.

If a fuel contains carbon it produces carbon dioxide
when it burns.

If a fuel contains hydrogen it produces water vapour
when it burns.

Many fossil fuels such as coal and oil contain a little
sulphur. If a fuel contains some sulphur, it produces
sulphur dioxide gas when it burns.

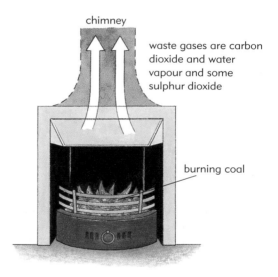

chimney

waste gases are carbon
dioxide and water
vapour and some
sulphur dioxide

burning coal

2 Copy the table. Use the information from the pictures
   to complete the table.

Name of the fuel	Gases produced when the fuel burns	What the fuel contains
charcoal		
coal		
butane		

3 Copy and complete the word equation for burning
   some camping gas.

   _____ _____ _____

   + _____ ⟶ _____ + _____ + ⚡energy⚡
   oxygen   _____ _____

waste gases are carbon
dioxide and water vapour

burning gas

camping gas cooker

butane gas

What other reactions release energy?

Many chemical reactions happen in solutions.
These reactions may also release some energy.

Look at the diagrams.

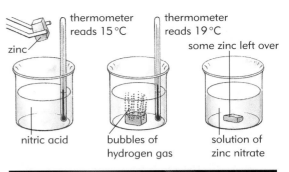

thermometer reads 15 °C
thermometer reads 19 °C
zinc
some zinc left over
nitric acid
bubbles of hydrogen gas
solution of zinc nitrate

4 How do you know that this reaction releases energy?

5 Copy and complete the word equation for this reaction.

$$ \underline{\qquad} + \underline{\qquad} \longrightarrow \underline{\qquad} + \underline{\qquad} + \text{energy} $$

An <u>ex</u>it sign is where you go <u>out</u>.

Naming reactions that release energy

Chemical reactions that release energy are called **exothermic** reactions.

6 Copy and complete the following sentences.

'Ex' means _____.

'Therm' means something to do with _____.

So 'exothermic' means _____ going _____.

A <u>therm</u>ometer tells you how <u>hot</u> something is.

A <u>therm</u>os flask keeps the <u>heat</u> in.

Other types of energy released by chemical reactions

Some chemical reactions release different kinds of energy. Look at the diagrams.

7 What other kinds of energy do these chemical reactions release?

A stone quarry.

What you need to remember [Copy and complete using the **key words**]

Getting energy out of chemicals

Charcoal, coal, gas and wood are all _____.
When we _____ them they release energy in the form of _____.
Many other chemical reactions also release _____ into the surroundings.
We call reactions like this _____ reactions.

These ideas, together with those from Patterns of chemical change 13, are extended, for Higher Tier students, in Patterns of chemical change H2 to H4 on pages 186–191.   167

Do chemical reactions always release energy?

Many chemical reactions release energy.

1 Write down <u>two</u> examples of chemical reactions that release energy.

2 Copy and complete the following sentence.

A reaction that releases heat energy is called an _____ reaction.

Other reactions will happen only if we **supply** energy. We call these **endothermic** reactions.

You have to supply energy to cook the egg.

3 Write down <u>one</u> everyday example of an endothermic reaction.

■ Using heat to make reactions happen

We can make some chemical reactions happen by supplying energy in the form of **heat**. This is why a Bunsen burner is so useful; it supplies heat energy.

4 Look at the diagrams.

Copy and complete the word equations for the <u>two</u> endothermic reactions.

copper _____ + ⚡energy⚡ ⟶ copper _____ + _____

lead oxide + _____ + ⚡_____⚡ ⟶ _____ + _____

_____

> ### REMEMBER
> When fuels burn or when metals react with acids, heat energy is released. We say that these reactions are exothermic.

carbon dioxide gas

changes to give

copper carbonate

copper oxide

heat

carbon dioxide gas

changes to give

mixture of lead oxide and carbon

beads of lead metal

some lead oxide or carbon left over

heat

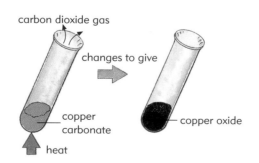

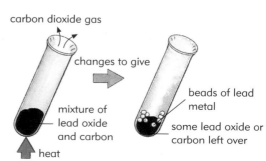

Using electricity to make reactions happen

We can make some chemical reactions happen by supplying energy in the form of **electricity**.

We can use electricity to obtain copper metal from a solution of copper chloride.

5 Copy and complete the word equation for this reaction.

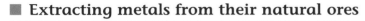

Extracting metals from their natural ores

You need to supply energy to extract metals from ores.

6 Copy and complete the following sentence.

The chemical reactions we use to extract metals from their ores are _____-thermic reactions.

7 How do you supply the energy you need to extract aluminium from aluminium ore?

8 How do you supply the energy you need to extract iron from iron ore in a blast furnace?

Reactions that use light energy

When you take a photograph, **light** energy changes the chemicals in the film. Films contain silver halides.
The word equation is:

silver halide + ⚡energy⚡ ⟶ silver metal + halogen

9 Copy and complete the following sentence.

In photography _____ energy changes silver halides into _____ _____ and the halogens.

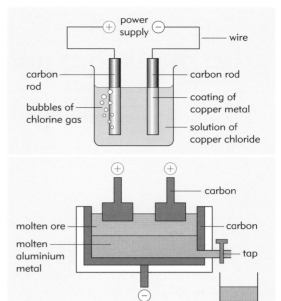

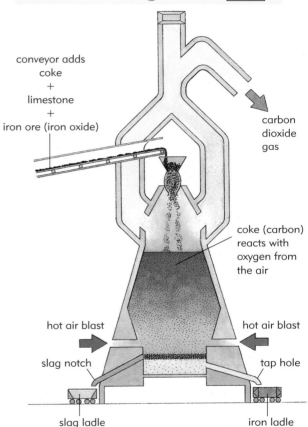

What you need to remember [Copy and complete using the **key words**]

Do chemical reactions always release energy?

To make some chemical reactions happen you must _____ energy.
We call these reactions _____ reactions.
We must supply energy to extract metals from their ores.
We can supply this energy in the form of _____ or _____.
The chemical reactions in photography use _____ energy.

These ideas are extended, for Higher Tier students, in Patterns of chemical change H2 to H4 on pages 186–191.

14

Reactions that go forwards and backwards

In <u>most</u> chemical reactions:

substances at the   new substances at
start of the reaction ⟶ the end of the reaction

reactants   ⟶   products

In <u>some</u> reactions, the products can change back into the original reactants.

$$A + B \rightleftharpoons C + D$$

reactants $\rightleftharpoons$ products

> This sign means that the reaction can go both ways. It is reversible.

This kind of reaction can go in both directions.
So we call it a **reversible reaction**.

■ What happens when we heat ammonium chloride?

1 Look at the pictures. When you heat ammonium chloride it decomposes to form two colourless gases. What are they?

2 Copy and complete the equation:

ammonium _____ $\rightleftharpoons$ **ammonia + hydrogen**
[_____ solid]   **chloride**
               [colourless gases]

3 Look at the hazard warning label for the two gases. What do you need to do to heat ammonium chloride safely?

4 What does the symbol $\rightleftharpoons$ in the equation tell you?

> **REMEMBER**
>
> Exothermic reactions give out energy into the surroundings.
>
> **Endothermic** reactions take energy from the surroundings.

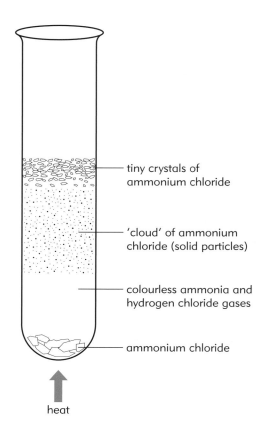

- tiny crystals of ammonium chloride
- 'cloud' of ammonium chloride (solid particles)
- colourless ammonia and hydrogen chloride gases
- ammonium chloride

heat

Ammonia and hydrogen chloride gases are both irritant.

What happens when we heat copper sulphate?

Look at the photographs of the two forms of copper sulphate.

It is easy to change one into the other.
So this change is reversible.

These crystals of copper sulphate have water molecules in them as well as copper sulphate. We say that they are hydrated.

5 Copy the equation.
The spaces are there for you to write in the colours.

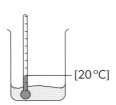

hydrated   **anhydrous**

copper sulphate + energy ⇌ copper sulphate + water

[_____]   [_____]

6 Is making anhydrous copper sulphate this way an exothermic or an endothermic reaction?
Explain your answer.

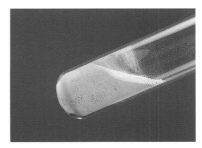

These crystals are anhydrous copper sulphate. This means that they have no water in them.

The diagrams show what happens when you add water to anhydrous copper sulphate.

7 Describe the energy transfer when you add water to anhydrous copper sulphate.

So energy is transferred <u>to</u> the surroundings when you add water to anhydrous copper sulphate. The **same** amount of energy <u>from</u> the surroundings is needed to drive water out of the hydrated crystals.

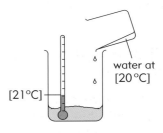

Crystals of anhydrous copper sulphate [20 °C].

Crystals of hydrated copper sulphate [21°C].

REMEMBER

We can use anhydrous copper sulphate as a test for water.

What you need to remember

Reactions that go forwards and backwards

In some chemical reactions the products react to form the original reactants.

A + B ⇌ C + D

We call this sort of reaction a _____ _____.

ammonium chloride ⇌ _____ + _____ _____
[white solid]   [colourless gases]

If a reversible reaction is exothermic in one direction it is _____ in the opposite direction. The amount of energy transferred is the _____.

_____ copper sulphate + [energy] ⇌ _____ copper sulphate + water
[blue]   [white]

15

What use is nitrogen?

The biggest part of the air is made from a gas called nitrogen. Nitrogen is an unreactive gas. Our bodies don't use the nitrogen in the air, but it is really useful to us in other ways. Chemists can make it into many useful substances.

Name of gas	How much there is in air
nitrogen	**78%**
oxygen	21%
other gases	1%

1 Look at the table.

(a) How much of the air is nitrogen?

(b) Is this about $\frac{1}{2}$, $\frac{2}{3}$ or $\frac{4}{5}$ of the air?

2 Look at the diagrams.

Write down <u>four</u> things that chemists can make with nitrogen.

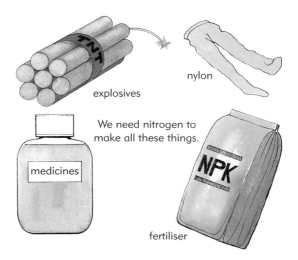

explosives

nylon

medicines

We need nitrogen to make all these things.

NPK

fertiliser

■ Plants need nitrogen

To grow healthy plants we must give them more than just water. Plants need **nitrogen** to help them grow well.

Plants can't use the nitrogen gas that we find in the air. The nitrogen must be joined with other elements in substances called **nitrates**. These nitrates dissolve in water. Plants can then take them in through their roots.

The pictures show what happens to a plant if it doesn't get enough nitrogen.

3 Copy and complete the following sentences.

Plants need nitrogen to grow healthy _____ and _____. Plants take in nitrogen through their _____ in the form of substances called _____.

4 What does the plant look like that had too little nitrogen?

Plant grown with plenty of nitrogen. Leaves and stem are healthy.

Plant grown with too little nitrogen. Small, yellow leaves and weak stem.

Why do farmers need fertilisers?

Fertilisers are important to farmers. Plants take nitrates out of the soil when they grow. Farmers often use the same fields year after year. It is important for the farmer to put nitrates back into the soil again.

Chemists can turn the nitrogen from the air into nitrates. This can happen in nature too. Farmers buy nitrates for fertiliser.

5 Look at the fertiliser labels. Write down

(a) <u>one</u> way in which fertilisers A and B are the same

(b) <u>two</u> ways in which the fertilisers are different.

Preparing to spread fertiliser on to fields.

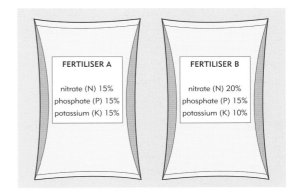

FERTILISER A	FERTILISER B
nitrate (N) 15%	nitrate (N) 20%
phosphate (P) 15%	phosphate (P) 15%
potassium (K) 15%	potassium (K) 10%

Big is best!

Farmers want to grow the best crops possible. The **yield** is the amount of crops that a farmer can grow. Farmers can increase the yield of their crops by using fertilisers.

6 (a) Copy this table.
Use the diagram to help you fill it in.

Mass of fertiliser used on field (kg)	Average height of crop (cm)

(b) What happens to the height of the crop as more fertiliser is used? Answer as carefully as you can.

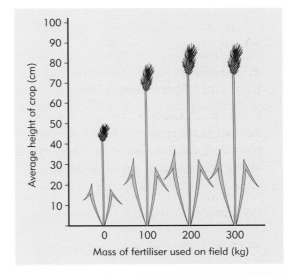

What you need to remember [Copy and complete using the **key words**]

What use is nitrogen?

Plants need _____ for healthy growth.

About _____ of the air is nitrogen but plants can't use nitrogen gas directly.

Instead, the plants take in _____ through their roots.

Farmers add nitrogen to the soil by using _____.

This increases the _____ of their crops.

16 Catching nitrogen to feed plants

Plants need nitrogen to grow properly but they can't use nitrogen from the air. The nitrogen has to be changed into nitrate.

Chemists make nitrate fertiliser in several steps. In the first step they change nitrogen into a chemical called **ammonia**. They do this using the **Haber process**.

1 (a) Why is the process chemists use to make ammonia called the Haber process?

   (b) How much fertiliser is made each day using this process?

   (c) How much fertiliser is made each year?

■ Making ammonia by the Haber process

In the Haber process
nitrogen + hydrogen $\rightleftharpoons$ ammonia

2 What does the symbol $\rightleftharpoons$ in the equation tell you about the reaction?

The reaction is reversible. So not all the nitrogen and hydrogen change to ammonia. Chemists and chemical engineers had to work out how to get a reasonable yield of ammonia as quickly and cheaply as possible.

For the reaction to produce ammonia most economically, it must be at a high temperature (about 400 °C) and a high pressure (about 200 times the pressure of the atmosphere).

Hot iron is the catalyst for the reaction.

3 Look at the diagram.

   (a) What two gases react to produce ammonia?

   (b) Where do these two gases come from?

4 Write down three things that help to produce ammonia faster.

Not all of the nitrogen and hydrogen react.

5 How is the ammonia separated from the unreacted nitrogen and hydrogen?

6 What then happens to the unreacted nitrogen and hydrogen?

REMEMBER

A chemical reaction $A + B \rightleftharpoons C + D$ is a reversible reaction.
We use a catalyst to speed up a reaction.

This is Fritz Haber. He developed the process for making ammonia from nitrogen and hydrogen. Thanks to him we make over 60 million kilograms of fertiliser containing nitrogen each day.

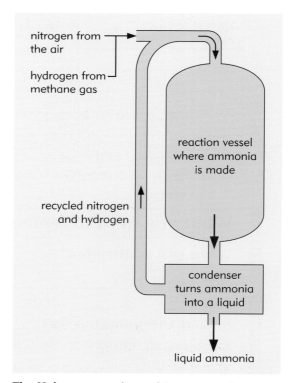

The Haber process for making ammonia.

Making nitric acid

Some ammonia from the Haber process is then changed into **nitric** acid. The diagram shows how this is done.

7 Copy and complete the following sentences.

When we heat the ammonia with oxygen we make a gas called _____ _____. We react this gas with water and oxygen to make _____ _____.

The first stage of the process is called an **oxidation** reaction.

8 What do we do to make the ammonia and oxygen react more quickly?

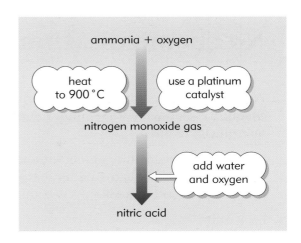

ammonia + oxygen

heat to 900 °C   use a platinum catalyst

nitrogen monoxide gas

add water and oxygen

nitric acid

And finally …

Farmers can't put corrosive nitric acid on the soil!

9 Why not?

We can change the acid into **ammonium nitrate**. Ammonium nitrate is the most common fertiliser. We make it by adding the nitric acid to more ammonia. We call this reaction **neutralisation**. The ammonia neutralises the nitric acid.

10 Copy and complete the word equation for this reaction.

_____ + _____ ⟶ _____ _____

Ammonium nitrate fertiliser.

What you need to remember

Catching nitrogen to feed plants

The flow chart shows how we can make ammonium nitrate fertiliser from the nitrogen in the air.

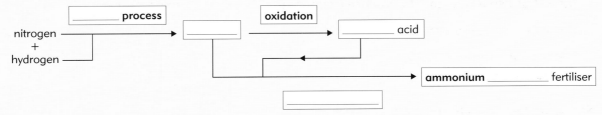

Copy the flow chart and fill in the boxes using the **key words**. Some of the boxes have been filled in for you.

You also need to know the equation in question 10.

These ideas are extended, for Higher Tier students, in Patterns of chemical change H5 to H7 on pages 192–197.

No chemicals, thank you

We make fertilisers such as ammonium nitrate in chemical factories. So we say that ammonium nitrate is an <u>artificial</u> fertiliser.

But we can grow healthy plants without using artificial fertilisers. Some people use natural fertilisers to put the nitrogen back into the soil.

Look at the diagrams.

1 Write down <u>three</u> natural ways we can put nitrogen back into the soil.

Natural fertilisers do the same job as artificial fertilisers, because they contain similar chemicals. However, if they just relied on natural fertilisers, farmers wouldn't be able to grow enough food for us all. There just isn't enough natural fertiliser to grow all of the crops that we need.

A compost heap makes fertiliser from rotting waste.

Animal manure is rich in nitrogen and makes a good fertiliser.

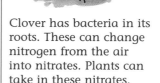

Clover has bacteria in its roots. These can change nitrogen from the air into nitrates. Plants can take in these nitrates.

■ A problem with fertilisers

Many fertilisers contain **nitrates**. Nitrates are good for plants because they contain **nitrogen** that makes plants grow well. But if the nitrates don't stay in the soil then we have a problem. Rain can wash them into our rivers and ponds.

2 Copy and complete the following sentences.

Fertilisers contain _____. If these get into our drinking _____ then they can cause problems.

3 What can happen if you swallow nitrates?

4 What can happen if nitrates get into rivers and lakes?

If you swallow nitrates, they can get into your blood. Your blood then cannot carry oxygen around your body properly.

Nitrates in lakes and rivers can cause the plants and animals to **die**.

■ So are fertilisers good or bad?

There are two sides to every argument.

Look at the different things that people say about fertilisers.

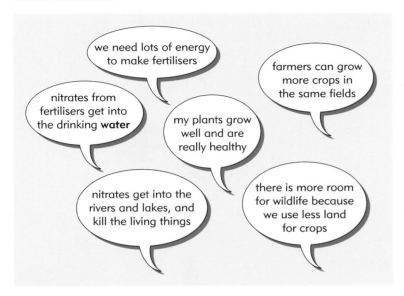

we need lots of energy to make fertilisers

nitrates from fertilisers get into the drinking **water**

my plants grow well and are really healthy

farmers can grow more crops in the same fields

nitrates get into the rivers and lakes, and kill the living things

there is more room for wildlife because we use less land for crops

5 Draw a table like this one and fill it in.

Advantages of using fertilisers	Disadvantages of using fertilisers

6 Imagine that you are an environmental health officer. It is your job to make sure that the environment doesn't harm people's health. You have just read the two newspaper articles. What should you now do?

My best crop ever!

Farmer William Mitchell cannot believe his luck this year. At Mill Farm he has had a bumper wheat harvest in spite of the poor weather.
'I can only think it must be the new fertiliser that I used. These ears of wheat are enormous, they have to be seen to be believed.'

Poisoned water

Three children in Mill St. Newbarton have been admitted to hospital this week. They were all suffering from nitrate poisoning. They were all swimming in the lake by Mill Farm earlier this week.

What you need to remember [Copy and complete using the **key words**]

No chemicals, thank you

Fertilisers contain chemicals called _____.

These chemicals give plants the _____ that they need.

Nitrates can cause problems if they get into the _____ supply because they are poisonous.

If nitrates get into rivers and lakes then they can cause many of the living things to _____.

How heavy are atoms?

■ Size of units

We choose units of measurement that make the numbers easy – not too big and not too small.
For example, we measure the length of a piece of paper in centimetres. We measure the length of a room in metres and the length of a journey to the next town in kilometres.

A person.

1 Which units (centimetres, metres or kilometres) would you use to measure the length of

(a) an air journey

(b) a picture frame

(c) a garden?

Sweets.

2 Match up the mass units below with the three things in the drawings. We would use:

(a) grams to measure the mass of _____

(b) kilograms to measure the mass of _____

(c) tonnes to measure the mass of _____

A large ship.

■ Can we weigh atoms?

Atoms are the very **small** particles that make up all of the elements. Atoms of different elements have different masses.

Atoms are so small that you can't weigh them even with the best scientific balance.

3 Copy and complete the following sentences.

The element made with the heaviest atoms is called _____.

One atom of this element has a mass of _____ g.

Numbers as small as this are not easy to write down or use in calculations.

4 Why do we not usually measure the mass of an atom in grams?

Atoms of uranium are the heaviest atoms that we find in nature. Even so there is a huge number of atoms in just 1 gram of uranium. There are lots of dots in this box.

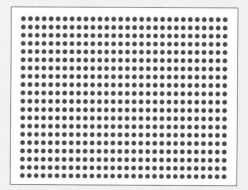

But in 1 gram of uranium, there are over 4 million, million, million times more atoms than dots in the box.

This means that one uranium atom has a mass of 0.0000000000000000000004 g.

Inventing a scale of mass for weighing atoms

Chemists can't weigh separate atoms. But they can compare how heavy different atoms are.

For example, a carbon atom weighs 12 times as much as a hydrogen atom. So if we say that the lightest atom, **hydrogen**, has a mass of **1 unit**, then a carbon atom has a mass of (12 × 1 units =) 12 units.

We call the mass of an atom in these units its **relative atomic mass**. We use the symbol A_r for short.

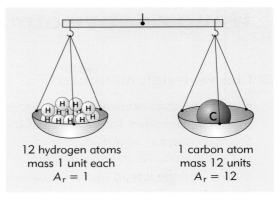

12 hydrogen atoms
mass 1 unit each
$A_r = 1$

1 carbon atom
mass 12 units
$A_r = 12$

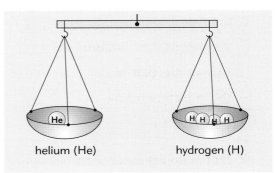

helium (He)   hydrogen (H)

5 Copy and complete the following sentence.

A_r is a quick way of writing _____ _____

_____.

6 Copy and complete the table.

Atom	A_r
hydrogen	
	12
helium	

7 Work out the relative atomic masses of the atoms shown in the diagram below.

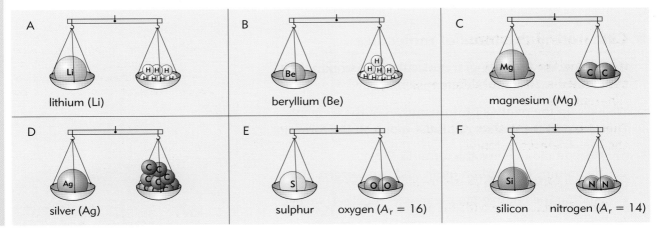

A   lithium (Li)

B   beryllium (Be)

C   magnesium (Mg)

D   silver (Ag)

E   sulphur   oxygen (A_r = 16)

F   silicon   nitrogen (A_r = 14)

What you need to remember [Copy and complete using the **key words**]

How heavy are atoms?

Atoms are far too _____ to be easily weighed in grams.

We compare the masses of atoms with each other. This is called _____ atomic mass or _____ for short.

The lightest element is _____. It has an A_r of _____ **unit**.

19

Using relative atomic mass

Can we weigh molecules?

In molecules, atoms are joined together. Substances are called compounds if their molecules are made from atoms of different elements.

1 Copy the picture of the two molecules. Write for each molecule whether it is an element or a compound.

2 Copy and complete the following sentences.

The formula for ammonia is _____.

This means that in one molecule of ammonia there are _____ hydrogen atoms and _____ nitrogen atom.

The formula for nitrogen is _____.

This means that it contains 2 _____ of nitrogen.

We use the relative atomic mass scale to compare the masses of different molecules.

We call the mass of the molecule its relative molecular mass, M_r.

Calculating the mass of molecules

If we know the formula of a molecule then working out the relative molecular mass is easy.

We look up the relative **atomic** masses of the elements. Then we **add** the masses of all the atoms in the formula.

(i) Carbon dioxide has the formula CO_2.
It contains one carbon atom and two oxygen atoms.

Adding the relative atomic masses together, we get:

$$\begin{array}{cccc} C & O & O & CO_2 \end{array}$$
Relative molecular mass = $12 + 16 + 16 = 44$

(ii) A molecule of oxygen, formula O_2, has got two oxygen atoms in the molecule.
Each oxygen atom has a mass of 16.
Therefore the two oxygen atoms have a total mass of 32.

$$\begin{array}{ccc} O & O & O_2 \end{array}$$
Relative molecular mass = $16 + 16 = 32$

REMEMBER

We <u>compare</u> the masses of different atoms by using the relative atomic mass (A_r) scale.

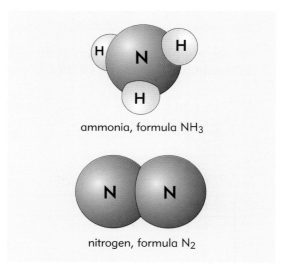

ammonia, formula NH_3

nitrogen, formula N_2

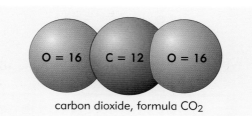

carbon dioxide, formula CO_2

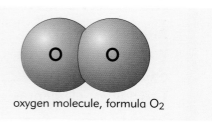

oxygen molecule, formula O_2

3 (a) Draw a molecule of ammonia.

(b) Write the relative atomic mass of each atom on your diagram.

(c) Now work out the relative molecular mass (M_r) for ammonia.

4 Calculate the relative molecular mass, M_r, for nitrogen in the same way.

Calculating more relative molecular masses

Here are some rules for reading a chemical formula.

Each element has a chemical symbol (e.g. H = hydrogen, O = oxygen).

A chemical symbol without a number stands for one atom of that element. So in H_2O (water) there is one atom of oxygen.

The little number to the right of a symbol tells you how many atoms there are of that element only. So, in water there are two hydrogen atoms.

5 The formula for copper sulphate is $CuSO_4$. It has four atoms of oxygen but only one atom each of copper and sulphur.

(a) How many atoms of copper does it have?

(b) How many atoms of sulphur does it have?

(c) How many atoms of oxygen does it have?

The number to the right of a bracket gives us the number of atoms of every element inside the bracket.

So, in $Ca(OH)_2$ there are two atoms of oxygen and two atoms of hydrogen.

6 Now calculate the relative molecular mass for each compound shown in the diagram opposite.

The relative atomic masses of some elements.

Element	Symbol	A_r
aluminium	Al	27
bromine	Br	80
calcium	Ca	40
carbon	C	12
chlorine	Cl	35.5
copper	Cu	64
helium	He	4
hydrogen	H	1
iron	Fe	56
krypton	Kr	84
magnesium	Mg	24
nitrogen	N	14
oxygen	O	16
sulphur	S	32

You need some of these to answer question 6.

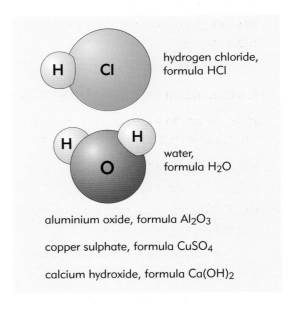

hydrogen chloride, formula HCl

water, formula H_2O

aluminium oxide, formula Al_2O_3

copper sulphate, formula $CuSO_4$

calcium hydroxide, formula $Ca(OH)_2$

What you need to remember [Copy and complete using the **key words**]

Using relative atomic mass

To work out a relative molecular mass (_____ for short):
- look up the relative _____ masses of the elements,
- then _____ together the masses of all the atoms in the formula.

These ideas are extended, for Higher Tier students, in Patterns of chemical change H8 & H9 on pages 198–201.

Elementary pie

Think about an apple pie you buy from the supermarket. There is usually a table of information on the packet. This tells us how much carbohydrate, fat and protein there is in each 100 g of the pie.

1 Write down how much of each type of food substance there is in 100 g of the pie. Write the list in order starting with what there is most of.

Apple pie Nutritional information Average values per 100 g	
protein	3 g
carbohydrate	54 g
fat	11 g

Telling you how much of everything there is in each 100 g makes it easy to compare different foods.

2 How do the amounts of protein and fat in the apple pie compare with the amounts in the bread?

Bread Nutritional information Average values per 100 g	
protein	8 g
carbohydrate	31 g
fat	2 g

Another way of saying 8 g out of 100 g is to say 8 per cent. Per cent means 'out of one hundred'.

■ How much of an element is in a compound?

We can easily see how many units of mass of **elements** are in a compound.

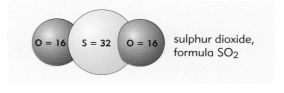

sulphur dioxide, formula SO_2

For example, sulphur dioxide is SO_2.

M_r = mass of S atom + mass of 2 O atoms
(relative = 32 + 2 × 16
molecular = 32 + 32
mass) = 64

Sulphur gives 32 units of mass out of 64 for sulphur dioxide. Oxygen gives the other 32 units of mass.

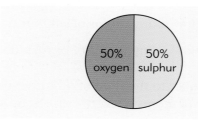

This means that sulphur dioxide is 50 per cent sulphur and 50 per cent oxygen by mass.

Half is the same as 50%.

3 Now work out the percentage by mass of carbon and hydrogen in methane one step at at time, like this:

methane, formula CH_4

(a) What is the mass of all the hydrogen atoms?

(b) What is the mass of the carbon atom?

(c) What is the relative molecular mass of methane?

(d) What is the percentage by mass of hydrogen in methane?

(e) What is the percentage by mass of carbon in methane?

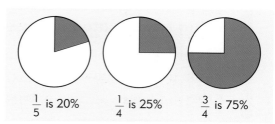

$\frac{1}{5}$ is 20% $\frac{1}{4}$ is 25% $\frac{3}{4}$ is 75%

How to calculate percentages

Percentages don't usually work out as easily as they do for sulphur dioxide and methane.

In water, for example, 2 parts out of 18 are hydrogen.

To calculate this as a %

> press the number 2
> then press ÷
> then press the numbers 1 then 8 (18)
> then press %

4 What is 2 out of 18 as a percentage?

You can work out other awkward percentages in a similar way.

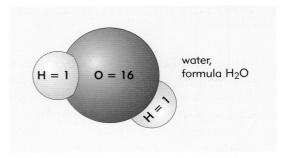

water, formula H_2O

The percentages by mass of elements in ammonia

The diagram shows an ammonia molecule.

5 Work out:

(a) the total mass of hydrogen atoms in the molecule

(b) the relative molecular mass, M_r, for the molecule

(c) the percentage by mass of hydrogen in the molecule.

6 Work out the percentage by mass of nitrogen in ammonia. (Hint: what percentage isn't hydrogen?)

ammonia, formula NH_3

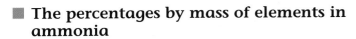

General percentage rule

The percentage by mass of an element in a compound

$$= \frac{\text{total mass of the element}}{\text{relative molecular mass of the compound}} \times 100$$

What you need to remember [Copy and complete using the **key words**]

Elementary pie

Chemical compounds are made of _____ (just as an apple pie is made of ingredients).

[You need to be able to work out the percentage by mass of each element in a compound, just like you have on these pages.]

These ideas are extended, for Higher Tier students, in Patterns of chemical change H10 on pages 202–203.

H1   This extends *Patterns of chemical change* 10 and 11 for Higher Tier students

Making the best use of enzymes

In good conditions, an enzyme molecule does the same job over and over again. But an enzyme is easily damaged. High temperatures or the wrong pH change the shape of an enzyme. We say that it is denatured. A denatured enzyme no longer works and it can't be repaired.

1 Make a copy of the graph. On your copy, mark

  (a) the part that shows the rate of reaction increasing

  (b) the optimum or best temperature for this reaction.

2 In an experiment, a sample of the same enzyme was kept at 55 °C. Then it was cooled to 35 °C and mixed with some starch. It didn't digest the starch. Explain this as fully as you can.

Carbohydrases from different microorganisms work best in slightly different conditions. Some enzymes are harder to damage than others. We say that they are more **stable**. Enzymes are expensive. So in industry, scientists choose the most stable enzymes. Then they keep them working by carefully controlling the conditions.

3 Write down <u>two</u> conditions that scientists control in processes that use enzymes.

> ### REMEMBER
>
> Enzymes are protein molecules made in living cells. They catalyse reactions inside cells. But we can extract them and use them outside cells too.

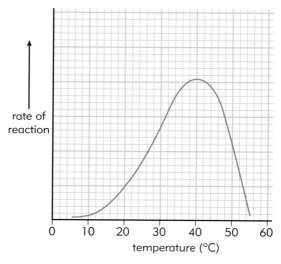

How temperature affects the rate of starch digestion by a carbohydrase.

■ Two kinds of industrial processes

Look at the flow chart about a batch process. In this kind of process, we make one batch of product. When that is finished, we start again. That's why we call it a **batch** process.

4 What is a batch process? Describe, as fully as you can, how beer is made by a batch process.

Making beer by a batch process

Each batch is fermented in a large vat. The raw materials are malt, sugar, hops and water. The enzymes that are used for the process are inside yeast cells.

Batch process

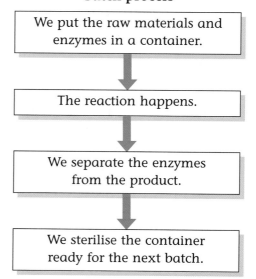

We put the raw materials and enzymes in a container.

↓

The reaction happens.

↓

We separate the enzymes from the product.

↓

We sterilise the container ready for the next batch.

Sometimes we can keep a process going for months. So we call it a **continuous** process. We do this by trapping the enzyme, then trickling a solution of the raw material over it. The reaction happens and the product trickles out. The enzyme stays trapped in the container.

5 Look at the diagram. Write down <u>three</u> ways that a continuous process is better than a batch process.

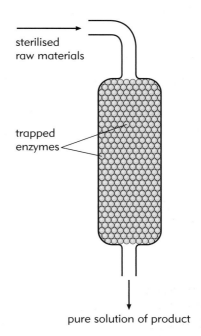

sterilised raw materials

trapped enzymes

pure solution of product

Trapped enzymes are
■ more stable
■ not lost

■ How do we trap the enzymes?

We trap enzymes in materials that don't affect the enzyme or the reaction. We say that these materials are **inert**. The enzymes can't move out of the materials. So we call them **immobilised** enzymes.

6 (a) What is an immobilised enzyme?

(b) Why do we use immobilised enzymes?

7 Look at the pictures. Write down <u>two</u> materials that we use to immobilise enzymes.

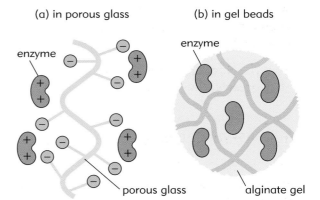

(a) in porous glass

(b) in gel beads

enzyme

enzyme

porous glass

alginate gel

Two ways of immobilising enzymes.

Using your knowledge

Look at the data for the reaction

$$\text{maltose} \xrightarrow{\text{carbohydrase}} \text{glucose}$$

	Concentration of glucose after 3 hours (%)
immobilised enzyme	6
non-immobilised enzyme	8

1 From this data only, which way of using the enzyme seems to be best?

2 After 3 months, the yield for the immobilised enzyme was twice as much as the yield for the non-immobilised enzyme. Explain this as fully as you can.

H2   This extends *Patterns of chemical change* 12 and 13 for Higher Tier students

What makes reactions exothermic or endothermic?

Chemical reactions that <u>give out</u> energy into the surroundings are called **exothermic reactions**. **Endothermic reactions** will only take place if energy is <u>taken in</u> from the surroundings.

Energy is transferred by chemical reactions because of the forces of attraction that hold atoms together. These forces of attraction between atoms are called **bonds**.

The chemical bonds between atoms in a molecule can be represented by lines:

- a **single bond** (one shared pair of electrons) is shown by –
- a **double bond** (two shared pairs of electrons) is =
- a **triple bond** (three shared pairs of electrons) is ≡

1 Copy the following diagrams of water, carbon dioxide and ammonia molecules. Below each one, draw a diagram to show the bonds between the atoms.

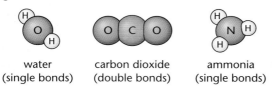

| water | carbon dioxide | ammonia |
| (single bonds) | (double bonds) | (single bonds) |

The diagrams in the box opposite show what happens when methane and oxygen react.

methane + oxygen → carbon dioxide + water
$$CH_4 + 2O_2 \rightarrow CO_2 + 2H_2O$$

For this chemical reaction to happen, the existing bonds in the methane and oxygen molecules must first be broken. New bonds can then be formed between different atoms to produce new substances, carbon dioxide and water.

2 Draw a similar set of diagrams to show the decomposition of ammonia into nitrogen and hydrogen.

ammonia   →   nitrogen   +   hydrogen

$$2NH_3 \rightarrow N_2 + 3H_2$$

Add captions to your diagrams to explain what is happening.

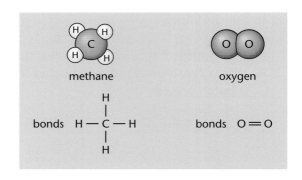

methane

bonds H — C — H

oxygen

bonds O = O

What happens when methane and oxygen react

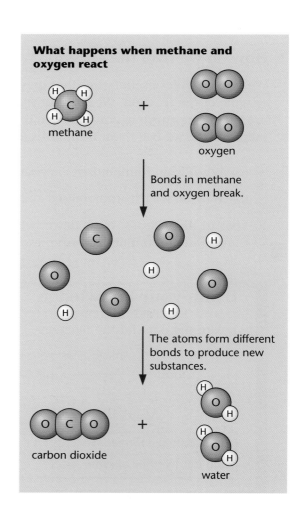

methane

oxygen

Bonds in methane and oxygen break.

The atoms form different bonds to produce new substances.

carbon dioxide

water

The table shows the bonds that are broken and the new bonds that are formed in the reaction between methane and oxygen.

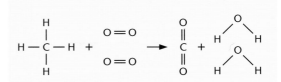

Reactants		Products	
Bonds broken		Bonds formed	
Bond	Number	Bond	Number
C–H	4	C=O	2
O=O	2	O–H	4

3 Copy the following.

$$H \quad \diagdown \quad H \qquad H \quad \diagdown \quad H \qquad\qquad H - H$$

[diagram: two ammonia-like molecules with N bonded to three H, combining to form N≡N plus three H—H]

Now make a table showing the bonds broken and the bonds formed during this reaction.

To break bonds, energy must be <u>supplied</u> (taken in). When new bonds are formed, energy is <u>released</u> (given out).

If more energy is needed to break bonds than is released when new bonds are formed, the overall reaction takes in energy. It is <u>endothermic</u>.

If more energy is released when new bonds are formed than was needed to break existing bonds, the overall reaction gives out energy. It is <u>exothermic</u>.

4 Explain in terms of the breaking and forming of bonds:

(a) what makes a reaction exothermic;

(b) what makes a reaction endothermic.

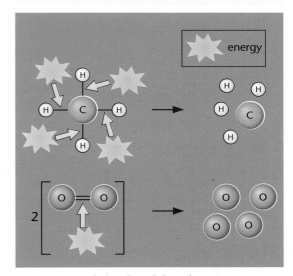

Energy is needed to break bonds in reactant molecules.

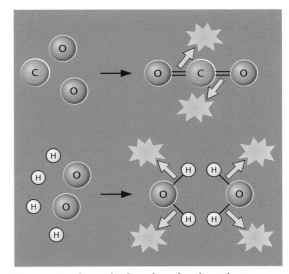

Energy is released when bonds of product molecules are formed.

Using your knowledge

1 $2H_2 + O_2 \longrightarrow 2H_2O$

(a) Write an equation for this reaction, showing the bonds between the atoms.

(b) Make a table that shows the bonds that are broken and the new bonds that are formed in the reaction.

Calculating energy changes in reactions

In a chemical reaction, energy is needed to break bonds. Energy is released when new bonds form. The energy change in a reaction is the difference between the two. We call this difference ΔH (delta aitch).

$$\Delta H \;=\; \begin{matrix}\text{energy needed to}\\\text{break bonds}\end{matrix} \;-\; \begin{matrix}\text{energy released when}\\\text{new bonds form}\end{matrix}$$

In an exothermic reaction, more energy is released when new bonds form than is needed to break existing bonds, so ΔH is negative (–).

Bond	Energy needed (or released) when bond is broken (or formed) (kJ per formula mass)
C–C	347
C=C	612
C–H	413
C=O	805
N≡N	945
O=O	498
H–O	464
H–H	436
H–N	391

> ### Example
>
> $$\Delta H = -55 \text{ kJ}$$
>
> The minus sign tells you   This is how much energy is transferred
> the reaction is exothermic.   for a formula mass of bonds. (kJ = kilojoule)

In an endothermic reaction, more energy is needed to break bonds than is released when new bonds form, so ΔH is positive (+).

1 Copy and complete the following.

ΔH = _____ – _____

If ΔH is positive (+), the reaction is _____.
If ΔH is negative (–), the reaction is _____.

The overall energy change in a chemical reaction (the net energy transfer) can be calculated by using **bond energy values**. These values are the amounts of energy needed to break bonds, or the amounts released when new bonds form.

2 (a) Which of the bonds in the table is the strongest (that is, needs the most energy for it to break)?

   (b) How does the bond energy of a C=C bond compare with that of a C–C bond?

The examples show how to calculate the energy needed (or released) to break (or form) bonds.

3 Calculate the energy released when a formula mass of water (18 g) is formed.

The formula mass is the relative molecular mass in grams.
For example, for methane, CH_4, it is

$$[12 + (4 \times 1)] = 16 \text{ grams}$$

For carbon dioxide CO_2 it is

$$[12 + (2 \times 16)] = 44 \text{ grams}$$

Example 1 (breaking bonds in methane)

$$H-\overset{\overset{\displaystyle H}{|}}{\underset{\underset{\displaystyle H}{|}}{C}}-H = 4 \text{ [C–H] bonds broken for 1 formula mass of } CH_4$$

Energy needed to break bonds
        = 4 × 413
        = <u>1652 kJ</u> per formula mass

Example 2 (forming bonds in carbon dioxide)

O=C=O = 2 [C=O] bonds formed for 1 formula mass of CO_2

Energy released when bonds formed
        = 2 × 805
        = <u>1610 kJ</u> per formula mass

Energy transfers in a complete reaction

Follow these steps if you need to find the net energy transfer in a reaction. The box on the right gives a worked example.

Step 1. Write down the balanced symbol equation for the reaction.
(You may be given this.)

Step 2. Write down the reaction using structural formulas to show the bonds in the reactants and the products.

Step 3. Show the bonds broken and formed and the number of each.

Step 4. Look up the bond energies for each type of bond.

Work out the energy needed to break the bonds of the reactants and to form the bonds of the products.

Step 5. Work out the net energy transfer in the reaction (ΔH).

Step 6. Write down your conclusion.

Example

Work out the net energy transfer in the reaction:

methane + oxygen → carbon dioxide + water

Is the reaction endothermic or exothermic?

$$CH_4 + 2O_2 \rightarrow CO_2 + 2H_2O$$

Reactants:

$$H - \underset{\underset{H}{|}}{\overset{\overset{H}{|}}{C}} - H \ + 2[O=O]$$

Products:

$$O=C=O + 2[H–O–H]$$

Bonds broken		Bonds formed	
Type	Number	Type	Number
C–H	4	C=O	2
O=O	2	O–H	4

Energy needed to break the bonds (reactants):
C–H $= 413 \times 4 = 1652$
O=O $= 498 \times 2 = 996$
Total $= \underline{2648 \text{ kJ}}$

Energy released when the products form:
C=O $= 805 \times 2 = 1610$
O–H $= 464 \times 4 = 1856$
Total $= \underline{3466 \text{ kJ}}$

$\Delta H = \begin{matrix} \text{energy needed} \\ \text{to break bonds} \end{matrix} - \begin{matrix} \text{energy released when} \\ \text{new bonds form} \end{matrix}$

$= 2648 - 3466 = -818 \text{ kJ}$

Because ΔH is negative, the reaction is exothermic.

Using your knowledge

1 Calculate the net energy transfer when water is decomposed into hydrogen and oxygen:

$$2H_2O \longrightarrow 2H_2 + O_2$$

(Work it out for <u>one</u> formula mass of water.) Use your results to find ΔH for this reaction and say whether it is exothermic or endothermic.

2 Repeat this exercise for the decomposition of ammonia:

$$2NH_3 \longrightarrow N_2 + 3H_2$$

Using diagrams to show energy transfers

The energy changes that take place in a chemical reaction
can be represented on an **energy level diagram**.

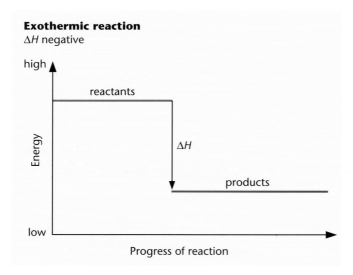

Exothermic reaction
ΔH negative

In an exothermic reaction, the reaction mixture loses
thermal energy to the surroundings. This means that
the energy level of the products of the reaction is less
than the energy level of the reactants.

Endothermic reaction
ΔH positive

In an endothermic reaction, energy is taken in from
the surroundings. So the energy level of the products
is greater than the energy level of the reactants.

When showing a particular reaction, we write
the names of the reactants and products on the
energy level diagram. For example, the diagram
on the right is for the reaction between methane
and oxygen.

1 Draw and label an energy level diagram for
the following reaction:

sodium
hydroxide $+$ hydrochloric
acid $\rightarrow$ sodium
chloride $+$ water

NaOH $+$ HCl $\rightarrow$ NaCl $+$ H$_2$O

$$\Delta H = -55 \, \text{kJ}$$

$$CH_4 + 2O_2 \longrightarrow CO_2 + 2H_2O \qquad \Delta H = -818 \, \text{kJ}$$

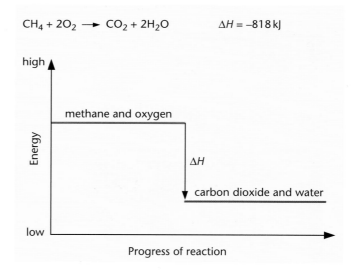

When you turn on the methane gas to a Bunsen burner, it does not begin to burn, no matter how long you wait. Only when you put a flame to the gas will it light.

For methane to react with oxygen, the existing chemical bonds between the atoms must first be broken. Putting a flame to the gas provides the energy that is needed to break some of these bonds and get the reaction started.

The energy needed to start a reaction is called the **activation energy**. It can be shown on an energy level diagram for the reaction.

2 (a) Why must we usually supply energy to get an exothermic reaction started?

(b) What do we call the energy we have to supply?

(c) An exothermic reaction will carry on by itself once it has been started. Explain why.

Some reactions will happen more quickly if a **catalyst** is used. Catalysts are substances that increase the rate of a chemical reaction but are not changed by the reaction.

Transition metals are often used as catalysts. For example, iron pellets are used as a catalyst in the manufacture of ammonia.

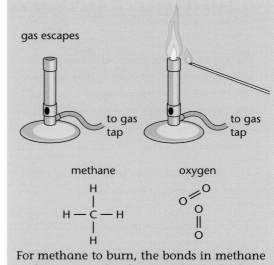

For methane to burn, the bonds in methane and oxygen molecules must first be broken.

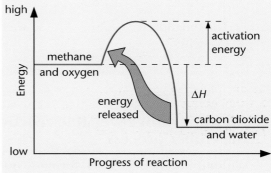

The energy released when new bonds form breaks more of the old bonds and keeps the reaction going.

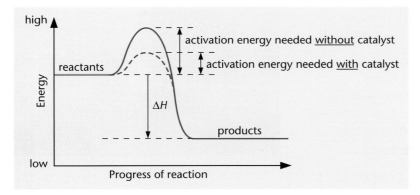

The thermal energy change (ΔH) for the reaction is unchanged, whether a catalyst is used or not.

Using your knowledge

1 Draw an energy level diagram for this reaction:

$2NH_3 \longrightarrow N_2 + 3H_2 \quad \Delta H = +93\,kJ$
(for the quantities shown in the balanced equation)

2 Hydrogen and oxygen will combine explosively if ignited by a spark, to form water (vapour).

$2H_2 + O_2 \rightarrow 2H_2O \quad \Delta H = -486\,kJ$

The activation energy for the reaction is 1370 kJ. Draw and fully label an energy level diagram for this reaction.

The Haber process – reversibility and equilibrium

In chemical reactions, the substances you start off with (the reactants) change into new substances (the products). But in some chemical reactions, the products can change back again into the original reactants. Reactions like this that can go in both directions are called **reversible reactions**.

> A forward reaction is: reactant(s) → product(s).
>
> A reverse reaction is: reactant(s) ← product(s).
>
> A reversible reaction can go both ways.
> It is shown like this: reactant(s) ⇌ product(s).

The diagram shows a reversible reaction that you have seen many times before.

1 Copy and complete the sentences.

To change litmus from red to blue, you add _____.

To change litmus from blue to red, you add _____.

The reaction is _____ so we can show it like this:

blue litmus ⇌ red litmus

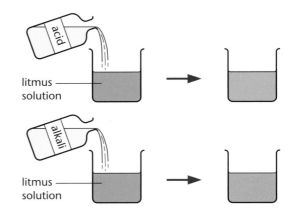

An important reversible reaction: the Haber process

Without nitrogen fertiliser, farmers couldn't produce so much food. The first step in making nitrogen fertiliser is to make ammonia from the nitrogen in the air, and hydrogen.

Almost all the ammonia used throughout the world is manufactured by the process developed by Fritz Haber at the beginning of the twentieth century. This and the next few spreads look at the Haber process in detail.

The reaction used in the Haber process is a reversible reaction. It can go both ways.

2 Look at the diagram on the right.
   For the Haber process:

   (a) write down the equation for the forward reaction;

   (b) write down the equation for the reverse reaction;

   (c) write down an equation which shows both reactions at the same time.

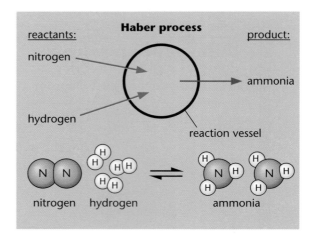

■ Equilibrium – a key idea

When the Haber process reaction begins, there will be many reacting molecules of nitrogen and hydrogen but few ammonia molecules. This means that the forward reaction will be fast, but the reverse reaction will be slow.

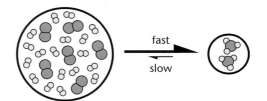

As the reaction continues, the number of nitrogen and hydrogen molecules will decrease and the number of ammonia molecules will increase. So the rate of the forward reaction will decrease and the rate of the reverse reaction will increase.

Eventually a point is reached where the rate of the forward reaction and the rate of the reverse reaction are equal. This point is called **equilibrium**.

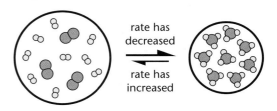

3 Copy and complete the sentences.

At equilibrium, the _____ of the forward and reverse reactions are equal. For the reactants and products to reach equilibrium, they must be in a _____ system.

At equilibrium, in the Haber process reaction vessel there will be three substances: _____, _____ and _____.

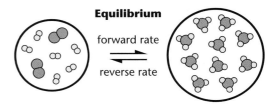

At equilibrium the rates of the forward and reverse reactions are the <u>same</u>.

How much of the product there is in the mixture at equilibrium depends on the particular reaction and on the reaction <u>conditions</u> (that is, the temperature and pressure).

In the Haber process, we need to know what conditions will give a good **yield** of ammonia.
The next spread looks at this.

> Under normal temperature and pressure (25 °C and 1 atmosphere), the amount of ammonia at equilibrium is about 1%.

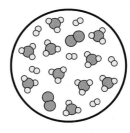

Equilibrium is reached only if both reactants and products are prevented from leaving the reaction vessel. We call this a <u>closed system</u>.

Using your knowledge

1 This word equation shows a reversible reaction:

iron + steam ⇌ iron oxide + hydrogen

(a) Explain what is meant by a reversible reaction.

(b) When the reaction begins, the reverse reaction (right to left) is slow. Explain why.

(c) In a closed system, the reaction will reach equilibrium. Explain what is happening at equilibrium.

Changing the position of equilibrium

The reaction used in the Haber process is reversible:
$N_2 + 3H_2 \rightleftharpoons 2NH_3$

Like other reversible reactions, this reaction reaches an equilibrium in a closed system.

At equilibrium, the forward and reverse reactions occur at the same rate.

In a reversible reaction such as the Haber process, it is possible to change the position of equilibrium by changing the conditions under which the reaction takes place.

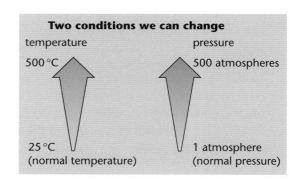

Two conditions we can change

temperature   pressure

500°C   500 atmospheres

25°C   1 atmosphere
(normal temperature)   (normal pressure)

1   Write down <u>two</u> ways in which we can change the conditions inside the reaction vessel used in the Haber process.

In the Haber process, ammonia is produced in the forward reaction:

$N_2 + 3H_2 \rightarrow 2NH_3$

2   Copy and complete the sentence.

   To produce more ammonia, we need to choose conditions that will favour the _____ reaction.

If the pressure is increased, the reaction mixture changes so as to reduce it again. The pressure is reduced if there are fewer molecules in the reaction vessel. The forward reaction forms <u>two</u> ammonia molecules for every <u>four</u> reactant molecules (one nitrogen and three hydrogen). So <u>more</u> forward reaction <u>reduces</u> the pressure.

■ Increasing the pressure

If we increase the pressure on an equilibrium mixture of nitrogen, hydrogen and ammonia, the rate of the forward reaction increases more than the rate of the reverse reaction. So a new equilibrium is reached which contains more ammonia than before.

3   (a) Which reaction in the Haber process, forward or reverse, is favoured by raising the pressure?

   (b) Why is this reaction favoured?

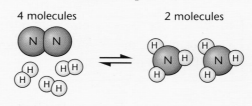

4 molecules   2 molecules

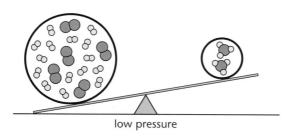

low pressure

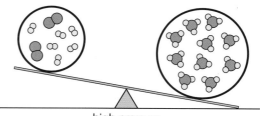

high pressure

Increasing the temperature

The energy changes in a reversible reaction are also reversible:

$N_2 + 3H_2 \rightarrow 2NH_3 \quad \Delta H = -93\,kJ$

$N_2 + 3H_2 \leftarrow 2NH_3 \quad \Delta H = +93\,kJ$

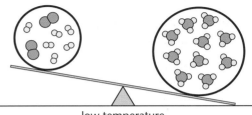

If we <u>increase</u> the temperature of an equilibrium mixture of nitrogen, hydrogen and ammonia, the equilibrium will shift so as to <u>reduce</u> the temperature. So the rate of the <u>endothermic</u> reaction is increased.

low temperature

4 (a) Which reaction in the Haber process, forward or reverse, is favoured by increasing the temperature?

   (b) Why is this reaction favoured?

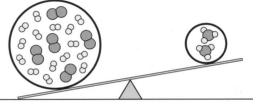

high temperature

Putting it all together

The graph shows the percentage of reacting gases converted into ammonia, at different temperatures and pressures.

5 (a) From the graph, under what conditions of temperature and pressure is the yield of ammonia greatest?

   (b) Suggest a combination of temperature and pressure that would give an even higher yield.

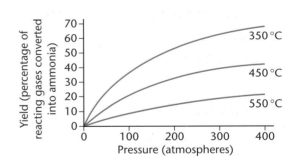

Using your knowledge

1   Copy this table and complete it for the reaction used in the Haber process.

Conditions for the reaction	Effect on rate of forward reaction compared with reverse reaction (increased or decreased)	Yield of ammonia (high or low)
high temperature		
low temperature		
high pressure		
low pressure		

2   If a forward reaction is endothermic, what is the effect of increasing the temperature on the yield of the product? Explain your answer.

H7 This extends *Patterns of chemical change* 16 for Higher Tier students

Economic and environmental considerations

All manufacturers try to make their products as economically as possible. Ammonia is usually manufactured at a temperature of about 400 °C and a pressure of about 200 atmospheres.

1 (a) How do these conditions compare with those for highest yield as shown on the graphs?

(b) Estimate the yield under these conditions.

The reasons for using these conditions are mainly economic.

The reaction vessel is made from reinforced steel and may be 20 metres high with a mass up to 200 tonnes. The cost of making the reaction vessel is high, but it would be much higher if it was built to withstand higher pressures. It would need to be even thicker and stronger.

Running costs would be greater at higher pressures, as the reacting gases would have to be pumped to a higher pressure.

Operating at a higher pressure also increases safety risks.

For these reasons, an **optimum pressure** of 200 atmospheres is used. ('Optimum' means the most favourable when all factors are considered.)

2 Explain why 200 atmospheres is the optimum pressure.

Although the yield of ammonia is higher when the temperature of reaction is lower, the <u>rate</u> of reaction is also lower. Slow production increases the costs of manufacture considerably.

For this reason, an **optimum temperature** of 400 °C is used.

3 Explain why 400 °C is the optimum temperature.

An iron catalyst is used to increase the rate of reaction. The catalyst increases the rates of both forward and reverse reactions equally in this reversible reaction.

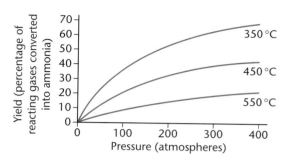

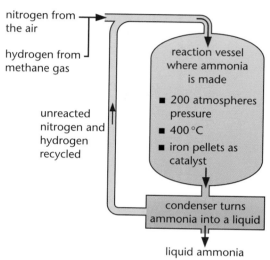

Manufacturing ammonia economically

Ensure the <u>pressure</u> is:

- not too high, or the costs are too high;
- not too low, or the yield is low.

Ensure the <u>temperature</u> is:

- not too high, or the yield is low;
- not too low, or the reaction is too slow.

A catalyst ensures that equilibrium is reached more quickly, but it does not affect the equilibrium position.

---

4 Copy and complete the sentences.

To raise the _____ above 200 atmospheres or to reduce the_____ below 400°C, would mean that the _____ in running costs would outweigh the advantages of the _____ yield.

Looking at the whole process

Reactants are put in and products are removed continuously over a long period of time. So we call this a continuous process.

Energy released from the exothermic reaction, and from hot ammonia leaving the system, is used to heat up incoming reactants and produce steam to drive turbines.

The plant can be operated by a small number of staff.

The ammonia plant and other plants which use ammonia for manufacture of nitric acid and fertilisers are usually on the same site. This reduces transport costs and delivery times.

Research is carried out into more-efficient processes, so making energy savings.

5 The hydrogen used in the reaction is expensive to produce. How does the process ensure that none of it is wasted?

Environmental considerations

If manufacturers are not careful, some processes can damage the environment and be a danger to health.
So, environmental considerations are important.

safe disposal of waste

design of plant to make it low, little seen and unobtrusive

regular safety checks/slam-shut valves in emergency

reduced gas emissions

selection of suitable site for plant

reduced noise levels

annual shut-down for safety checks

warning and evacuation procedures for local community and schools

Sometimes reducing damage to the environment increases manufacturing costs.

Using your knowledge

1 The table shows the yield of ammonia as a percentage at different temperatures and pressures in the Haber process.

Pressure (atm)	100°C	300°C	500°C
25	91.7%	27.4%	2.9%
100	96.7%	52.5%	10.6%
400	99.4%	79.7%	31.9%

(a) Under what conditions (shown in the table) would the maximum yield of ammonia be obtained?

(b) At room temperature and pressure the yield of ammonia is only about 1%. Describe and explain how the yield is affected by the conditions used in the manufacturing process.

(c) Why is the pressure used lower than the pressure that gives the maximum yield?

H8 This extends *Patterns of chemical change* 19 for Higher Tier students

Using chemical equations to calculate reacting masses

A balanced symbol equation is a useful shorthand way of describing what happens in a chemical reaction.

1 What does this equation tell you?

$$CH_4 + 2O_2 \rightarrow 2H_2O + CO_2$$

(CH_4 is the formula for methane.)

An equation does <u>not</u> tell us about the conditions necessary for the reaction, the rate of reaction, energy changes, and so on. However, we <u>can</u> use a balanced symbol equation to work out the masses of substances which react together and the masses of the products.

These are the steps to follow.

Step 1. Write down the balanced symbol equation.

Step 2. Decide what each formula tells you about the numbers of each kind of atom. That is, decide how many of each kind of atom is shown in each formula. (You may find it helpful to write this down.)

Step 3. Write in the relative atomic masses.

Step 4. Work out the reacting masses and product mass. (Note that the mass of reactant(s) equals the mass of product(s). This is because all the same atoms are still there.)

Step 5. Write in words what this means. (You can use <u>any</u> units. Normally, you should use the units given in the question.)

2 Follow steps 1–4 to work out the masses of reactants and products in these two chemical reactions.

(a) $C + O_2 \rightarrow CO_2$

(b) $CH_4 + 2O_2 \rightarrow 2H_2O + CO_2$

Set out the answers as in the example in the box.

Element	Symbol	A_r
aluminium	Al	27
carbon	C	12
iron	Fe	56
magnesium	Mg	24
oxygen	O	16

Relative atomic masses (A_r) of some atoms.

Example

Magnesium reacts with oxygen to form magnesium oxide. Work out the reacting masses and the product mass.

$$2Mg + O_2 \quad \rightarrow \quad 2MgO$$

2 magnesium atoms → 2 magnesium atoms
+ 2 oxygen atoms   + 2 oxygen atoms

$(2 \times 24) + (2 \times 16) = (2 \times 24) + (2 \times 16)$
  48   +   32   =   48   +   32
  48   +   32   =   80

For the product, work out the inner ( ) brackets first.

$$48 + 32 \rightarrow 80$$

48 grams of magnesium react with 32 grams of oxygen to form 80 grams of magnesium oxide.

You may be asked to calculate the mass of a product from a given mass of reactant in a chemical reaction.

Use only the quantities of the substances about which you are asked.

Example 1 shows how you should set out your answer so that what you are doing is clear.

3   Calculate the mass of calcium oxide (CaO) that is produced from heating 10 g of limestone ($CaCO_3$).

$$CaCO_3 \rightarrow CaO + CO_2$$

Set out your answer as in Example 1.

Sometimes you will be asked to calculate the mass of one of the reactants.

Again, use only the quantities about which you are asked.

Example 2 shows how you should set out your answer so that what you are doing is clear.

4   $CuO + H_2 \rightarrow Cu + H_2O$

How much copper oxide (CuO) is needed to produce 16 kg of copper in this reaction?
Set out your answer in a similar way to Example 2.
(But this time the calculation isn't exactly the same.)

Example 1

$$2Al + Fe_2O_3 \rightarrow Al_2O_3 + 2Fe$$

In this reaction, what mass of iron is produced from 8 grams of iron oxide (Fe_2O_3)?

$$Fe_2O_3 \rightarrow 2Fe$$

2 iron atoms + 3 oxygen atoms → 2 iron atoms

$$[(2 \times 56) + (3 \times 16)] \rightarrow (2 \times 56)$$
$$[112 + 48] \rightarrow 112$$
$$160 \rightarrow 112$$

So 160 g of iron oxide produces 112 g of iron.

So 1 g of iron oxide produces $\frac{112}{160}$ g of iron.

So 8 g of iron oxide produces $\frac{112}{160} \times 8 = 5.6$ g of iron

---

Example 2

$$2Al + Fe_2O_3 \rightarrow Al_2O_3 + 2Fe$$

How much aluminium is needed to react completely with 8 kg of iron oxide in this reaction?

$$2Al + Fe_2O_3$$

2 aluminium atoms   2 iron atoms + 3 oxygen atoms

$$(2 \times 27) \qquad [(2 \times 56) + (3 \times 16)]$$
$$54 \qquad\qquad [112 + 48]$$
$$54 \qquad\qquad\qquad 160$$

So 160 kg of iron oxide reacts with 54 kg of aluminium.

So 1 kg of iron oxide reacts with $\frac{54}{160}$ kg of aluminium.

So 8 kg of iron oxide reacts with

$$\frac{54}{160} \times 8 = 2.7 \text{ kg of aluminium}$$

Using your knowledge

1   $Fe_2O_3 + 3CO \rightarrow 2Fe + 3CO_2$

In this reaction in the blast furnace, how much iron oxide would be needed to react with 42 tonnes of carbon monoxide? How much iron would be produced?

More calculations using chemical equations

Experiments with gases show that at a given temperature and pressure, equal numbers of molecules of all gases occupy the same volume.

For example, the diagram shows water being split up into hydrogen and oxygen gases by passing an electric current through it.

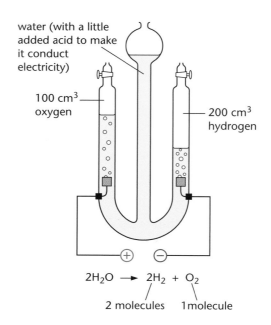

water (with a little added acid to make it conduct electricity)

100 cm^3 oxygen

200 cm^3 hydrogen

$2H_2O \longrightarrow 2H_2 + O_2$

2 molecules   1 molecule

1 (a) How many times more hydrogen molecules are produced than oxygen molecules?

(b) How many times more cm^3 of hydrogen are produced than oxygen?

(c) What do your answers to (a) and (b) tell you?

■ Calculating the volume of a gas in a reaction

The **relative formula mass** (M_r), in grams, of any gas has a volume of 24 000 cm^3 (24 litres), at 25°C and 1 atmosphere.

> **Calculating the relative formula mass of gases**
>
> Hydrogen (H_2) $M_r = (2 \times 1) = 2$
> 2 grams of hydrogen has a volume of 24 000 cm^3.
>
> Oxygen (O_2) $M_r = (2 \times 16) = 32$
> 32 grams of oxygen has a volume of 24 000 cm^3.

You can use this information about volumes of gases to calculate the volumes of gases in a chemical reaction.

The example on the right shows how you can do this.

2 Mg + 2HCl → MgCl$_2$ + H$_2$

What volume of hydrogen is produced when 0.072 g of magnesium reacts with hydrochloric acid?
Set out your answer as in the example on the right.

> **Example**
>
> What volume of carbon dioxide is produced when 6 g of carbon burns in oxygen?
>
> $$C + O_2 \rightarrow CO_2$$
>
> A_r for carbon is 12
>
> so 12 g → one formula mass
> of carbon   of carbon dioxide
>
> that is 12 g → 24 000 cm^3
>
> So 1 g → (24 000 ÷ 12) cm^3
>
> So 6 g → (24 000 ÷ 12) × 6
>
> = 12 000 cm^3
>
> 6 g of carbon produces 12 000 cm^3 of carbon dioxide.

Calculating the masses and volumes of substances produced during electrolysis

In the electrolysis of potassium bromide (KBr), reactions take place at the two electrodes.

You can calculate the amount of chemical change at one electrode if you are given information about the change at the other electrode.

For example, during an experiment to electrolyse molten potassium bromide, the mass of potassium released at the negative electrode was 1.56 g. You can calculate the volume of bromine given off at the positive electrode like this.

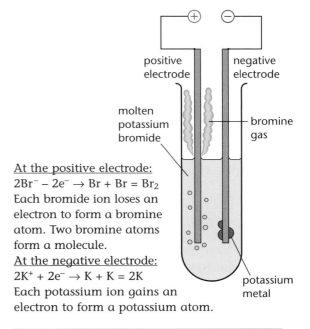

Step 1. Write down the two balanced half-equations (these will be provided for you in questions of this type).

Step 2. Write in words what happens at each electrode.

Step 3. Work out the unknown quantity using the information about the other amount.

At the positive electrode:
$2Br^- - 2e^- \rightarrow Br + Br = Br_2$
Each bromide ion loses an electron to form a bromine atom. Two bromine atoms form a molecule.

At the negative electrode:
$2K^+ + 2e^- \rightarrow K + K = 2K$
Each potassium ion gains an electron to form a potassium atom.

Example

Positive electrode: $2Br^- - 2e^- \rightarrow Br_2$
Negative electrode: $2K^+ + 2e^- \rightarrow 2K$

One molecule (two atoms) of bromine is released at the positive electrode for every two potassium atoms that are deposited at the negative electrode.

M_r Br_2 (g) has a volume of 24 000 cm³.
A_r K is 39, so 2K is 78.

So volume of bromine displaced while 1.56 g of potassium is formed is

$\frac{1.56}{78} \times 24\,000 = 480 \text{ cm}^3$

3 During the electrolysis of molten sodium chloride, 9.2 g of sodium is formed at the negative electrode. What volume of chlorine is formed at the positive electrode at normal temperature and pressure?

The half equations are:
At the positive electrode:
$\qquad 2Cl^- - 2e^- \rightarrow Cl_2$

At the negative electrode:
$\qquad 2Na^+ + 2e^- \rightarrow 2Na$

[Set out your answer as in the example.]

Using your knowledge

1 The equation shows the reaction between sodium metal and water.

$2Na + 2H_2O \rightarrow 2NaOH + H_2$

Calculate the mass and volume of hydrogen produced when 4.6 g of sodium reacts with water.

A_r for copper = 63.5

2 1.92 g of copper were deposited at the negative electrode during electrolysis of a solution of copper sulphate. What volume of oxygen at 25 °C and 1 atmosphere were formed during the experiment?

The half-equations are as follows:
$4OH^- - 4e^- \rightarrow O_2 + 2H_2O$
$2Cu^{2+} + 4e^- \rightarrow 2Cu$

Working out the formulas of compounds

The formula of a compound tells you how many of each kind of atom there are in a compound.

1 What is the ratio of the atoms (or ions) in:

   (a) an ammonia molecule, formula NH_3;

   (b) a methane molecule, formula CH_4;

   (c) the compound magnesium oxide, formula MgO;

   (d) the compound aluminium oxide, formula Al_2O_3?

You can find the masses of the elements that combine by careful weighing in experiments. Using this information, you can find the ratio of atoms in a compound.

The example below shows how to do this.

The formula for carbon dioxide is

$$\underset{\text{1 carbon atom}}{\underbrace{}}\ CO_2\ \underset{\text{2 oxygen atoms}}{\underbrace{}}$$

The ratio of carbon to oxygen atoms in a carbon dioxide molecule is 1 : 2.

The formula for sodium chloride is

$$\underset{\text{1 sodium atom}}{\underbrace{}}\ NaCl\ \underset{\text{1 chlorine atom}}{\underbrace{}}$$

Sodium chloride is an ionic compound.

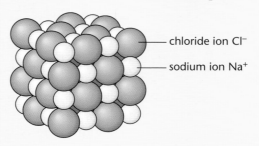

chloride ion Cl^-

sodium ion Na^+

The ratio of sodium atoms (ions) to chlorine atoms (ions) is 1 : 1.

Example

A chemist found that 0.12 g of magnesium combined with 0.8 g of bromine. What is the ratio of magnesium to bromine atoms in the compound magnesium bromide?

Step 1. Write down the ratio of the masses combining (from information in the question).

Step 2. Write down A_r for each element.

Step 3. Divide each mass by A_r to get the ratio of the atoms of each element.

Step 4. Work out the simplest whole-number ratio (in this case divide the larger number by the smaller).

magnesium	:	bromine
0.12 g	:	0.8 g
$A_r = 24$	:	$A_r = 80$
$0.12 \div 24 = 0.005$	:	$0.8 \div 80 = 0.01$
1	:	2

The ratio of magnesium to bromine atoms is 1 : 2.
The ratio Mg : Br is 1 : 2.
The simplest formula for the compound is $MgBr_2$.
This is called the **empirical formula**.

2 1.28 grams of an oxide of sulphur contain 0.64 g of sulphur and 0.64 g of oxygen. Find the ratio of sulphur to oxygen atoms and work out the empirical formula for this compound.
[Set out your answer as in the example on the opposite page. A_r sulphur = 32; A_r oxygen = 16]

■ Finding a formula by experiment

The diagram shows an experiment to find the empirical formula of copper oxide. The results (weighings) taken are shown in the table.

3 (a) Copy the table of results and then complete it.

   (b) Use the results to work out the empirical formula for copper oxide.
   [Set out your answer as in the example on the opposite page.
   A_r copper = 63.5]

   Note. You do not usually get exact whole-number ratios from the results of an experiment. So if, for example, you get a ratio of 2.1 : 1, you would assume that the correct answer is 2 : 1.

Finding the formula of copper oxide

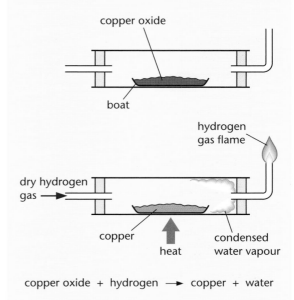

copper oxide + hydrogen ⟶ copper + water

Results	
Mass of boat	= 15.43 grams
Mass of boat + copper oxide	= 23.38 grams
Mass of boat + copper	= 21.78 grams
Mass of copper oxide	=
Mass of copper	=
Mass of oxygen in the copper oxide	=

Using your knowledge

1 In an analysis of potassium oxide, a student found that 1.17 g of potassium combines with 0.24 g of oxygen. Find the ratio of potassium to oxygen atoms and the simplest (empirical) formula for potassium oxide. [A_r potassium = 39]

2 An experiment shows that 13.5 g of aluminium combine with 12.0 g of oxygen. Find the ratio of aluminium to oxygen atoms and work out the empirical formula for aluminium oxide.

3 A hydrocarbon consists of 75% carbon and 25% hydrogen by mass. Find the ratio of carbon : hydrogen atoms and the simplest (empirical) formula for the hydrocarbon. [A_r carbon = 12; A_r hydrogen = 1]

Handling data

In tests and examinations, you will be asked to interpret scientific data. This data may be presented in several different ways.

■ Pie charts

The gases in air
The pie charts show how much there is of the main gases in air.

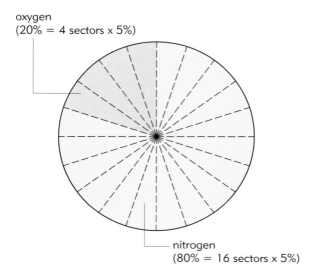

oxygen
(20% = 4 sectors x 5%)

nitrogen
(80% = 16 sectors x 5%)

Approximate figures.

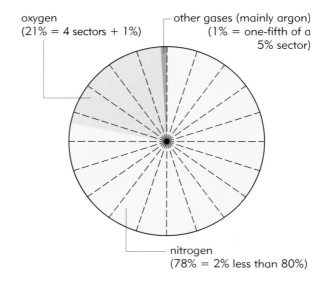

oxygen
(21% = 4 sectors + 1%)

other gases (mainly argon)
(1% = one-fifth of a
5% sector)

nitrogen
(78% = 2% less than 80%)

More accurate figures.

You may be asked to <u>compare</u> the amounts of nitrogen and oxygen in the air.

You could say that there is <u>more</u> nitrogen than oxygen.

A better answer is to say that there is (about) <u>four times as much</u> nitrogen as oxygen.

You may be asked to complete a pie chart.

Remember:

■ to draw thin, straight lines through the centre of the circle

■ to mark off each 1% in some of the sectors if you need to, like this

■ to add labels, or use a key like this

nitrogen	
oxygen	
other gases	

■ Bar charts

Comparing the strengths of metals

The bar chart shows the force you need to break wires of different metals by stretching them. The wires are all the same thickness.

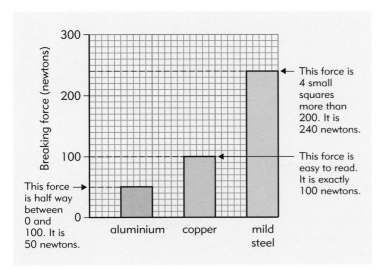

You may be asked to put the figures into a table like this:

Metal	Breaking force in N
aluminium	50
copper	100
mild steel	240

You may be asked to draw bars on a bar chart.

Remember:

■ to look carefully at the scale

■ to draw the bars the same thickness and equally spaced out

■ to draw the top of each bar with a thin, straight line

■ to label each bar or colour the bars and draw a key like this

aluminium	
copper	
mild steel	

■ Sankey diagrams

Where does the candle wax go?

The diagram shows what happens to each 100 g of wax when a candle burns.

Remember, all the candle wax must go somewhere:

$$80\,g + 15\,g + 5\,g = 100\,g$$

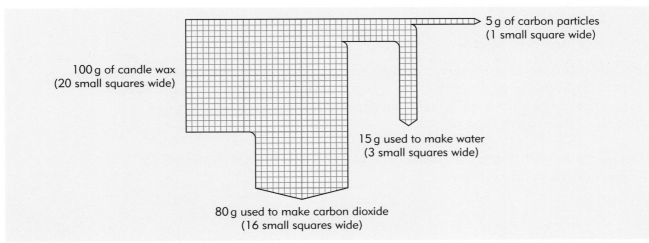

100 g of candle wax
(20 small squares wide)

5 g of carbon particles
(1 small square wide)

15 g used to make water
(3 small squares wide)

80 g used to make carbon dioxide
(16 small squares wide)

■ Interpreting line graphs

When you are reading off values from a graph:

- ■ check the scales on the axes so that you know what each small square on the grid represents;
- ■ remember to quote units in your answer. [You can find these on the axis where you read off your answer. You can still quote the correct units even if you don't understand what they mean!]

Be as precise and accurate as you can:

- ■ when describing trends or patterns
  [in the example, both reactions are fastest at the start, gradually slow down and eventually stop];
- ■ when specifying key points
  [in the example:
  saying that both reactions stop when 4 g of carbon dioxide has been produced is better than simply saying that both reactions produce the same amount of carbon dioxide;
  saying that the reaction stops after 80 seconds with the small pieces and after 120 seconds with the larger pieces is better than simply saying that the reaction stops sooner with the smaller pieces].

Get plenty of practice interpreting graphs, etc. as indicated above until you do it perfectly with as little effort as possible.

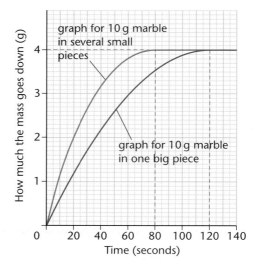

The graphs show the results of an experiment on rates of reaction. Marble reacts with acid and releases carbon dioxide gas. You can measure the rate of reaction by weighing. Carbon dioxide escapes into the air during a reaction, so the mass of what is left goes down.

■ Drawing line graphs

- ■ Choose sensible scales for the axes. [You should use <u>more than half</u> of the available squares along each axis.]
- ■ Label the axes [e.g. Volume of hydrogen (cm³)].
- ■ Mark all the points neatly and accurately
  like this   or like this

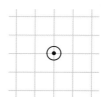

- ■ If the points are close to being a straight line or smooth curve, then draw the 'best fit' straight line or smooth curve. Use a pencil so you can rub your line out if you don't get it right first time. If there's an <u>obviously</u> wrong point, <u>ignore</u> it and indicate that you've done so.

Get plenty of practice doing these things so that you'll do the right thing even if you're nervous in an examination.

Revising for tests and examinations

■ Stage 1

See if you know which words go into the **What you need to remember** boxes for the pages you are revising.

Try to do this <u>without</u> looking at the text or diagrams on the pages.

Then, if there is anything that you can't do, read the text and look at the diagrams to find the answer.

Remember

■ the key words are printed like this

So we can put them into the **reactivity** series of metals.

■ you can check your answers at the back of the book (pages 214–223).

If you are taking the Higher Tier tests or examinations, you will also need to make sure that you can answer the questions that occur at various points in the text on the extension pages.

But you don't just have to <u>remember</u> the scientific ideas.

You also need to be able to <u>use</u> these ideas.

You may be asked to do this in a situation you haven't met before.

■ Stage 2

See if you can <u>use</u> the ideas you have revised.

There are lots of questions in the text which ask you to do this. Higher Tier students will find questions of this type at the ends of the extension pages.

Your teacher should be able to give you some extra questions.

Some of these may have been used in examinations in previous years.

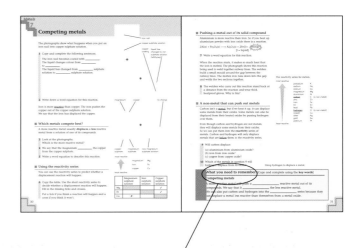

What you need to remember [Copy and complete using the **key words**]

Competing metals

A more reactive metal will push a ____less____ reactive metal out of its compounds. We say that it ___displaces___ the less reactive metal.
We can also put carbon and hydrogen into the ___reactivity___ series because they can displace a metal less reactive than themselves from a metal oxide.

Example
Most metals corrode in damp air.

If you join two metals together:

■ the more reactive metal corrodes even faster

■ the less reactive metal doesn't corrode until all the other metal has corroded.

(a) Why are magnesium blocks attached to the iron pipes that carry North Sea gas?

(b) Why should you not use copper washers with iron bolts?

Answers
(a) The magnesium corrodes more quickly. This stops the iron pipe corroding.

(b) Using copper washers would make the iron bolts corrode more quickly.

How to write good answers in GCSE Science examinations

■ Short answer questions

Here is an example of this type of question:

> limestone $\xrightarrow{\text{heat}}$ quicklime $\xrightarrow{\text{add water}}$ slaked lime
>
> What is the chemical name for quicklime?

If you're not sure of the answer to this type of question, you might be tempted to write down <u>several</u> answers in the hope that one of them is right. This is a bad idea. In most cases you'll automatically get <u>no</u> marks.

If you wrote *calcium oxide or calcium hydroxide* as your answer to this question you would score 0 marks even though calcium oxide is the right answer.

> You must make up your mind what you think is the most likely answer. If you change your mind later, you can cross out the old answer and write the new one.

■ Questions that require longer answers

It's easy to tell when you are expected to give a longer answer to a question. There will be lots of space for your answer and the question paper will indicate that you can score more than one or two marks for your answer. For example:

> Explain what it is about the east coast of South America and the west coast of Africa that supports the idea of 'continental drift'.
>
> This tells you the number of marks available $\longrightarrow$ (4)
> $\longrightarrow$ or (4 marks)

When answering these questions, don't just write down the first thing you think of and then leave it at that. You should include <u>all</u> the relevant ideas that you can remember. But you should be sure that the ideas you write down really are relevant.

<u>Don't</u> write down things that you just hope might possibly be relevant. That's a sure way to lose marks because, if they're not relevant, it tells the person marking your answer that you don't really understand the question. This means that you will probably lose marks.

When answering the above question about continental drift, for example, you should be as specific as possible.

You should refer to the shapes of the continents <u>fitting together</u> quite closely. [Note that it is not correct to say that they are the <u>same</u> shape]. You should also refer to the fact that when the continents are fitting together, the types of rocks and the types of fossils in the rock <u>also match up</u>. [This is better than simply saying that there are similar types of rocks and fossils in the two continents.]
Finally you should say that the evidence you have mentioned suggests that the two continents were once joined together and have since moved (drifted) very slowly apart.

You should also try to <u>organise</u> your answer. This means putting all your ideas into a sensible order and then linking them together in a way that shows you really understand what's going on.

A few words like this in your answer:

> First of all ... then ... because ...
> This means that ... So, on balance, ...

can help a lot.

> Don't rush into writing down your longer answers.
>
> Decide what the relevant ideas are and jot them down in pencil.
>
> Then decide what order to write them down in and how you are going to link them together.

■ Science 'stories'

GCSE Science consists mainly of many separate ideas which, once you've understood them, you'll probably remember. But there are also some longer scientific 'stories' that you're expected to remember, for example:

- explaining the evidence for continental drift (see page 208);
- describing the sequence of reactions etc. in a blast furnace;
- explaining how the percentage of carbon dioxide and/or oxygen in the Earth's atmosphere has changed since the Earth was formed;
- describing the chemical reactions involved in the production of nitric acid and ammonium nitrate fertiliser from ammonia;

and, for Higher Tier students,

- describing and explaining the magnetic reversal patterns in parts of the oceanic crust;
- describing and evaluating the scientific and economic factors associated with the conditions under which ammonia is made in the Haber process;
- explaining the properties of <u>substances</u> in terms of the particular <u>particles</u> from which they are made (as with the low boiling point of pentane, or when explaining the different properties of diamond and graphite).

Very few candidates can <u>correctly</u> remember <u>all</u> the details of these stories that GCSE syllabuses require them to know.

Try setting out the stories in different ways, for example as a list of points in the correct order or in the form of a flow diagram. You will then find out which is the best way for <u>you</u> to remember them.

Finally, <u>practise</u> remembering the stories until you can remember them accurately.

How to write good answers (continued)

■ Calculations

Some chemistry questions on examination papers include calculations. Some of the data you need to know and/or be able to use to work out these calculations are listed on page 213 of this book.

Even if you get the wrong answer to a calculation, you can still get quite a lot of the marks. To gain these marks, you must have gone about the calculation in the right way. But the person marking your answer can only see that you've done this if you write down your working neatly and set it out tidily so it's quite clear what you have done.

You should:

■ be sure to calculate the quantity you are asked for
(for example, you are sometimes asked to calculate the <u>mass</u> of a gas produced in a chemical reaction, and sometimes asked to calculate the <u>volume</u>);
■ follow the steps for each type of calculation as shown in the examples in this book;
■ write down the answer, with the units where relevant.

You should <u>not</u> alter incorrect figures. Instead, cross them out and write them again.

Example

Calculate the percentage of hydrogen, by mass, in water.

You should set out your answer like this:

Water has the formula H_2O

Relative atomic masses (A_r*) $H = 1$ $O = 16$

Relative molecular mass of water $2 \times 1 + 16 = 18$

So water $\frac{2}{18}$ hydrogen (by mass)

i.e. water is $\frac{2}{18} \times 100 = \underline{11.1\% \text{ hydrogen}}$

You get credit
for these steps
⟵ even if you
⟵ don't get the
⟵ correct answer

* [This information will be given in the question itself or on a Data sheet.]

Always set out your classwork and homework calculations as in the example above so that you get into good habits. Then you'll still do calculations in the right way even under the pressure of examinations.

Chemical data

You will be expected to be able to use the data on these pages. In GCSE Science examinations, you will be given the information on a Data Sheet or in the question.

■ Reactivity series for metals

[Elements in *italics*, though non-metals, have been included for comparison.]

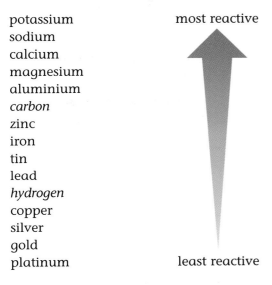

potassium   most reactive
sodium
calcium
magnesium
aluminium
carbon
zinc
iron
tin
lead
hydrogen
copper
silver
gold
platinum   least reactive

■ Names and formulas of some common ions

Positive ions

hydrogen	H^+
sodium	Na^+
silver	Ag^+
potassium	K^+
lithium	Li^+
ammonium	NH_4^+
barium	Ba^{2+}
calcium	Ca^{2+}
copper(II)	Cu^{2+}
magnesium	Mg^{2+}
zinc	Zn^{2+}
lead	Pb^{2+}
iron(II)	Fe^{2+}
iron(III)	Fe^{3+}
aluminium	Al^{3+}

Negative ions

chloride	Cl^-
bromide	Br^-
fluoride	F^-
iodide	I^-
hydroxide	OH^-
nitrate	NO_3^-
oxide	O^{2-}
sulphide	S^{2-}
sulphate	SO_4^{2-}
carbonate	CO_3^{2-}

The Periodic Table of the elements

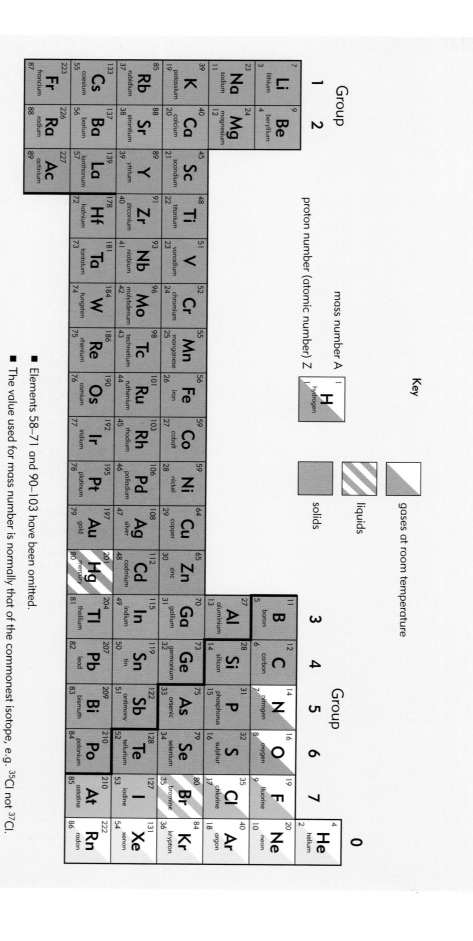

Key

mass number A
proton number (atomic number) Z

1		
H		
hydrogen		

gases at room temperature

liquids

solids

Group

Group 1

7	
Li	
lithium	
3	

23
Na
sodium
11

39
K
potassium
19

85
Rb
rubidium
37

133
Cs
caesium
55

223
Fr
francium
87

Group 2

9
Be
beryllium
4

24
Mg
magnesium
12

40
Ca
calcium
20

88
Sr
strontium
38

137
Ba
barium
56

226
Ra
radium
88

(Transition metals and remaining groups as shown in table)

- Elements 58–71 and 90–103 have been omitted.
- The value used for mass number is normally that of the commonest isotope, e.g. ^{35}Cl not ^{37}Cl.
- Bromine is approximately equal proportions of ^{79}Br and ^{81}Br.
- The relative atomic mass is the average mass of isotopes in the proportions they are normally found. (You will be given relative atomic masses wherever you need them for calculations.)

Chemical information you are expected to know

You are expected to know the following.

■ Chemical tests

You should be able to describe simple laboratory tests for:

> carbon dioxide
> chlorine
> hydrogen
> water
> oxygen (re-lights a glowing splint)
> pH (i.e. whether a solution is acidic, alkaline or neutral)

and, for Higher Tier students only,

> alkenes

Use the **Glossary/index** if you need to look up the details of any of these tests.

■ Type of reaction

You should be able to describe and give examples of the following types of chemical reaction:

> thermal decomposition (including cracking)
> neutralisation
> displacement
> electrolysis
> oxidation (as addition of oxygen)
> reduction (as removal of oxygen)
> exothermic reactions
> endothermic reactions
> reversible reactions

and, for Higher Tier students only,

> oxidation (as the loss of electrons)
> reduction (as the gain of electrons)
> redox

Use the **Glossary/index** if you need to look up the details of any of these tests.

■ Molecular formulae

You should know the formulae of the molecular substances mentioned in the syllabus, i.e.:

Elements			Compounds		
	hydrogen	H_2		water	H_2O
	oxygen	O_2		methane	CH_4
	nitrogen	N_2		ammonia	NH_3
	chlorine	Cl_2		carbon dioxide	CO_2
	bromine	Br_2		carbon monoxide	CO
				sulphur dioxide	SO_2
				nitrogen oxides	NO_X*
				hydrogen chloride	HCl

and, for Higher Tier students,

ethene C_2H_4

*[i.e. the formulae of different nitrogen oxides are <u>not</u> required]

Metals

1 How many metals are there?

About three-quarters of the elements are **metals**. Metals are mainly in **Groups** 1 and 2 of the Periodic Table and in the block of elements called **transition elements**.

[Remember that you also need to know the information in the box about the Periodic Table on p17.]

2 Making things from metals

Many things are made from transition metals because they have all the usual **properties** of metals. Copper, for example, is used to make electrical **cables**. This is because it is a good **conductor** of electricity and is easily shaped into wires. The most widely used structural metal is **steel**. This is because it is tough, **strong**, cheap and is easily shaped. (One transition metal, however, is a liquid at room temperature. This is **mercury**.) A widely used metal that is <u>not</u> a transition metal is **aluminium**. It is a very **lightweight** metal and is also a very good **conductor** of electricity. Aluminium can be mixed with other metals such as magnesium. This makes an alloy that is **stronger**, **harder** and **stiffer** than aluminium.

3 The alkali metals – a chemical family

The elements in Group 1 are called the **alkali metals**. We need to keep them under oil because they are very **reactive**. Alkali metals react with water to produce **hydrogen** gas. A colourless solution of the alkali metal **hydroxide** is also produced. An indicator shows that the solution is **alkaline**. Alkali metals react with some **non-metals**, such as oxygen. For example:

sodium + oxygen → **sodium oxide**

4 Colours and catalysts

Most transition metal compounds are **coloured**. If a transition metal compound dissolves in water it forms a coloured **solution**. Alkali metal compounds are white. They dissolve to form **colourless** solutions. Transition metal oxides are used to make coloured glass and pottery **glazes**. Some transition metals are used as **catalysts**. They speed up chemical reactions.

5 Making salts of alkali metals

Acid + alkali → **salt + water**

The acid and alkali **neutralise** each other. This is called a **neutralisation** reaction. To make:

■ a sodium salt you neutralise **sodium** hydroxide with an acid
■ a potassium salt you neutralise **potassium** hydroxide with an acid
■ a chloride you neutralise **hydrochloric** acid with an alkali
■ a nitrate you neutralise **nitric** acid with an alkali
■ a sulphate you neutralise **sulphuric** acid with an alkali.

6 Making salts of transition metals

Transition metal oxides and hydroxides are **insoluble** in water so they cannot produce alkaline solutions. But they can still neutralise acids to produce **salts** and water. All substances which can do this are called **bases**. Alkalis are **soluble** bases. To make sure that all of an acid has been neutralised, you must keep on adding an insoluble base until no more will **react**. You can then **filter** off any unreacted base. Ammonia dissolves in water to produce an alkaline solution of ammonium **hydroxide**. This will neutralise acids to produce **ammonium** salts.

7 Competing metals

A more reactive metal will push a **less** reactive metal out of its compounds. We say that it **displaces** the less reactive metal. We can also put carbon and hydrogen into the **reactivity** series because they can displace a metal less reactive than themselves from a metal oxide.

8 Where do metals come from?

Metals are found in the Earth's **crust**. Most metals, except gold, are found joined with other **elements** as compounds. Compounds of metals and oxygen are called **oxides**. Rocks containing metal compounds are called **ores**. Copper and iron are extracted from their oxides by heating them with **carbon**. Removing the oxygen from a metal oxide is called **reduction**. Aluminium oxide can only be reduced using **electricity**.

9 How do we get all the steel we use?

Iron is extracted from iron ore in a **blast** furnace. The ore is called **haematite**. The high temperature needed is produced by burning **coke** in the hot **air** that is blasted into the furnace. This makes carbon **dioxide** gas. The carbon dioxide then reacts with more carbon to make carbon **monoxide** gas. Carbon is more **reactive** than iron, so carbon monoxide takes the oxygen from iron oxide. This gives the metal iron and a gas called carbon **dioxide**. The iron oxide has been **reduced**. The carbon monoxide has been **oxidised**. Solid waste materials in the iron ore react with **limestone** to make **slag**. The furnace is so hot that the iron and slag both **melt** and run down to the base of the furnace.

10 Using electricity to split up metal compounds

Electrically charged atoms are called **ions**. You can split up a metal compound by passing **electricity** through it. You can do this only if you **melt** the compound by heating it, or **dissolve** the compound in water. This means that the ions in the compound can **move** about. Using electricity to split up a compound is called **electrolysis**. We say that the compound has been **decomposed**. The metal ions in a compound have a **positive** charge. During electrolysis, the metal ions move towards the **negative** electrode.

11 How do we get all the aluminium we need?

We can extract aluminium from an ore called **bauxite**. This contains the compound aluminium **oxide**. To pass electricity through aluminium oxide we need to **melt** it. This only happens at a very high temperature. So that we can use a lower temperature, the aluminium oxide is added to molten **cryolite**. The electrodes are made of **carbon**. Since the temperature is high and oxygen is given off, the **positive** electrode burns away. Aluminium is produced at the **negative** electrode. Molten **aluminium** collects at the base.

12 Which ores should we mine?

Many rocks contain metal, usually in the form of metal **compounds**. If a rock contains enough metal it can be used as an **ore**. If a rock contains too little metal, it is **uneconomic** to extract the metal from it. A rock containing only a small amount of metal may still be used as an ore if the metal is **valuable** enough. The metal compound in the ore may need to be **concentrated** before the metal is extracted.

[You should also be able to comment on the environmental aspects of producing metals as you did on page 41.]

13 Preventing corrosion

Iron and steel tend to **corrode** (rust) quite quickly. One way of preventing this is to connect the iron or steel to a more **reactive** metal. This method of preventing corrosion is called **sacrificial protection**. Steel which doesn't rust is called **stainless** steel. It is an alloy of iron, **nickel** and **chromium**. Aluminium is a reactive metal but it does not corrode very quickly because a layer of **aluminium oxide** forms on the surface. This is **tough** and prevents water and **oxygen** from reaching the aluminium underneath.

15 Making very pure copper

Copper is purified by a process of **electrolysis**. The positive electrode is a large block of **impure** copper from a furnace. The negative electrode is a thin sheet of **pure** copper. The electrodes are placed in a solution containing copper **ions**. During the electrolysis, copper is transferred from the **positive** electrode to the **negative** electrode. The **impurities** in the copper fall to the bottom of the container.

Earth materials

1 Limestone – a useful rock

Limestone is a common **rock**. We get limestone from **quarries**. Limestone is very useful for **buildings** because it is easy to cut into blocks. The chemical in limestone is **calcium carbonate**. When we heat limestone strongly in a kiln it breaks down into **quicklime** and **carbon dioxide**. We call this kind of reaction **thermal decomposition**. The chemical name for quicklime is **calcium oxide**.

2 What can we do with quicklime?

When you heat limestone, it decomposes into **quicklime** and carbon dioxide. Many other **carbonates** decompose in a similar way when you heat them. Quicklime (calcium oxide) **reacts** with cold water to form **slaked lime** (calcium hydroxide). Slaked lime is an **alkali**, it can neutralise acids. We can use slaked lime to neutralise the **acidity** in lakes and soils. Most plants do not grow well in acidic soils.

3 Other useful materials made from limestone

We heat limestone and clay together in a hot kiln to make **cement**. A mixture of cement, sand, rock and water gives **concrete**. The water **reacts** with the cement and makes the concrete set solid. Glass is a very useful material. You need to heat a mixture of limestone, sand and **soda** to make glass. Soda has the chemical name **sodium carbonate**. We can melt old glass and use it again. We say that the glass has been **recycled**.

4 How crude oil is split up into parts

When you heat a liquid it **evaporates** to form a vapour. When you cool a vapour it **condenses** to form a liquid. Evaporating a liquid and then condensing it again is called **distillation**. Separating a mixture of liquids like this is called **fractional distillation**. The liquids in the mixture must have different **boiling points**. Crude oil is separated into fractions in **fractionating towers**.

5 What are the chemicals in crude oil?

Substances that contain more than one kind of atom are called **compounds**. Most of the compounds in crude oil are made from two kinds of atoms. These are **hydrogen** atoms and **carbon** atoms. We call these compounds **hydrocarbons**. The smallest part of each hydrocarbon is called a **molecule**. Hydrocarbons with the highest boiling points have the **largest** molecules.

6 Different hydrocarbons for different jobs

Small hydrocarbon molecules can:

- evaporate quickly (we say they are very **volatile**)
- catch fire easily (we say they are very **flammable**)
- pour easily (we say they are not very **viscous**).

Larger hydrocarbons do <u>not</u> have these **properties** and so they are not very good **fuels**. Large hydrocarbon molecules can be split up into smaller molecules that are more useful. We call this **cracking**; it is a **thermal decomposition** reaction.

7 More about cracking hydrocarbons

In a refinery, we heat large hydrocarbon molecules so that they **evaporate**. We pass the vapours over a hot **catalyst**. The large molecules **split up** to make smaller ones. We use the small molecules as **fuels** and to make new materials such as **plastics**. We make plastics by joining lots of **small molecules** together. We call these big molecules **polymers**.

8 Plastics from oil

Bottles can be made from a plastic called **poly(ethene)**. Crates and ropes can be made from a different plastic called **poly(propene)**. Most plastics are not broken down by **microorganisms**. We say that they are <u>not</u> **biodegradable**. This means that plastics can be a problem in the environment.

[You should also be able to comment on the impact on the environment of plastic waste disposal as you did on page 69.]

9 Burning fuels – where do they go?

When fuels burn they react with **oxygen** from the air. The new substances that are produced are mainly **gases** that escape into the air. The atoms in fuels join up with oxygen atoms to form compounds called **oxides**.

When hydrocarbons burn:

- hydrogen atoms join up with oxygen atoms to make **water** molecules
- carbon atoms join up with oxygen atoms to make **carbon dioxide** molecules.

Sometimes fuels contain sulphur. Sulphur atoms join up with oxygen to form **sulphur dioxide**.

10 It's raining acid

Acid rain can harm buildings and living things. When we burn fuels that contain sulphur we make the gas called **sulphur dioxide**. This gas dissolves in water droplets to make **sulphuric** acid. The heat from burning fuels makes oxygen and **nitrogen** from the air react together. This makes gases called **nitrogen oxides**. These gases dissolve in water to produce **nitric** acid.

11 The Earth's changing atmosphere

The Earth's atmosphere now is about $\frac{4}{5}$ **nitrogen** and $\frac{1}{5}$ **oxygen**. Other gases in it are **carbon dioxide** and **noble** gases. The Earth's early atmosphere was made of gases that came out of volcanoes. It was mainly **carbon dioxide** with some **nitrogen** and **water** vapour. There were small amounts of methane. Water vapour condensed to form the **oceans**. Microorganisms removed carbon dioxide and from the atmosphere and added **oxygen**.

12 More oxygen, less carbon dioxide

Plants evolved and colonised the Earth's surface. They released **oxygen** into the atmosphere. Oxygen reacted with **methane** and **ammonia**, removing them from the air. Most of the carbon from the carbon dioxide in the atmosphere became 'locked up' in sedimentary rocks as **fossil fuels** and **carbonate** rocks.

13 The Earth

The Earth is shaped like a ball. We say it is nearly **spherical**.

14 The present gives us clues to the past

Often clues such as **ripple marks** tell us about how rocks were formed. A new layer in a sediment shows that there has been a **break** in deposition.

With sedimentary rock, normally:

- the layer at the bottom is the **oldest**,
- the layer at the top is the **youngest**.

This is usually true even when the rocks have been moved.

15 Evidence for Earth movements

Large forces act on the Earth's crust. So the crust is **unstable**. Sometimes layers of rock are tilted, **faulted** or **folded**. Sometimes they are even turned upside down. We can use **fossils** to tell us the age of each layer of rock. Then we know whether or not the layers are the right way up.

16 Movements that make mountains

Weathering and **erosion** wear mountains away. Large-scale movements of the **Earth's crust** over millions of years cause new mountains to form. Mountain-building involves high **temperatures** and **pressures**. So **metamorphic** rocks form at the same time as new mountain belts. Earthquakes and **volcanic eruptions** happen in places where there are Earth movements or **tectonic** activity.

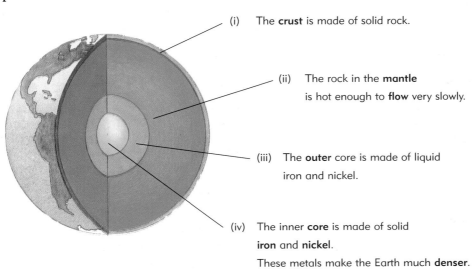

(i) The **crust** is made of solid rock.

(ii) The rock in the **mantle** is hot enough to **flow** very slowly.

(iii) The **outer** core is made of liquid iron and nickel.

(iv) The inner **core** is made of solid **iron** and **nickel**. These metals make the Earth much **denser**.

17 Why are some parts of the Earth's crust more unstable than others?

The Earth's crust is cracked into large pieces. We call these **tectonic plates**. The plates **move** very slowly, just a few **centimetres** each year. Millions of years ago, South America and Africa were next to each other. We know this because:

- their **shapes** fit together well
- they have rocks containing the same **fossils**.

In some places, tectonic plates push together. This forces some rocks upwards and makes new **mountains**.

18 What keeps the Earth's crust moving?

Tectonic plates move because of **convection** currents in the **mantle** below the Earth's lithosphere. The energy that produces the currents comes from **radioactive** substances inside the Earth.

19 Changing ideas about the Earth

[You should be able to:

- describe the 'shrinking Earth' model of how mountains are formed;
- explain why this model has been replaced by the idea of the Earth's crust being made up of moving plates;
- explain why the idea of moving continents was not accepted by most scientists until about 50 years after Wegener suggested it, just as you did on pages 92–93.]

Structure and bonding

1 Elements and compounds

All substances are made from tiny **atoms**. If the substance has atoms that are all of one type, we call it an **element**. Substances made from atoms of different elements joined together are called **compounds**. We use letters to stand for elements. We call these **symbols**. The **formula** of a compound tells us which atoms are in the compound.

[Remember that if you are given the formula of a compound, you should be able to say how many atoms there are of each element in the compound.]

2 How to describe chemical reactions

We can describe a chemical reaction using a **word equation**. The substances that react are the **reactants**. The new substances that are produced are the **products**. We can replace the names of each reactant and product by writing its **formula**. The equation for the reaction is now called a **symbol equation**. In a symbol equation, (s) stands for **solid**, (l) stands for **liquid**, (g) stands for gas, (aq) stands for aqueous solution.

[You should be able to:

■ write word equations for reactions you know about
■ explain what a symbol equation means in words.]

3 Where did the idea of atoms come from?

[You need to be able to interpret information you are given in the same sort of way that you did in this topic on pages 106–109.]

4 Two families of elements

Elements can be listed in order of the mass of their atoms (their **relative atomic mass**). The list can then be arranged in rows to make a **Periodic Table**. In this table, elements with similar properties are all in the same **Groups**. The elements in Group 1 of the Periodic Table are called **alkali metals**. They all react with water to produce an **alkaline** solution of the metal **hydroxide**. The elements in Group 0 of the Periodic Table are called **noble gases**. They are **unreactive**. This makes **helium** a safe gas to use in balloons and airships, and **argon** a suitable gas to fill the bulbs of filament lamps. The atoms of noble gases do not pair up to form **molecules**. So we say noble gases are **mon**atomic.

5 The halogens – another chemical family

The elements that are 'salt makers' are called **halogens**. These elements are all in **Group 7** of the Periodic Table. Atoms of the halogens join up in pairs. We call these pairs **molecules**. Halogens react with metals to form compounds we call **halides**. These compounds are part of a family of compounds called **salts**. Halogens also react with other **non-metals** such as hydrogen and carbon.

6 Differences between elements in the same Group

The further down Group 1 you go:

■ the lower the **melting points** and the **boiling points** are, and
■ the more **reactive** the metals are.

The further **down** Group 7 you go:

■ the higher the melting points and boiling points are, and
■ the halogens become less **reactive**.

A more reactive halogen **displaces** a less reactive halogen from its compounds.

7 How the Periodic Table was discovered

[You need to be able to interpret information you may be given about earlier versions of the Periodic Table. You also need to be able to compare earlier tables with the modern Periodic Table.]

8 What are atoms made of?

The centre of an atom is called the **nucleus**. This can contain two kinds of particle:

■ particles with a positive charge called **protons**
■ particles with no charge called **neutrons**.

Atoms of the same element always have the same number of protons. So every element has its own special **proton** number. The total number of protons and neutrons is called the **mass** number. Atoms of the same element that have different numbers of neutrons are called **isotopes**. Around the nucleus there are particles with a negative charge called **electrons**.

9 The modern Periodic Table

In the modern Periodic Table the elements are listed in order of their **proton numbers**. This number also tells you the number of **electrons** in each atom. This is what gives an element its particular **properties**. Argon then comes before **potassium**, where it fits best.

10 Why are there families of elements?

In atoms the electrons are arranged in certain **energy levels**. The first level has the **lowest** energy. The lowest level can take up to **two** electrons. The second and third energy levels can each take up to **eight** electrons. Elements in the same Group have the same number of electrons in their **top** energy level. This number is the same as the Group number e.g. Group 7 elements have **7** electrons in their **top** energy level.

[You should be able to show how the electrons are arranged in the first 20 elements of the Periodic Table.]

11 Why elements react to form compounds

When a metal reacts with a non-metal, the metal atoms always give away **electrons**. They form ions that have a **positive** charge. The non-metal atoms take electrons. They form **ions** that have a **negative** charge. Both ions then have electron structures like **noble** gases. The substances produced when metals react with non-metals are called **ionic** substances.

[You should be able to show the arrangement of electrons in the ions for sodium chloride, magnesium oxide and calcium chloride. See pages 124–125.]

12 How atoms of non-metals can join together

Atoms of non-metal elements can join by **sharing** electrons. When atoms join together in this way they form a **molecule**. Substances made of molecules are called **molecular** substances.

[You should know the formula of each molecule shown on pages 126–127.]

13 Why different types of substances have different properties

Molecular substances have **low** melting points and boiling points. This is because they are made of individual **molecules** that are easy to separate from each other. Ionic substances form **giant** structures of ions that are held together by strong forces of **attraction** between ions of opposite charges. This is why they have **high** melting points and boiling points. Ionic compounds will conduct electricity if the ions are free to **move**. This can happen if we **dissolve** the compounds in water or **melt** them.

14 Salt – a very useful substance

The chemical name for salt is **sodium chloride**. It contains the alkali metal **sodium** and the halogen **chlorine**. We find salt dissolved in the **sea** and buried **underground**. A solution of salt in water is called **brine**. **Electrolysis** of brine produces useful new substances. At the positive electrode we get **chlorine**, which **bleaches** damp indicator paper. At the negative electrode we get **hydrogen**, which **burns** with a squeaky pop. The solution left at the end contains **sodium hydroxide**.

15 Using the chemicals we make from salt

The three useful materials made by passing electricity through salt water are **chlorine**, **hydrogen** and sodium hydroxide.

Chlorine is used:

- in substances that kill **bacteria**
- to make a plastic called **PVC**
- to make **bleach**, which removes stains and fades colours.

Hydrogen is used:

- to make **ammonia**, which can be turned into fertiliser
- to change vegetable oils into **margarine**.

Paper, ceramics and soap are all made using **sodium hydroxide**. Hydrogen reacts with chlorine to make **hydrogen chloride**. This dissolves in water to make hydrochloric **acid**. Other compounds of hydrogen and halogens (hydrogen **halides**) also dissolve in water to make acidic solutions.

16 The chemicals we use to make photographs

Silver chloride, silver bromide and silver iodide are all silver **halides**. Light can change silver halides into **silver metal**. We say that light **reduces** silver halides to silver metal. Silver halides are also reduced by **X-rays** and the radiation from **radioactive** substances. We use silver halides to make photographic **film** and photographic paper.

17 How to write balanced symbol equations

[You need to be able to remember the formulas of the molecules shown on p213. You need to be able to work out the formulas of ionic compounds and to write balanced symbol equations as you did on pages 136–137.]

Patterns of chemical change

Knowing when to be careful

> You will need to <u>use</u> this information throughout your course.
> It will be <u>examined</u> with the module 'Patterns of chemical change'.

Some substances have warning signs on them called **hazard symbols**. If a material catches fire easily it is **highly flammable**. If a material helps other substances to burn by supplying oxygen, we say it is an **oxidising** substance. We say that substances that can kill you are **toxic**. Less dangerous substances are called **harmful**. The skin can be destroyed or burned by **corrosive** substances. Substances that can redden the skin or make you cough are **irritants**.

1 Using heat to speed things up

Chemical reactions go at different speeds or **rates**. Chemical reactions go faster at **higher** temperatures. At low temperatures, chemical reactions **slow down**.

2 Making solutions react faster

When you dissolve a substance in water you get a **solution**. A solution that contains a lot of dissolved substance is a **concentrated** solution. To make a concentrated solution react more slowly, you can **dilute** it. To make gases react faster, you need a **high** pressure.

3 Making solids react faster

A solid can react with a liquid only where they touch. The reaction is on the **surface** of the solid. If we break up the solid, we increase the total **surface area**. This means that smaller pieces react **faster**.

4 Substances that speed up reactions

A substance that speeds up a chemical reaction is called a **catalyst**. The catalyst increases the rate of reaction but is not **used up**. You can use catalysts **over** and **over** again. Each chemical reaction needs its own **special** catalyst. Useful materials such as margarine and sulphuric acid **cost** less to make when we use catalysts.

5 Investigating the speed of reactions

[You should be able to explain information that you are given about rates of reaction just as you did on pages 152–153.]

6 What makes chemical reactions happen?

For substances to react:

- their particles must **collide**;
- the particles must have enough **energy** when they do this.

The smallest amount of energy they need is called the **activation** energy. If you increase the temperature, reactions happen faster. This is because the particles collide more **often** and with more **energy**. Breaking solids into smaller pieces, making solutions more concentrated and increasing the pressure of gases all make reactions **faster**. All these things make the collisions between particles more **frequent**.

7 Living things can do our chemistry for us

We can use **living cells** to help us make new substances. Examples of living things we can use in this way are **yeasts** and **moulds**. When we make wine and beer, we use yeast cells to turn **sugar** into **alcohol**. We call this reaction **fermentation**. Yeast also makes the gas called **carbon dioxide**. The bubbles of this gas help bread to rise.

8 More cells that will work for us

The type of living cells that make yogurt are called **bacteria**. They feed on the **sugar** in the milk and turn it into **lactic acid**. To speed up their chemical reactions, living cells contain **enzymes**. These need to be warm to work well, but must not get too hot as they are made from **protein**. Protein **changes** when it is heated and cannot be changed back again.

9 Not too hot and not too cold

Food goes bad when **living cells** feed on it. We can keep food fresh for longer by keeping it in a **fridge** or a **freezer**. This is because living cells use **enzymes** to speed up their reactions. These work slowly if the temperature is **low**. Useful living cells like yeast work best at temperatures around **35** to **40°C**. Different enzymes work best at different **pH** values.

10 More uses of enzymes

It is important to use biological washing powders at low temperatures because high temperatures damage the **enzymes** in them. The washing powders contain **proteases** to digest proteins and **lipases** to digest fats. Some industries use high **temperatures** and **pressures**. This is expensive. Enzymes carry out reactions at **normal** temperatures and pressures.

[When you are given information about using an enzyme to bring about a reaction, you should be able to explain the advantages and disadvantages of using the enzyme as you did on page 163.]

11 Enzymes in the food industry

Job	Enzyme
break down starch into glucose	carbohydrases
change glucose to a sweeter sugar called fructose	isomerase
to 'pre-digest' the proteins in some baby foods	proteases

12 Getting energy out of chemicals

Charcoal, coal, gas and wood are all **fuels**. When we **burn** them they release energy in the form of **heat**. Many other chemical reactions also release **energy** into the surroundings. We call reactions like this **exothermic** reactions.

13 Do chemical reactions always release energy?

To make some chemical reactions happen you must **supply** energy. We call these reactions **endothermic** reactions. We must supply energy to extract metals from their ores. We can supply this energy in the form of **heat** or **electricity**. The chemical reactions in photography use **light** energy.

14 Reactions that go forwards and backwards

In some chemical reactions the products react to form the original reactants.

A + B $\rightleftharpoons$ C + D

We call this sort of reaction a **reversible reaction**.

Ammonium chloride $\rightleftharpoons$ **ammonia + hydrogen chloride**
    [white solid]   [colourless gases]

If a reversible reaction is exothermic in one direction it is **endothermic** in the opposite direction. The amount of energy transferred is the **same**.

hydrated copper sulphate + [energy] $\rightleftharpoons$ **anhydrous** copper sulphate + water
      [blue]   [white]

15 What use is nitrogen?

Plants need **nitrogen** for healthy growth. About **78%** of the air is nitrogen but plants can't use nitrogen gas directly. Instead, the plants take in **nitrates** through their roots. Farmers add nitrogen to the soil by using **fertilisers**. This increases the **yield** of their crops.

16 Catching nitrogen to feed plants

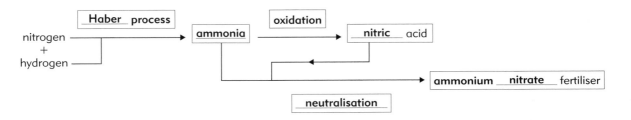

Answer to Q10

ammonia + nitric acid → ammonium nitrate

17 No chemicals, thank you

Fertilisers contain chemicals called **nitrates**. These chemicals give plants the **nitrogen** that they need. Nitrates can cause problems if they get into the **water** supply because they are poisonous. If nitrates get into rivers and lakes then they can cause many of the living things to **die**.

18 How heavy are atoms?

Atoms are far too **small** to be easily weighed in grams. We compare the masses of atoms with each other. This is called **relative** atomic mass or A_r for short. The lightest element is **hydrogen**. It has an A_r of **1 unit**.

19 Using relative atomic mass

To work out a relative molecular mass (M_r for short):

■ look up the relative **atomic** masses of the elements,
■ then **add** together the masses of all the atoms in the formula.

20 Elementary pie

Chemical compounds are made of **elements** (just as an apple pie is made of ingredients).

[You should be able to work out the percentage by mass of each element in a compound as you did on pages 182–183.]

Glossary/index

carbon: a non–metal *element* that is found in living organisms and in *fossil fuels* such as *crude oil*   31, 33, 39, 141–142

carbon dioxide: a gas produced when substances containing *carbon burn*, and during *fermentation*   53, 70, 72, 76–77, 97, 157 (test)

carbon monoxide: a gas produced when there isn't enough *oxygen* for *carbon* to *burn* completely; the *reducing agent* in a *blast furnace*   34

catalysts: substances, including *enzymes*, that increase the *rates* of chemical reactions without being used up in the reaction   150–151, 191

cement: made from *limestone* and clay; used to make *concrete*   57

chlorides: *salts* made from *hydrochloric acid*   25

chlorine: a *toxic* gas; a *halogen* in *Group* 7 of the *Periodic Table*   113, 131 (test), 132

coke: a form of *carbon* used in the *blast furnace*   34

compound: a substance made from *atoms* of different *elements* joined together by chemical bonds   103, 124–127

concentrated solution: a *solution* with a lot of dissolved substance in it   146–147

concrete: artificial stone made using *cement*   56–57

condense, condensation: when a gas is changed to a liquid by cooling   60–61, 100

conductor: a substance that allows electricity, or thermal (heat) energy, to pass through it easily   12, 18–20

convection currents: movements that occur in materials that can flow because of differences in temperature between different parts   90, 98

copper: a useful *metal* because it is a good *conductor* and not very reactive   18, 36, 44, 51

core: the part of the Earth nearest to its centre   80

corrosion: when *metals* react with oxygen and/or other substances from the atmosphere to form *compounds*; When *iron* or *steel* corrodes, rust is formed   42–43

corrosive substances: substances such as *acids* that dissolve or eat away other materials   11

covalent bonds: chemical bonds formed between *atoms* because they share one or more pairs of *electrons*   140–141

cracking: splitting *large hydrocarbon* molecules into smaller ones   65–67

crude oil: a liquid mixture of *hydrocarbons* found in the Earth's *crust*; a *fossil fuel*   58–59, 60–63

crust: the outer layer of the Earth, made of solid rock   32, 78–93

cryolite: a *compound* of *aluminium* that is *melted* and then used to dissolve *bauxite* so that it can be *electrolysed* at a lower temperature   38–39

D

Dalton, John: first developed the *atomic* theory that is the basis of chemistry   106–109

diamond: a very hard form of the *element carbon*   141–142

diatomic: the *molecules*, formed from pairs of atoms, of *elements* that are gases, but <u>not</u> *noble gases*   111

dilute solution: a weak *solution* containing very little dissolved substance   146

displace, displacement: when one *element* is pushed out from one of its *compounds* by another, more reactive element   30–31, 34–35

distil, distillation: when a liquid is evaporated and then condensed again to make it purer   60

double bond: a *covalent* bond in which two pairs of *electrons* are shared between *atoms*   94–95, 186–187

E

earthquakes: shaking of the Earth's *crust* caused by shock (seismic) waves produced by movement of adjacent *tectonic plates*   87–88, 98

electrodes: these supply an electric current to a *melted* or dissolved *ionic compound* so that *electrolysis* can occur; the products of the electrolysis form at the electrodes   36–37, 39, 46

electrolysis: when a dissolved or *molten ionic compound* is *decomposed* by having an electric current passed through it 36–37, 38–39, 44, 143, 201

electrolyte: a *molten* or dissolved *ionic compound* that will allow an electric current to pass through it 49

electronic structure: the arrangement of *electrons* in *atoms* into different energy levels (or shells) 122–126, 138–139

electrons: *particles*, with a negative electric charge and very little mass, that surround the *nucleus* of an *atom* 118–119

electron transfer: the losing and gaining of *electrons* between *atoms* when *ionic compounds* are formed 48–51

element: a substance that is made of only one type of *atom* 16–17, 102, 106–107

empirical formula: the simplest *formula* for a *compound* 202–203

endothermic reaction: a chemical reaction that takes in energy from its surroundings 168–169, 186–189

energy level diagram: a type of graph that shows the energy transfers to and from the surroundings that occur during a chemical reaction 190

enzymes: *catalysts* that are found in living cells 158–165

equilibrium: the point in a *reversible reaction* when the rate of the forward reaction (*reactants* → *products*) exactly balances the rate of the reverse reaction (reactants ← products); usually represented by ⇌ 170–171, 193–195

evaporate, evaporation: when a liquid is changed into a gas or a vapour 60–61, 100–101

exothermic reaction: a chemical reaction that gives out energy to the surroundings 166–167, 186–189

F

ferment(ation): a reaction in which *yeast* produces *alcohol* and *carbon dioxide* from sugar 157

fertilisers: substances put into soil to make crops grow better 173, 175–177

flammable substances: substances that catch fire easily 10

formula: the *symbols* and numbers that tell you the number of *atoms* of each *element* in a *compound* 103–104

fossil fuels: *fuels* formed in the Earth's *crust* from the remains of living things, for example *crude oil* 59

fossils: the remains, in rocks, of plants and animals from long ago 85, 89

fraction: one part from a mixture of liquids separated by *fractional distillation* 60–61, 63

fractional distillation: the separation of a mixture of liquids, for example the *hydrocarbons* in *crude oil*, by *distillation* 60–61, 63

fuels: substances that are *burned* to release energy 65, 70–73

G

(g): short for gas; used in *symbol equations* 29, 105

giant structures: structures which consist of a large, usually three-dimensional lattice of *atoms* or *ions* held together by *covalent* or *ionic bonds* 141–142

graphite: a form of *carbon* that is a *conductor* of electricity 141

Group: a family of similar *elements* in the same column of the *Periodic Table* 110–112

H

Haber process: a process for making *ammonia* from *hydrogen* and *nitrogen* 174, 192–197

haematite: a form of iron *oxide*; the main *ore* of iron 34

half-equations: show what happens at each *electrode* during *electrolysis* 143, 201

molten substance: a substance that has been *melted*   34–35, 38–39

monatomic: *atoms* that exist singly, e.g. those of the *noble gases*   111

monomers: small *molecules* that can link together to form long chain molecules called *polymers*   95

N

neutral solution: a *solution* that is neither *acidic* nor *alkaline*; it has a *pH* of 7   14, 24

neutralise, neutralisation: when an *acid* reacts with an *alkali* or insoluble *base* to make a *neutral solution*   24–27, 175

neutrons: *particles* in the *nucleus* of an *atom* that have no electrical charge; they have the same mass as *protons*   118–119

nitrates: *salts* produced from *nitric acid*; important in *fertilisers*   25, 172, 175–177

nitric acid: an *acid* made by reacting *ammonia* with *oxygen* and *water*; can be used to produce *salts* called *nitrates*   175

nitrogen: a not very reactive gas that makes up about $\frac{4}{5}$ of the air   73–76, 96, 172, 174–175

nitrogen oxides: *compounds* of *nitrogen* and *oxygen* that help to cause *acid rain*   73

noble gases: unreactive, or **inert**, gases in *Group* 0 of the *Periodic Table*   111, 127

nucleus: the central part of an *atom*; made of *neutrons* and *protons*   118

O

oceanic ridge: mountainous ridge of *igneous rock* formed on the ocean bed as *magma* rises between *tectonic plates* that are moving apart   93, 99

oil: see *crude oil*

optimum temperature and pressure: the best temperature and pressure to use for a particular chemical reaction, e.g. the *Haber process*   196–197

ore: a *compound*, often an *oxide*, from which a *metal* is extracted   32–35, 38, 40–41

oxidation, oxidise:
1 *oxygen* combining with another *element* usually to form an *oxide*   48, 175
2 when an *atom* loses *electrons*   49, 51

oxides: *compounds* of *oxygen* and another *element*   28, 32–33, 40–41, 70–71

oxidising substance: a substance that readily makes *oxygen* available and so allows things to *burn* very readily   10

oxygen: a gas making up about $\frac{1}{5}$ of the air; when substances *burn* they react with oxygen to produce *oxides* of the *elements* they contain   21, 28, 34, 48, 70–71, 76

ozone screen: a layer in the Earth's atmosphere containing ozone gas which filters out some of the harmful *ultraviolet radiation* from the Sun   96

P

particles: the very small bits that scientists think that everything is made of   100–101

Periodic Table: a table of the *elements*, arranged in order of their mass or their *proton number*, that has similar elements placed in the same column or *Group*   16–17, 110–117, 120–121

pH: a scale that tells you how *acidic* or *alkaline* a *solution* is   15, 161

plastics: *compounds* usually made from *oil*; they are *polymers*   67–69

polymers: substances such as *plastics* which have very long *molecules*   68–69

poly(ethene): a *plastic* or *polymer* made from the *monomer* ethene   68, 95

poly(propene): a *plastic* or *polymer* made from the *monomer* propene   68, 95

polythene: the everyday name for *poly(ethene)*   68

potassium: a very reactive *alkali metal*   20

products: the new substances that are produced in chemical reactions   104

properties: what substances are like, e.g. chemically reactive or *tough*   12–13, 18–19, 64

proteases: *enzymes* that digest proteins   165

proton number: the number of *protons* in the *nucleus* of an *atom*   118–120

protons: *particles* found in the *nucleus* of an *atom* that have a positive electrical charge; they have the same mass as *neutrons*   118–119

Q

quicklime: a substance made by heating *limestone*; its chemical name is calcium oxide   53–54

R

rate of reaction: how fast a chemical reaction happens   144–145

reactants: the substance(s) that you start off with in a chemical reaction   104

reactivity series: a list of *elements* in order of how reactive they are   28–29, 30–31, 114–115, 138–139

redox reactions: reactions in which both *oxidation* and *reduction* occur   48–49

reduce, reduction:
1 the process of obtaining a *metal* from its *ore*, usually by removing the *oxygen* with which the metal is combined   33–34
2 when an *atom* gains *electrons*   48–49

reducing agent: a substance that is used to bring about *reduction*   33–34, 48–49

relative atomic mass: the mass of an *atom* compared to other atoms   178–181

relative formula mass: another name for *relative molecular mass*

relative molecular mass: you get this by adding together the *relative atomic masses* of all the *atoms* in the *formula* for a *compound*   180–182, 200

reversal patterns: magnetic stripe patterns in the Earth's *crust* caused by the alignment of iron–rich minerals with the alternating direction of the Earth's magnetic field   99

reversible reactions: chemical reactions that can go both ways, i.e.

reactants → products   or   reactants ← products

rock cycle: the way that the materials which make up rocks are continually being recycled in the Earth's *crust* and *mantle*   78–79

S

(s): short for solid; used in *symbol equations*   29, 105

sacrificial protection: the protection of one *metal* against *corrosion*, by using a second more reactive metal in contact with it that corrodes first   42, 50

salt:
1 a *compound* that you get when you *neutralise* an *acid* with an *alkali* or an insoluble *base*   24–27
2 the everyday name for common salt or sodium chloride   113, 130–131

saturated: a *hydrocarbon molecule* in which all the *carbon atoms* are joined by *single bonds*; saturated hydrocarbons, e.g. *alkanes*, are fairly unreactive   94

sea–floor spreading: caused by *tectonic plates* that are moving apart; new crust is formed as *magma* rises to fill the gap and then solidifies   99

sediment: small bits of solid that settle at the bottom of a liquid   78, 82

sedimentary rocks: rocks formed from layers of *sediment*   78, 82–83, 85

silver halides: *compounds* of silver and a *halogen*; they are *reduced* to silver by light   134–135

single bond: a *covalent* bond where one pair of *electrons* is shared between two *atoms*   186

slag: the *molten* waste produced in a *blast furnace*   35

slaked lime: a substance used to make soil less *acidic*; its chemical name is calcium hydroxide   54–55

sodium: a very reactive *alkali metal*   20–21

sodium chloride: the chemical name for ordinary (common) *salt*   113, 130–131

sodium hydroxide: a strong *alkali* that is used to make many other chemicals   21, 133